SPORT

and American
Mentality

D0171287

SPORT

and American Mentality, 1880–1910

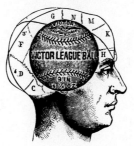

Donald J. Mrozek

THE UNIVERSITY OF TENNESSEE PRESS / KNOXVILLE

Copyright © 1983 by The University of Tennessee Press / Knoxville
All rights reserved
Manufactured in the United States of America
First edition

Clothbound editions of University of Tennessee Press books are printed
on paper designed for an effective life of at least 300 years, and bind-
ing materials are chosen for strength and durability.

Library of Congress Cataloging in Publication Data
Mrozek, Donald J.
   Sport and American mentality, 1880–1910.
   Bibliography: p.
   Includes index.
   1. Sports—United States—History. 2. Sports—
Social aspects—United States. 3. National character-
istics, American—History. 4. Social values—History.
I. Title.
GV583.M76   1983   796'.0973   83-3667
ISBN 0-87049-394-9
ISBN 0-87049-395-7 (pbk.)

For my parents

Contents

Illustrations

Acknowledgments

I am grateful to the friends and colleagues who have helped me personally and academically. Lloyd C. Gardner and Warren I. Susman of Rutgers University taught me more than they may realize and more than I show. Guy Lewis of the University of Massachusetts early encouraged my interest in sport history, and my colleagues in the Department of History at Kansas State University have been consistently supportive. Many of the ideas presented in this work were first discussed at departmental seminars, and my colleagues saved me from many errors, while proposing more profitable lines of inquiry. I appreciate especially the suggestions I received from Burton I. Kaufman, Albert N. Hamscher, Joseph M. Hawes, Robert D. Linder, and Leroy E. Page on specific chapters. Judith Sealander, now of Wright State University, offered generous advice concerning women and sport. Peter Levine of Michigan State University carefully read an earlier draft, and his critical responses sharpened my own sense of what I was intending with this project. David K. Wiggins of the Department of Physical Education, Dance and Leisure Studies at Kansas State University endured many long discussions with me during the drafting of several chapters, and his reaction often forced me to reconsider my ideas. I also owe a deep personal debt to James C. Carey, Lorna Carey, George M. Kren, Margo Kren, and Samuel Bertsche for their kindnesses and care while I was working on this study.

I am happy to thank the National Endowment for the Humanities for its generous support during my year as a fellow in 1980–81. Also, Kansas State University's Faculty Research Awards

Committee provided grants during several years prior to my fellowship with the Endowment, as well as a summer fellowship which freed time for writing. The physical preparation of the manuscript was overseen in its earlier drafts by Mrs. Betty Bailey, whose efficient assistance is surpassed only by her friendliness; later drafts were typed by Mrs. Nedra Sylvis, whose reliability and intelligent care have saved me time and grief. In addition, the staff and readers of the University of Tennessee Press pointed helpfully toward areas where revisions proved beneficial.

To my family and especially to my parents, Joseph W. and Mildred B. Mrozek, go my thanks for everything. I am sure that they know what I mean.

October 1982   —D.J.M.
Manhattan, Kansas

Preface

IN the forms that Americans presently take for granted, sport came to prominence toward the end of the nineteenth century. The play, games, and spectacles of earlier generations lacked many features now deemed common in sport — an emphasis on standardized rules and procedures, a quest to set records, a reliance on experts in games and their management, and many others. Most of all, sport acquired a "preexistence," when the sheer number of sporting events and their arrangement into schedules, leagues, teams, and seasons gave it a crucial institutional tone. Like the truisms "church on Sunday" and "business as usual," sport became a standard part of the American scene instead of a spectacle, an oddity, or even a special ritual event reserved for a few days during the year. Sporting clubs proliferated during the nineteenth century, and already respected agencies such as colleges and churches gradually accommodated themselves to the increasingly numerous and organized games of their charges. As a result of these and other occurrences, sport itself developed a measure of institutional permanence and autonomy.[1]

Sport's rise to prominence hinged on its attainment of respectability among the middle and upper classes, whose support did not dictate what character sport must have but whose opposition could have frustrated and slowed the emergence of sport while pressuring it into different forms. To Americans at the beginning of the nineteenth century, there was no obvious merit in sport — certainly no clear social value to it and no sense that it contributed to the improvement of the individual's character or the society's moral or even physical health. Significantly, even antebellum health reformers rarely promoted what later Americans considered to be real sport, concentrating instead on various calisthenic and exercise programs. Even those captivated by skating and pedestrianism, or road-running, played without benefit of bureaucratic organization, usually as individuals even when in the midst of crowds. Antebellum clubs rarely formed regional associations, let alone national ones; and the scope and tone of physical activity remained limited. Although laws such as those imposed by the Quakers to suppress many sports and amusements had been lifted or lightened, the whole realm of sport and physical contest remained mired in a netherworld of violence, bloodletting, and theatricality. Bullbaiting, ratting, and cockfighting remained among the most visible and revolting examples of what "sport" might be; and boxing stood barely one link up the "chain of being," as primitive sluggers bloodied each other for the titillation of an audience composed of near-criminals and respectable types slumming in the haunts of the wicked. Even the great horse races of the antebellum years enjoyed popularity for reasons that later seemed ancillary or even improper, including sectional rivalry and betting; and racing was a "sport" that even focused on an animal as the key performer, leaving unanswered the question of whether a man of the decent sort could properly be an athlete. As an early twentieth-century commentator said of rowing in the antebellum years, "Gentlemen did not row, but, sitting in the stern, satisfied their sporting instincts by making up scratch races with the barges that they met in the course of their excursions." The men pulling the oars were just a propulsion system, and the point of the whole exercise was the mere diversion of the gentleman.[2]

By the end of the century, however, the sporting scene and the sense of its significance bore little resemblance to the sometimes tawdry and eccentric displays of earlier years. Sport remained complex and confusing, more open to description than to definition. But it enjoyed a generally higher moral tone, partly because of changes imposed on its conduct during the intervening decades, yet also because of a new interpretation of its utility to society. No more unified and coherent than such other institutions as religion or business, sport now seemed to parallel them in exerting effects on the public and thus in its claims for

social esteem and recognition. This change in sport's meaning
and significance did not come automatically, and it demands detailed explanation. Far more than a way of passing "leisure time,"
sport aspired to provide answers to pressing societal concerns.[3]

The people who claimed this role for sport were varied, and
they understood sport in different ways. Distinct but overlapping constituencies developed, not always distinguished from
each other by common social and economic interests but sometimes primarily by sentiment and sensibility. Even within a single group definable in terms of class, wealth, and social ties,
differences in attitude sometimes spawned opposing views about
sport, as well as about the nature and future of American society and culture more broadly. Although mentality is affected
by class and wealth, it also varies over time. Thus the changing
composition of ideas within a "middle class," a "gentry," a "traditional governing elite," or an "ultra-rich" depends not only
on socioeconomic characteristics but also on how the people
within each group reconceive their own lives and destinies.
Shortly before the Civil War, for example, Thomas Wentworth
Higginson argued that the moral power and social effectiveness of the "saints" on earth depended on the strength of "their
bodies"; and he sensed that both the body and the human personality were processes rather than fixed entities, subject to
change by the force of human will. Prophetic as this notion
was of thinking among late nineteenth-century Americans, Higginson was rare — even a bit odd — among contemporaries of his
own background. His injunction that Emily Dickinson would
write "stronger" poetry if she lifted weights invited wonder,
if not derision; and, to be sure, the counterpoint between Higginson and Dickinson suggests how deeply sensibility can differ
even if class is substantially the same. So, then, although social
and economic characteristics played a part in shaping sport and
the attitudes toward it, disagreements over the meaning of the
changes taking place in American life also affected thinking
about sport. Constituencies formed around concrete social and
economic interests, but also around sentiments.[4]

The fragmented actions of the many different advocates of
sport combined to generate a climate that sustained it, even
though the sharp and often vocal disagreements among the pro-

ponents attracted greater attention at the time. Those mouth-
ing the rhetoric of the declining code of gentility, for example,
expressed dismay at encroachment by commercial entrepreneurs
— and they defined commercialization so broadly that they frequently disparaged the whole coterie of professionals emerging
in collegiate and club sport. Never strictly defined in economic
or even in social terms, the "gentry" itself seemed to be disinte-
grating in a rapidly changing environment. Yet for many the attractiveness of the genteel sensibility lingered, affecting their
sense of propriety and, by extension, of the appropriate way to
pursue sport. Moreover, genteel sentiments proved engaging,
or at least convenient, to some whose professional and economic
interests might easily have suggested a different loyalty. Physical educators, for example, objected to the daemonic quest for
victory that drove the paid coach, and so they cooperated with
traditionally inclined families despite the common status of educators and coaches as expert professionals. Yet even the paid
coaches served roles that could be turned to advantage by traditionalists; these latter thought that, through participation in
well-managed sport, students might gain habits of efficiency
that were needed for victory in business, politics, and international relations. In the former case, a similarity on the level of
sentiment and sensibility obtained; in the latter, a conformity
in the material results expected. Meanwhile, the new industrial
and financial rich drew attention to sport and gave it their highly
visible sanction, even though educators normally deplored the
behavior of the rich as frivolous and unconstructive.[5]

Cutting across all classes and sentiments, however, several
major changes in American culture affected the perception of
sport and altered the context in which its suitability and respectability could be measured. One was the emergence of a
national consciousness in America, another was the changing
role of women in society, and the third was a rising disposition
in favor of an energetic, dynamic style in all aspects of life.
After the Civil War, America became a unitary political entity;
and many leaders sought a unitary culture to ensure its continuity. This search led toward the promotion of sports that were
national in scope and "Americanizing" in effect. Meanwhile,
the social contributions of women were in flux, as work was

relocated, reorganized, and redefined; and as familial responsibilities underwent significant reappraisal. Changes in the roles
of women affected what roles sport could play in their lives.
Lastly, the growing disposition to value energy, activity, and
movement deeply influenced the whole sense of style that Americans brought to every area of work and play. To cite only one
example, "relevant style" explained Americans' preference for
baseball and their intolerance of cricket. Such broad issues helped
to define what was deemed necessary and appropriate in American culture, and sport's respectability depended in part on its
ability to adapt to all three trends.[6]

The complex of interactions among various groups, within
the context of broad changes in the whole national point of
view, left a crucial residue of belief. Whatever differences they
had about what sport was and what it should become, advocates came to assume its worth in a general, unqualified sense.
The final acceptability of sport, then, transcended the disputed
criteria and purposes set out by groups that never could have
agreed completely on these matters in any case. The diversity
of sport thus became a source of its vulnerability to criticism
as different constituencies squabbled over its future. But it also
ensured sport's potential strength as an institution, multiplying
its sources of strength and its audiences, and thus contributing
to its appearance of autonomy.

The liveliness and energy of late nineteenth-century American culture all but necessitated that its "search for order" would
be accompanied by a search for meaning. Although the yearning for spiritual fulfillment remained, supernatural forces faced
impeachment in a century of rapidly accumulating scientific
discoveries, many of which ran counter to traditional sources
of spiritual guidance. For a Christian who felt compelled to
respond to Darwinism, for example, the world became the unfolding creation of a God whose presence was continuously
shown in matter. Ultimately, however, this made the world itself the true statement of creation and the Bible a metaphor.
In philanthropy and the work of the "social Gospel," the material world displaced the unseen realm as the arena of theology;
and spiritualism sought links between the material and spiritual
realms, presuming the interpenetrability of the two. Although

very much an age of materialism, the late nineteenth century also ached for the comfort and assurance of the religious sensibility, even as specific creeds fell and denominations dissembled. The need for renewal — on an emotional and spiritual level perhaps even more than a physical one — may have been even stronger beneath the surface than its public expressions, in the face of challenges from science and skepticism, suggested. Hinting at a resolution, Henry Adams perceived a parallel between medieval man's veneration of the mediatrix of graces and his contemporaries' devotion to the machine—"the dynamo and the Virgin." He sensed a new understanding of transcendent power as the mystical merged with the mechanical and resided within it.[7]

The relationship between matter and spirit or, more concretely, mind and body that so preoccupied certain articulate Americans was basically a personalized version of the search for connections between ideas and action; and the human body emerged as the cogenerator of both. Admittedly, there was much room for confusion and error, as in the loss of distinction between intention and instinct. Yet the basic thrust in the world of sport paralleled that in other areas of the culture. The emphasis that many Americans placed on developing willpower in the individual through the crucible of sport was quite analogous to the quest for greater power and control over the forces of nature, much as raw ores are turned into steel. Best of all, the crucible was concrete. As Howard Mumford Jones has put it, late nineteenth-century Americans came to the "profound conviction that the visible world exists." Speaking of the governing classes of the same period, Christopher Lasch recognized this aspect of American mentality. "They appealed," Lasch argued, "only to the unmediated authority of the fact. They asked not that the citizen or worker submit to legitimate authority but that he submit to reality itself." As Elting Morison has suggested, the critical question in industrial culture may well be "how much abstraction man can stand, how much removal from first causes, how much action at a distance, how much translation of personal experience into attenuating resemblances or symbols, before he gets beside himself in the shadows?" The middle- and upper-class Americans who came to accept and promote sport increasingly challenged that "abstraction." To legitimize sport was, from this vantage point, to revalidate the authenticity of their own experience and, even more, their tactile sense of experience itself.[8]

Undergirding this structure of thoughts and sensibilities was the sweeping architecture of experimentalist philosophy. The pragmatism developed by Charles Sanders Peirce, William James, and John Dewey required an acceptance of the material world as the sole available and verifiable basis for thought. But it also led toward the assertion of the inseparability of thought and action, raising experience in the physical world and the specific experiences of each human being to a new and remarkable eminence. The patterns that these actions assumed came to constitute a form of thought, as experience and ideas relied on each other in an indivisible and continuous process. Each act thus pretended to importance because it affected the whole of one's experience by interacting with it. This highly tactile philosophy accorded well with the emphasis that the new experts in the study of the body placed upon the mutuality of mind and matter. Physical educators, promoters of sport, nutritionists, physiologists, and others saw the human being as a double-faced entity whose parts could be separated only as an analytical convenience. For them, processes deposed fixed states as the common model for describing and interpreting experience. Coherence with and absorption in the world replaced any desire to reject or even transcend it. In particular, the body became the inescapable and magnificently suitable organism in which the form and function of all thought and deed revealed themselves as one.

This experimentalist disposition, which assumed that only practice made perfect and that truth, like matter, was in motion, led directly toward the belief that values (which sociology was reducing to custom) were conditioned by behavior and were consequently always open to change. Even though there were constraints on the degree to which change was possible, such as the slowness in the rate of bodily evolution, the contingency of moral values on physical conditions encouraged a thorough reconsideration of all sorts of activity. In such an environment, the perception that sportive and athletic behavior contributed to the shaping of attitudes and values followed an irrepressible logic. In at least one respect, sport appealed with special force to the contemporary passion for the deed, since it offered a way of learning through the senses and of expressing oneself through action.[9]

The broadest implications of sport's attainment of respectability did not reveal themselves until the emergence of a mass leisure-culture in the twentieth century. The commercialization of baseball hinted at this future, and the ambiguous reaction of workers to the regulated sport favored by their industrial managers should have served warning that the elaborate rationales for sport might not have lasting pertinence. Yet mass leisure-culture as it later emerged was hardly what most of sport's articulate proponents had in mind at the turn of the century, and even an entrepreneur such as Albert Spalding did not envision that the masses should in any sense call the shots. The immediate significance of the various constituencies attracted to sport lay in their defection from the lists of its potential opponents and in their lending it the mantle of respectability. What others did with it later was another story. They were less the creators of mass sport than the inventors of a mythology that outlived the real world that created it.

It has been pointed out — and wisely so — that to study a maturing people is to observe the interaction of culture and experience. However, for late nineteenth- and early twentieth-century Americans, there seems to have been a sense that experience was, practically speaking, identical to culture. The reconciliation that was needed was between one's vision of one's own experience in life with one's sense of experience in the broader sense and the grand scale — the systematized behavior of the society as a whole. On that level of personal reconciliation to a public interpretation of experience, sport supplied a sense of renewal through the medium of action. The various understandings of this role are the themes running through this study.

SPORT
and American
Mentality

CHAPTER 1

Strategies of Regeneration

THE constituent groups which favored sport did so out of need. In different ways, each found in sport a strategy for regeneration and renewal. Specific visions of regeneration — what it entailed and how it could be achieved — grew out of their distinctive experiences. Some saw physical improvement as the paramount goal, while others claimed spiritual effects from physical training; and still another group doubted the validity of distinguishing between body, mind, and spirit. Certain advocates of sport sought consciously to use it as a means of regeneration, while others left the renewing role of sport masked beneath mundane rhetoric. In either case, sport entered the complex of concerns that formed the real life-experiences of Americans.

Every culture has its own strategies of regeneration — beliefs, rituals, and mechanisms for personal and social renewal. Basic questions bring forth these different approaches. What is the place of man in the world? How can man exert any control or, less ambitiously, some influence over the forces of nature? Failing that, how can man reconcile himself to his weakness? What does death suggest about the meaning of life? The issues face all cultures. But they take special shape in each, altering in form and impact over time. Thus, modes of renewal vary even in the same culture; and the meaning of regeneration itself can change. Although it can be tempting to label such strategies "illogical," the adjective reflects differences in culture more than the objective features of the phenomena described. The rationality and logic of regenerative behavior depends essentially on the correspondence

3

between a society's intent and the actual social result of the behavior the society uses to attain it.[1]

During the nineteenth century, the mode in which individuals and society expected regeneration changed; and sport became an American strategy for renewal. Although spiritual regeneration remained desirable, the spiritual consequences of physical renewal seemed even more critical. In a secular and materialist age, sport began to encroach upon the renewing role of religion and even seized some of its aura and tone. Although sport was not a religion or even a quasi religion, it offered a means to fulfill, at least temporarily, the needs that religion had difficulty in meeting.[2]

RELIGIOUS RENEWAL AND THE IMPORTANCE OF THE BODY

Although hardly the mainstream of European religion in the seventeenth century, New England Puritanism drew on some aspects of that tradition; and it was rooted in common cultural experiences. In this sense, early American religion—whether in New England or elsewhere, Puritan or not—sought to give convincing answers to the compelling questions of life. Religious meetings and rituals took place predictably and with accustomed frequency, adding to the appeal of religion and its persuasiveness as a mode of renewal. Religious regeneration within Christian cultures depended primarily upon physical sacramentalism, particularly in the Roman Catholic and Orthodox traditions, or else upon an inner experience of spiritual conversion. Sacrifice and expiation were thus deeply rooted in both main channels of Christianity—each a means of asserting some measure of control over both one's world and one's eternal destiny. The Puritan emphasis on conversion placed the locus of expiation squarely in Christ, while their Arminian counterparts came to value the works of man as a means of invoking Christ's sacrificial merit. The relaxation of this tenet of New England Puritanism allowed a growing conviction in the worth of man's discipline, sacrificial action, orderly behavior, and gradual "improvement" as the source of regeneration. At the very least, these became its proximate cause. As religion increasingly became a realm of sentiment, under the impact of the Enlightenment and Romanticism, its more disciplined and rig-

4

orous features began to fall away from it and into other institutions. Important beneficiaries included the natural and physical sciences, the human health professions, and the new "sciences of the body." Some of sport's attractiveness, despite its novelty as an institution, derived from its capitalizing on many of these qualities that were bogged in equivocation in much of religion.[3]

While other ages had passionately attended to the salvation of the soul, the nineteenth century increasingly cared about the salvation of the body in this life as well as the next. The preservation and resurrection of the body became a major concern in disciplines such as religion, medicine, nutrition, and physical education, albeit in markedly different ways. Moreover, self-help emerged meaningfully in the regenerative process — man would assume greater responsibility for his own destiny. Within regenerative strategies that relied heavily on the material world, the Arminian sense that man could greatly assist the working of his own salvation on earth strengthened. At the same time, the intense concern over the survival of the body softened the threat in the growing suspicion that physical explanations accounted for the workings of the soul. If thought, emotions, and morals were not commanded by man's "immortal half," then they might at least be conditioned by one's mortal whole. In practice, both doctrines had their adherents and were frequently mixed. But the residual belief in the influence of the soul yielded much ground to a newer conviction in the moral power of the body. The body claimed more attention as a vehicle for right conduct in this world and, increasingly, as the model of life in the next. The growing expectation of an afterlife patterned after life on earth, but raised to unfathomed perfection, reflected this new focus on the value and role of the human body.

Because of the growing importance of scientific and medical research, the appeal of religion as a means of gaining a sense of control over one's life and one's world suffered losses in the nineteenth century; and religion itself changed appreciably. For several decades around mid-century, most denominations had difficulty keeping pace with findings in the sciences; and many acquiesced as secular institutions attempted a limited dominion over the earth. The Puritan tradition, which had originated in the rejection of magic and in condemnation of the numerous rituals of both Roman Catholics and Anglicans as mere sorcery, provided that man could not cause his own improvement. This theological conviction of the exclusive saving effect of divine grace suggested, as its corollary, that human actions reflected the state of the soul but could not govern it. This opinion did little to foster medical research, for example; nor did it encourage rapid accommodation to medical and scientific findings as they emerged. The Arminian strain within the Puritan community, and especially outside it, was more promising in this regard. For it implied that conduct which in one sense only signified the level of a man's morality could, in a different sense, actually shape his moral character. This latter view substituted a moral determinism based on behavior for predestination; and it opened the door to belief in an incremental and increasingly secular salvation achieved largely by man himself, carefully regulating his own behavior and using his accumulated acts to shape his moral as well as physical character. Implications of perfectionism ran boldly through this view, and it invited a secular dogma of progress. Salvation by grace was an all-or-nothing proposition — saved or damned, all in a crucial moment of conversion, everything depending on God. Its emphasis on transformation of one's state was not easily reconciled with the notion of evolutionary gradualism that spread in the nineteenth century. Even when accepting the doctrine of salvation by divine grace, the Arminian tended to take responsibility for improving his own moral behavior and that of his society. Yet, while the triumph of Arminianism supported a view of regeneration rooted in progress and evolutionary improvement even on earth, it also risked losing the task of physical regeneration to secular agents, largely by sanctioning attention to the temporal world and its betterment. A shift in regenerative strategies in America, then, followed from a displacement of religion in man's quest for power over life and from a corresponding enhancement of competing secular institutions.[4]

The increasingly sympathetic understanding of the visible world probably contributed to the strains within religious doctrine, partly by encouraging curiosity about the condition of

6

the body after its promised resurrection. Not all Christian denominations were convinced that resurrection was even possible. Some doubted that a body could be reconstituted after its complete decay, while others questioned if the body were to be resurrected for all eternity. Still another group wondered, if the bodies of both the just and the unjust were raised, whether there would be room for the many millions of the sons of Adam, while others puzzled over the specific form of existence the body would enjoy after the Second Coming. Whatever equivocation and ambiguity existed on this subject began to disappear in the nineteenth century; and the specific nature of the answers offered to these questions reflected much of the positive sentiment for the body that was emerging at the same time. The notion that man was to become a disembodied spirit was generally rejected, and confidence in the value of the body as a vehicle of divine will was affirmed.

The regenerative appeal of Mormonism, whose theology of evolutionary progress aimed largely at resolving the uncertainness already noted, hinged on its assurance of perpetual existence for the human body and on its provision of some explanation of how matter and spirit were to coexist throughout eternity, continuing to enjoy purposeful action and to benefit from experience through the senses. In an age that emphasized energy and activity, death became a special horror, particularly since the Western religious tradition had conventionally made death the end of man's opportunity for moral choice and thus his clear capitulation to divine power. But death was also the end of man's physical strength; and it seemed to be the ultimate insult to people who aimed at establishing power over nature. The character of an afterlife and the status of the body after death consequently attracted religious denominations in the nineteenth century; and the growing belief in bodily resurrection, depending increasingly on the favorable attitude toward the material world, strengthened in turn the sentiment that the body was not an evil thing. For Mormons, the acquisition of bodies by spirits who had enjoyed preexistence before the creation of the earth was a happy event and a stage in their unfolding progress; and, as a result, the Mormons frequently termed the body a "tabernacle," worthy of decent treatment

7

and respect, and destined for a magnificently transformed existence after its death on earth. Thereafter, it would continue happily doing the work of the Lord. As a theology based on progress, Mormonism gutted death of much of its impact by insisting that death was only a transformation of status; and the specific doctrines through which Mormon elders made this assertion explicitly described the promised continuation of life. In the process of exerting their claim of theological power over death, the Mormons had specifically enhanced the moral worth and spiritual utility of bodily life in the material world. The body was a necessary part of the progress of God's created beings and thus a true vehicle of glory and renewal.[5]

Although not a typical religion, as suggested by the early persecution of the Saints and their later confrontation with the federal government, Mormonism was nonetheless distinctly a product of the nineteenth century. In this sense, it exemplifies the strong, new understanding that matter and spirit were linked. On the other hand, Mormonism was not unique. As a philosophical extension of Congregationalist and Unitarian thought, transcendentalism also encouraged a more benevolent view of the human body and the material world, though from a different place in the religious spectrum. Also like Mormonism, transcendentalism was distinctly a child of the age. Though muting the call of formal religion, transcendentalism encouraged a Romantic reverence for nature and, by positing an immanent spirit or "over-soul" in the universe, verged on a pantheistic celebration of matter as the expression of divinity. So, too, it shared an emphasis on self-help — secularized in Ralph Waldo Emerson's call to "self-reliance." Although transcendentalism may have discouraged social organization as a source of strength to the individual, it also reduced dependence upon God either for strength or for regeneration. Thus, transcendental thought enhanced the importance of the material world, encouraged suspicion of the whole realm of metaphysics, threw the individual into the toils of self-help, and brought the erosion of earlier Puritan doctrine to virtual fulfillment. Unlike Mormonism, however, transcendentalism offered little satisfaction to those who craved physical resurrection; and it was perhaps inevitable that many Americans would find an afterlife that was hardly more than a theoretical abstraction a very bitter pill to swallow.[6]

Many who failed to make death a necessary part of progress in the way the Mormons did veered sharply to avoid or "deny" death through a variety of practices. The inheritors of the Puritan tradition, including Unitarians and Congregationalists, became leading exponents of a consolation literature that described heaven as one's true home, in which familial warmth would be restored. So, too, they hoped for the physical perfection of the individual in an unflawed body. Aunt Winifred, a character who sees heaven as her real home in Elizabeth Stuart Phelps's *Gates Ajar* (1868), put it personally: in the afterlife, her hair would no longer be gray, and Heaven would look like Kansas. Thus, Aunt Winifred even anticipated the emphasis on youth — which increasingly characterized the denial of death and gradually became a hallmark of sporting culture. The rise of morticians in the late decades of the nineteenth century, particularly with their arts of embalming and cosmetic treatment of corpses, led to the presentation of the dead as if they were "sleeping"—that is, alive; and the embalmer sought to erase the signs of pain and roll back the years of the deceased. The use of metal caskets supposedly forestalled the normal processes of decay and the return of "dust to dust." The rural cemetery, meanwhile, which paralleled the Olmstedian contemplative park, encouraged the notion of continuous care by the living for the dead; and yet, by the turn of the century, such places shielded against the reality of death as much as inviting its contemplation. The harsh images of skulls and hourglasses common on gravestones of the seventeenth century had long since yielded to the gentle willow. Changes in the practices associated with death thus suggested a change in the American attitude toward life, notably that active life in the material world was something to be treasured. So deep was this concern for the present world and one's own life in it that funerary practices increasingly suggested a macabre quickening of the dead, restored to greater beauty and youth, even before they had been buried. Death was, for some, far too troubling to leave the business of resurrection to God. Man sought to take a hand in this vital matter — even if it was the illusory hand of embalming and cosmetics.[7]

9

Matters were potentially more grim for those who lacked conviction in any religious promise of restoration of the body to the soul after indefinite interment; and anxiety goaded them to search for some other solution that was grounded in the visible world. For such people, youth became much more important; and its prolongation became desirable as the dread of death spawned a fear of aging. Even those who accepted death as simply the fate of all men, as had been felt in early medieval culture, also saw benefit in making the most of one's time here on earth and making it as long as possible. Among the latter group was the philosopher and psychologist William James, who believed that his hiking brought him into direct contact with nature's power and who found organized sport a reasonable human vehicle for experiencing order, discipline, and sacrifice. Even without crude desperation, then, one could see physical exertion and sport as renewing. But when haunted by that desperation, the burden of sport became much heavier — a periodic bodily resurrection within the temporal realm that shaded somewhat one's vision of death and corruption to come. For, it must be understood, the secularization of death gave it an aching finality; and this in turn sharpened the urgency to assume individual responsibility for one's own physical renewal before the last moment came.

The turn toward "child's play," transformed by the genius of organization in the industrial age, projected sport's apparent youthfulness into adulthood, and in so doing it softened the boundaries between the various ages of life. Unlike activities that were tied to a particular period of one's life, sport was becoming functionally timeless.

It has been suggested that everyone, including those without a commitment to a specific religion, must develop a religious sensibility in some fashion or else risk psychological dysfunction.[8] Although the term "human nature" invites debate, the repeated behavior of mankind in different times and cultures suggests that certain concerns persist and questions about one's place in the world and the significance of human life recur. The behavioral qualities approved by American religions — including personal discipline, commitment to a system (such as the Covenant), and sacrificial devotion — did not, in themselves, answer any of those questions. But their repetition, even outside an explicitly religious framework, carried the aura of religion, or at least devotion, into an otherwise secular life. These approved qualities predated industrialization, even if they resembled the work habits deemed desirable in the factories and offices of the late nineteenth century. Their symmetry with virtuous religious practice ennobled the spirit with which people could pursue the other activities to which they were applied. In practice, though rarely in theory, sport became the religious ritual of the machine age — sacrifice without purpose, performance without magic, obsolescence without compensation, and value without meaning.

Sport simultaneously replicated and transformed the behavioral impulses of the era of industrial labor, and it did so at a time when the explanatory and didactic power of religion was somewhat muted. But sport added a sense of form and ritual of its own. Intending to show that sport could enslave the worker to the bourgeois manager, Theodor Adorno has suggested: "Modern sports, one will perhaps say, seek to restore to the body some of the functions of which the machine has deprived it. But they do so only in order to train men all the more inexorably to serve the machine." Yet, from another vantage, a religious vision is a vision of order; and, as the symbolic model of order in the industrial world, the machine had a kind of religious force. Sport may have reduced the human body to a machine, but those who valued the culture represented by the machine could see this treatment of the body as a benefit rather than a calamity. Such, in fact, was the case with the new experts in the "sciences of the body." Further, sport made the body a kind of ritual object — ennobled in the artificially elevated realm of sport, and rated so highly precisely because of its regimen and demands.

In an era of secularization, sport went far to supply Americans with a satisfying and suitable means of regeneration. In an era of specialization, a "priesthood" of experts formed quickly in its service. In an era of organization, this secularized renewal assumed institutional status. Most of all, even though the devotees of sport might avoid the vocabulary of religion when pursuing their favored activities, they could appropriate much of religion's benefit and comfort, since the structure of attitudes

11

in one burlesqued that in the other. For even where the substance of theology had become an exotic profession and where popular religion virtually jettisoned theology, deep sentiments and anthropologically identifiable needs remained — ritual, communion, time and cycle, regeneration and renewal. What altered was the sense of strategy to meet those needs.[9]

FOUNTAINS OF YOUTH, WELLSPRINGS OF HEALTH

A different form of regeneration had actually been lacking from the American scene altogether. This was the "total regenerative bath," and its conspicuous absence from America created a gap in which sport gained an image of moral and social purpose. As care of the soul focused more on the destiny of the body than it had before, the regeneration of the body shifted from restful leisure toward organized activity. Here the concept of self-help was broadened frequently to the context of the group, in which the individual worked toward his own renewal in the setting of secular society.[10]

An important tradition within human culture has linked care and regeneration of the body with the bath, not only as a matter of hygiene — and, indeed, sometimes not primarily for this purpose — but as a means of restoring energy and vitality to the bather. In fact, the bath as a leisurely restorative must be distinguished from cleansing, which is only one phase in the total bathing cycle, and especially from mere cleansing of the skin's surface, which is its last and least aspect. The most typical forms of the total regenerative bath include the steam bath (the Islamic or "Turkish" bath), the sweat bath (induced by dry heat as in Scandinavia, Amerindian cultures, or Russia), or variants using tubs and large pools which combine immersion with warm and humid air (as in the classical Roman bath and that of medieval northern Europe). All of them compel relaxation and ease, and all take time. Further, all seek to purify the person from the inside out. Cleansing, then, became internalized. By "expelling wastes," perspiration acquires a renewing purpose. This bathing format also parallels the numerous purification rites in so-called primitive religions, in which internal purity and renewal are essential; and, although European cultures in the modern era jettisoned this explicit connection between reli-

12

gion and the regenerative bath, vestiges of the impulse toward purification remained even after religious forms had changed and the bath had become secularized.[11]

Differences among regenerative baths (and also the decision to substitute mere surface cleansing) suggest differences in mentality and in the social goals set for the bath. Customarily, noblemen in medieval Europe conducted business in the bath, extending an aura of ease over the conduct of their affairs. The physical structure of the Islamic bath, to take another case, created a mood of calm beauty, intended to induce a hushed and relaxed manner in the bather as well as a contemplative mood. The Roman *thermae*, by contrast, were open to bright daylight and full sun. A brief consideration of two major types of regenerative bath suggests how the inclination toward one over the other (and their relationship to simple ablution) improved the chance of finding meaning and value in sport.

Both high Islamic culture and Roman culture shortly after Christ greatly emphasized the regenerative bath. The most notable difference between them was the fact that the Roman *thermae* did not need intense steam-laden air to stimulate perspiration since, unlike the Islamic baths, the *thermae* were physically connected to *palestrae* and *stadia* where the bathers had already brought on sweat through athletic exercise. The common ground between the Roman and Islamic baths was, most simply, sweat; but they grew out of different notions about how regeneration was effected. For the Romans, the bath was linked with athletic exercise and sport, and these became an intrinsic part of the regenerative process. As a corollary, the sporting activities gained a ritual and social purpose. Siegfried Giedion has suggested: "The obstinacy with which Rome and Byzantium, until their decline, and Islam, until the onset of mechanized life, clung to their total regeneration shows how deepseated in human nature is the need for such institutions." Equally significant, however, was the fact that it took specialized forms in different cultures. Some, as with Islam, adopted a basically passive, subdued approach; others, as with Rome, broke the regenerative process into identifiable parts, at least one of which — sporting activity — was expressive and active.[12]

The regenerative process typified by the Islamic bath ran afoul

13

of certain cardinal points in the creed of late nineteenth-century America. Correspondingly, it never achieved institutional success. For one thing, it violated the instinct toward "time-thrift." Whether one said that idleness was an invitation to the Devil or that time was money, it was difficult to see value in lying wrapped in towels in a dimly-lit steam-room for much of an afternoon while the world passed one by. In an age when activity was nearly a synonym for life, such a practice seemed to be the embrace of entropy.[13] The languid aura of the Islamic bath contradicted the energetic spirit of late nineteenth-century America and had the scent of self-indulgent evil. On the other hand, sweat itself attained a certain legitimacy. Indeed, it was an achievement of considerable importance when Americans began to question and reinterpret the long hostility toward the regenerative bath. Given their disposition to value work highly, Americans not surprisingly found a means of drawing virtue from the "sweat of the brow" of members of the middle and upper middle class, thus extending the protective rhetoric of the work-ethic over the active, physically strenuous life. But the Americans resolved the conflicts in their attitudes toward physical regeneration only by subjecting it to segmentation — breaking it into component elements, much as was being done in other aspects of the culture.

The very absence of the total bath as a common feature in American life invited the rise of some other, related mode of regeneration. More like the Romans than the Turks, the Americans separated the process of sweating from the immediate effect of cleansing, thus shifting the locus of regeneration to that which raised the sweat rather than to the sweating itself or the process of its removal. Thus, while cleansing was relegated to quickly executed surface ablution, as suggested by the rising emphasis on the shower bath and on technical terms such as "personal hygiene," regenerative effect was imputed to strenuous effort in work and play. Thus both work and sport seemed good for a man, since the two shared a certain kinship. The linking of athletic exercise to the superficial cleansing bath thus formed a package that compared in overall effect with what other civilizations got from the regenerative bath; and action assumed a regenerative role. The appeal of the "strenuous life," so often

14

associated with Theodore Roosevelt and his friends, did not lie in an egotistical triumph over demanding conditions alone, but also in the belief that it peculiarly refreshed the body and renewed the spirit. It was in the world of experience and action, then, that Americans could find their way to regeneration. After much vacillation, then, Americans settled on simple ablution, reinforced by the mechanized standardization of tubs and showers.[14] Ablution, however, tended toward privacy and left the social and public functions of regeneration to other institutions. In considerable measure, sport claimed it. The obsession with winning in athletics and the vocabulary and metaphors for discussing it are illustrative. For example, to say that losing is a little like dying is to imply that athletic victory is being born anew. As the athletic enterprise became increasingly social, winning became a means of social as much as personal renewal.

Yet, even as this happened, sport itself remained touched with the society's long ill-ease over the public display of muscle and the body. The confusion of nakedness with intimacy encouraged some traditionalists to discourage publicity about their sporting events and their athletes, and even to restrict attendance at games. The gradual standardization of sport-costumes into uniforms, aside from its obvious impact on sharpening an athlete's identification with his team, relieved some of this inner tension and made it far easier for sport to exert a social and socializing effect. To the extent that the degree of exposure of the body was a matter of social agreement and public sanction, the sports uniform became the expression and the vehicle for carrying that sanction into practice. As a conceptual matter, then, sport was being divorced from the conscious sense of physical intimacy and was neutralized so that its emotional content was contained and its sensuality masked by the cloak of discipline.[15]

Leisure and sensuality, then, were both held at arm's length by the emerging institution of sport; and the growing esteem of discipline, suggesting to later critics a perversion of the "play instinct," put sport under the socially respected aegis of order. Prominent among these later critics, Freudian Marxists have raised beneficial questions, while agreeing that sport serves a regenerative role, albeit a deplorable compensatory one. As Jean-Marie Brohm has concluded, for example, the worker's claim of a right to sport along with the right to work reflects sport's deep grounding in the ideology of capitalism, particularly in the alienation of labor and in the application of work-principles to all aspects of life. For the Freudian Marxist, sport becomes, by reduction, a sublimation of sexuality and a denial of sensual leisure, while free expression is transformed into a mimicry of work. The compensation which Brohm and others believe sport encourages enables the worker to relieve the nervous tension created by being, as Marx alleged, a mere appendage of the machine. Moreover, in arguing that sport relieves the potential for political unrest by sapping nervous energy and masking frustrations (a peculiar parallel to Paxson's application of the Turnerian "safety valve" to sport), the Marxist critics reinforce the assertion that sport strengthens the optimistic passivity of the working class and thereby extends the bourgeois order's lease on life.[16]

In another sense, however, critics have alleged that sport was aimed at the physical renewal of the worker, albeit for exploitative purposes. Sport called into being a whole new group of "technocrats of the body" whose business it is to promote a Stakhanovite assault on leisure time. These "recuperation technicians," as Brohm has called them, contribute to harmonious relations in industry and society by compensating for the fatigue of the factory with the therapy of sport, which is fatiguing in itself and thus simultaneously keeps the worker docile and fit. Thus, sport is a "fountain of youth for its wage slaves," who maintain higher productivity for a longer time. Absent the casual and sensual regenerative bath, presumably kept out of the scene as inappropriate to an industrial society, sport is a well of health to prolong the productive life of the workers.[17]

One unavoidable problem with sport, for the Freudian Marxist, is that it does not seem to be true leisure at all. Instead, in Brohm's terms, it is "an institutionalized celebration of the mortification of the flesh" which acts out a fundamentally sado masochistic ideology. In its "compulsive repetitiveness and sexual frustration," sport shows a pathologically obsessive commitment to "discipline and self-mastery." Thus, sport becomes a process of eagerly sought suffering wherein the individual pleasures himself through self-denial and the pursuit of sublimated death. The repression of the body is thus warped into a quasireligious phenomenon; and sport, much like religion (to which Marxists imply it is a partial successor), becomes the opiate of the masses.[18]

What never seemed palatable to the Marxist was the possibility that the workers, as well as the bourgeoisie, might genuinely value the mechanized society itself and even aspire to personal imitation of a machine. In the American context, the assertion that workers labored under "false consciousness" fails to account for the centuries-long fascination of Americans with machines and gadgets and the unsettling fact that it has historically been a compliment to suggest that an American has performed as efficiently as a machine. The Marxist description of how sport functions is not without foundation, and it even strengthens the view that sport has a regenerative role. But it founders on the complex motivations and interests of the athlete.[19]

The Marxist critique might be left a matter of historiography were it not for the symmetry between their analysis of sport (though not their verdict on it) and that of the industrial capitalists of nineteenth-century America. Because of this, the Marxist analysis suggests insights into the views of the industrialists. After all, the general legitimacy of sport in society and its specific claim to regenerative power depended more on the opinions of articulate members of the middle and upper classes than on the preferences of the workers. Despite the influence of the working class in the disposition of public parks and their impact on sports programs, the promotion of sport in the industrial context was primarily the burden of the managers. Although some forms of company-sponsored activities needed little sacrifice or discipline, industrial promoters of sport often favored athletic competition to generate desirable work habits. Business leaders were hardly shy about exerting influence over the lives of their workers — a lingering aspect of traditional paternalism, as well as a function of management under industrial capitalism. Consequently, unhampered by reluctance to give advice or to intrude on the privacy of their workers, company officials proclaimed the worth of sport as a remedy to unhealthy amuse-

17

ments, as a refreshment to the workers, and as a wellspring of order and discipline as much as health.[20]

The growing perception that sport encouraged the health of the body and spirit was a variant of the broader interest in therapeutic intervention. Pioneers, such as Vincenz Priessnitz who developed a famous water cure in Switzerland, often risked challenge as fakers and quacks in the early decades of the nineteenth century; but they helped to open a wide-ranging study of the effects of physical phenomena—such as water and electricity—on man's psychic as well as physical health. Later, experts in human health professions sought to solve problems and minister to the personal needs of their subjects, drawing on the long but inconsistent tradition of health-cures and fads. The advances in medicine during the century were little short of incredible, including major advances in surgery made possible by W.T.G. Morton's and C.T. Jackson's experiments with ether and anesthesia and Lister's advances in antisepsis. Simultaneous strides in the substance of medical knowledge, the quality of medical training, and the efficiency of medical organization created a much enhanced sense of the power of the physician over the human body—one who could dispel evils, and one whose inability to bring people back from the dead was compensated by his growing power to keep them from getting there in the first place. Changes in the quality of medical care encouraged hope of recovery. While mortality rates among victims of disease and trauma had previously been so high as to put the focus persistently on death, the growing strength of medicine permitted even the expectation of survival.[21]

Nutritionists contributed to the view that, by applying scientific principles, human life could be improved, personal vitality enhanced, efficiency increased, and life prolonged. Sylvester Graham's remarkably prescient instincts concerning food and diet in the antebellum period derived from a general spirit of reform; but he escaped some of its limits, suggesting a link between physical behavior (in this case, the intake of food) and moral character. By the late decades of the century, a scientific effort was mounted to upgrade the diet of Americans. Stellar figures such as Horace Fletcher emerged and popularized nutrition. But even more demonstrative of its place in general reform was the involvement of the U.S. Department of Agriculture, especially through its Office of Experiment Stations. Prominent businessmen such as Edward Atkinson contributed to the cause, and chemists-turned-nutritionists sought to found public kitchens in major cities. Meanwhile, extensive experiments tested the relationship between nutrition and human performance, as in the work of Russell Chittenden at Yale's Sheffield Scientific School.[22]

Not surprisingly, Chittenden was a physical educator; and he and his professional colleagues asserted sport's contribution to health perhaps even more vigorously than other groups. Despite the slogan *mens sana in corpore sano*, the physical educators' practical programs focused on the *corpus* and its work in the world. Dudley A. Sargent, one of the country's leading physical educators, added to the hint of man's secular perfectibility by emphasizing "corrective gymnastics," which would ensure the equal and symmetrically balanced development of the body. Unlike some of the other constituencies favoring sport, physical educators perceived sport only as a means to the fulfillment of human health, as an enrichment of the human spirit by transference from physical well-being, and never as an end in itself. In this way, physical education conformed to the doctrine of self-help and to the belief that man could attempt secular renewal.

Health care, in sum, was entering the realm of regeneration; and, if it did not absolutely demand optimism, it made it more reasonable. Increasingly credible as an attainable state, health risked displacing spiritual grace as a center of concern. Therapeutic intervention suggested something essential to the rise of sport — the increasing belief that life on earth could be a good thing, that disease and suffering were abnormal, and that a secularized heaven could be attempted in this world. Whatever their theological views may have been, health professionals thus contributed to an underlying sense that, whatever might happen at the Resurrection, renewal occurred on earth.

THE FEAR OF EXHAUSTION

The search for renewal came largely in reaction to the fear of exhaustion, and it became an open concern in society. Some

Americans explicitly sought new sources of strength and energy, admitting their fear that one's personal energy could be easily sapped. The obvious activity of society as a whole suggested the need for some means of replenishing the reserves. Meanwhile, the individual must conserve his own supply and hope for restoration. Seeing power in material and even physical terms, Americans readily opted for material and physical remedies for deficiencies observed, imagined, or predicted. Explicit connections between sport and the regeneration of the body ultimately appeared, notably in connection with the concept of spermatic economy. According to this theory, the human male possessed a limited quantity of sperm which could be invested in various enterprises, ranging from business through sport to copulation and procreation. In this context, the careful regulation of the body was the only path to conservation of energy. But discovery of an activity that would actually regenerate the body would be far better, making the body a renewable resource, rather like one of Gifford Pinchot's forests.[23]

The fear of limits and the desire to expand — this dread of running out of whatever stuff it was that had brought America to what it considered success — showed itself in many ways. As Elting Morison has observed, the sense that the rapid invention of machines was lowering the reservoir of knowledge led to the institutionalization of research. What applied in the physical and natural sciences also applied, in a parallel way, to social science and public behavior. In this sense, the newly created General Electric Laboratory compared with Yale's Sheffield Scientific Laboratory, which conducted experiments in human performance. Charles Steinmetz, as a searcher after new volumes of knowledge and understanding, had his match in Russell Chittenden or Dudley Sargent. In both cases, the search had begun to renew and refill the pool of American resources.[24]

It is hardly a mystery that a culture increasingly familiar with the vocabulary and processes of a mechanized world feared entropy. Nor was it odd, given the scientific efforts to establish mechanical models for the workings of physics and chemistry in organism, that machine and organism sometimes seemed identical. Capturing these themes in a single phrase, Brooks Adams observed in 1913: "Human society is a living organism, work-

20

ing mechanically, like any other organism." In a later essay about his brother Henry's contribution to American thought, Brooks referred to George Washington's vision of the national capital as organic (despite its rationalistic plan), with a university serving as "the brain of the corporeal system developed by the highways."[25] But the model of the organism had its perils. Henry Adams, for example, dismissed the notion of inevitable upward evolution as desperate, pathetic, and simply false. He denied the indestructibility of energy, thus charging human agents with the task of sustaining the social organism. The observation that organisms were affected by their environment harmonized with the fact that machines were shaped by will and altered by tinkering. But both models—either individually or working synergistically—brought visions of decay and anxiety about the need for new energy. After all, organisms died and machines wore out.

In his almost lyrical essay "The Dynamo and the Virgin," Henry Adams captured the love of the machine in industrial cultures and the dynamo's displacement of the Virgin Mother of God as the tie between humble earth and transcendent power. It was more than a matter of utility—it was faith, perhaps even passion, contained within the discipline of industrialism. Belief in the machine as the model, and the dynamo as the image, of power in society had its parallels outside the factory precincts. It appeared in certain mechanical health devices—electrical belts to cure kidney disease, electrical brushes to calm nervous disorders, and the like. It also appeared in sporting circles, where trainers increasingly used specially designed practice machines and where the team itself was thought to generate energy beyond the sum of its parts. Experimentation with electrical devices to cure exhaustion helped Americans move from a static sense of the body, which made depletion and exhaustion such a terror, toward a more dynamic sense of the body as capable of restoration.

Yet machinery could not supplant the human experts who now rose to professional status in physical education, athletic management, coaching, and training. Nor did the devices they employed teeter on the brink of quackery. The professionals shunned the "quick fix." Instead, they sought to improve their

21

charges by careful training and by developing teamwork. The very structure of a team made it seem a kind of energy-system requiring efficient performance from all players in order to generate current. In some descriptions of sporting events, even the spectators became a part of the system. Albert Spalding, seeking to give women a practical and creative role in baseball (which he thought they should never play), claimed that the team on the field could literally suck in power from the crowd in the stands. The spectators became a pulsing mechanism, set in motion by the triggering action on the field. The team and the crowd together became a kind of dynamo.[26]

Theodore Roosevelt did not comment specifically on Spalding's assertions, but he shared the commitment to producing energy with sport. Commenting on Brooks Adams's *The Law of Civilization and Decay* but dissenting from its pessimism, Roosevelt insisted that renewal must be possible through a combination of discipline and the "strenuous life." Reviewing the role of sport in the rise of the British empire, the American commentator Price Collier adopted a view much like Roosevelt's. In *England and the English from an American Point of View* (1916), he decried luxury as the "most insidious of all foes," much as Brooks Adams argued. The Americans should continue imitating the British to reap benefit, and the roughness of their sport would inculcate daring and dynamism. Costs would be high, he admitted. The British, for example, spent an estimated $200 million per year on sport during the 1910s. But Collier judged it a great investment, concluding that "the governing races of to-day are races of sportsmen. The peoples who are inheriting the earth to-day," he added with intentional irony, "are the peoples who play games, perhaps because their contests make them meek!"[27]

For Americans who feared that the New England stock was declining in numbers and social influence, sport came to be associated with sexual behavior — first as a means of guarding what they thought to be the limited sexual energy of the male, and later as a means of increasing his sexual potency and improving the woman's capacity to bear healthy children. The first of these interests tapped religious and moral belief but also merged with current notions about sexuality. As a religious matter, sexual intercourse won moral approval under the biblical injunction to be fruitful and multiply. At the same time, however, many practical problems such as the sharp decline in infant and child mortality made this earnest propagation of the faith a financially and socially straining proposition. The educated moralist was likely to urge restraint in sexual affairs and to encourage continence or even abstinence—much as Thomas Malthus did in England. Against this background, any morally acceptable prophylactic against unwanted sexual activity helped; and bodily exercise began gaining advocates among ministers and doctors even in the antebellum period. Their approval of exercise and sport seems to have depended on the understanding that they did not deplete "nervous energy." By contrast, sexual activity was widely seen as draining this reserve. (There was an alternative view pitting nervous excitability against reasoned restraint, but this limited sexual activity and invited sublimation through sport simply by inverting the reasoning.) Even the term applied to sexual dysfunction—"sexual neurasthenia"— suggested this, since "neurasthenia" was inexactly translated as "exhaustion." Exhaustion and depletion, then, were linguistically associated with nerves. On the other hand, work and sport (to the extent that the latter replicated the patterns of the former) placed demands on the body other than in its nervous functions. Thus, the Reverend John Todd, a prolific and influential writer of sexual guidance and antimasturbation literature at mid-century, advocated bodily exercise and hard manual labor as remedies for the dreaded "disease" of "secret vice."[28]

Generally, Todd suggested that intimacy with women drained male strength, while association with men might increase it. While the latter point was ambiguous, the former was absolute. Todd showed compulsive interest in exerting command over his study, his house, and his life; and he clearly saw his family as something of a nuisance, jeopardizing his unqualified control over his life by governing its conditions. Thus, in his *Student's Manual* (1835), he encouraged readers to embrace the world—but it was a world sex-typed as male. Todd claimed that the male gained energy by being thrown about with other men and compared the process to sport. He was as "a football among men, thrown wherever they please, and in the power of every man." The Reverend Todd thus helped to lay a foundation of thought which later proponents of football carried toward its logical reduction, when they asserted that it cultivated manly values. It was the shock of conflict, according to Todd, which generated an "electricity" that gave "all the powers of your mind new energy." Isolated from the other sex, men thus sought new power while protecting the old.[29]

Dr. Augustus Kinsley Gardner, an innovator in gynecological surgery and an author of moral and sexual guidance literature, pursued concerns much like Todd's and brought them more directly to back sport. In *Our Children* (1872), Gardner urged boys and young men to engage in athletics, insisting that such activity guarded the player from sexual vice (primarily masturbation) and inculcated desirable moral qualities. He faced the problem of time-thrift squarely, observing: "It takes time to be an athlete, and time is money." But he reconciled himself to sport because he believed that its social benefits exceeded its costs in time. Gardner's concern over the prospect of "race decline"— the shrinking in numbers of the old stock— made him eager to conserve sexual energy; and he concluded that physical education and athletics served this end, helping to "develope our bodies, or even our souls symmetrically." The survival of the traditional stock, the re-creation of conventional morals, and the balanced development of the body thus merged in his thinking; and sport was grasped by all three. With thoughtful guidance, Gardner concluded, there was no reason why "a physical culture, and consequent perfection similar to that of the Greeks should not take root in America." The doctor's discussions of physical development thus dipped into the vocabulary and conceptual baggage of the physical educator; but the focus of his concerns was somewhat different. The praise he heaped on sport was contingent on his view of the Anglo-Saxon as the carrier of morality; and so he judged that a boy who failed to develop the moral character that sport supposedly nurtured "had far better be dead."[30]

To the man who fulfilled his duty by limiting sexual activity to the minimum necessary to keep the race vital, there lay the promise of dominance and power — a promise made more convincing by Gardner's advocacy of military training for all males.

24

He thought this would help to counter the debilitating luxuries of urban living that America's economic successes made possible. In this respect, he anticipated Brooks Adams's repeated attacks on decadence and the corrosive impact of "economic man." "We are living in a hot-house," Gardner wrote in *Conjugal Sins,* "where our nervous energies are developed at the expense of our physique." The imperfect air and light of the city, coupled with the city-dweller's dangerously stimulating food and inaptness for exercise, encouraged one to pour out energy in sexual excess, which, in turn, merely worsened appetites and derangement. Always the exponent of sublimation, Gardner continued to rail against "physical excess" in copulation and advocated instead a devotion to physical culture. Even procreation was a danger, but copulation merely for pleasure undermined health. By contrast, a well-developed physique was evidence of a job well done (much like a pregnancy), and the pleasure of sport was skimmed off and turned into moral renewal.[31]

In the years during which Theodore Roosevelt made his pronouncements on behalf of the "strenuous life," Dr. George M. Beard, a practicing physician and writer of manuals in the tradition of Gardner (though with a far greater concentration on medical rather than moral guidance), continued praising the energetic type as the paragon of bodily health and sexual continence. In *Sexual Neurasthenia* (1898) he declared: "The strong, the phlegmatic, the healthy, the well-balanced temperaments — those who live out-doors and work with the muscle more than the mind — are not tormented with sexual desire to the same degree or in the same way as the hysterical, the sensitive, the nervous — those who live in-doors and use the mind much and muscle very little." It was far more likely, according to Beard, that "the delicate, finely-organized lads of our cities and of the higher civilization" would be driven to lurid excess and to the substitution of illicit cravings for morally positive social and commercial enterprise.[32] Nevertheless, there was an undertone of difference — at least in emphasis — between Beard and Gardner.

Writing later than Gardner and speaking to somewhat altered concerns, Beard answered the suspicion that sport might actually impair the player's sexual and bodily powers. This accounted for his urgency in citing the alleged ease with which

25

"savages and semi-savages," American blacks under slavery, and "the strong, healthy farming population in all civilized countries" triumphed over the annoyance of sexual desire "when they have no opportunities for gratification . . . ." The anxiety over sport's effect on sexual functions led some promoters to undertake what they considered scientific study to establish a definitive answer. If the prospect of "race decline" was a serious one and if sport interfered with male sexual potency, then the increasing popularity of sport in the colleges endangered the traditional elites. Fearing the worst, Dr. C.J. Engelmann conducted a study of alumni who had been varsity oarsmen at Harvard, expecting to find that their marriages were less satisfying, their children fewer, and their health uncertain. The depths of his fear added to his elation when he concluded the opposite. According to Engelmann, the oarsmen were superior "in the matter of perpetuating the best elements of the American race" and especially "in all points relating to the question of race decline." A larger than average percentage of oarsmen married, and they had more children. Infertile marriages were few. All but a handful of crew alumni reported themselves in unusually good health. Although Engelmann's research methods and logic were flawed, his results met a sympathetic reception. George L. Meylan of Columbia University reported the findings with unconcealed relief in the March 1904 issue of the *Harvard Graduates' Magazine*. After all, Meylan and others like him were rejoicing in news that affected them personally. Increasingly, at least for the male, anxiety that sport might limit sexual potency was yielding to a suspicion that it aided sexual renewal.[33]

It is clear that there were varying approaches toward the regeneration of body and spirit. In the American experience, the rise of one belief did not mean the demise of its logical contrary, nor did it require the complete disappearance of any other strategy of regeneration. What changed was the mix — the whole set of methods available to Americans. The novelties among the methods reflected whatever was institutionally novel in the culture as a whole. In this respect, sport entered the scene and forged links with other major forces — autonomous, but reciprocal.

The growing accommodation of Americans with their bodies

26

permitted them to adapt their traditions to the nineteenth century's special emphasis on the material world. Thus were born the various strategies of regeneration, tugged by the residual undercurrent of myth but appealing to the logic of self-help and applied science. Sport's growing capacity to carry myth itself suggested the shifting emphasis toward the body over the soul; and, with the confusion of physical discipline with moral character, Thomas Wentworth Higginson's phrase "saints and their bodies" gained new meaning and force. To a considerable extent, this positive attitude toward the body's role in renewal depended on creating, at the very least, a morally and emotionally neutral vision of the body itself. It was secularized as it lost its old identity as a source of sin and a sign of divine disfavor after the expulsion from Eden; and the body was treated as if it were the triumph of the industrial age — a machine. The rationalism of the age and the mystery of religious belief, each pulled some distance away from its originating institution, seemed joined in the attribution of regenerative functions to sport. The varying ways of identifying and promoting this role were the brain children of the several constituent groups advocating the rise of sport.

CHAPTER 2

Social Efficiency and the Spirit of Victory — The Ideas and Sporting Practices of Politicians and Military Officers

IN 1896, everybody loved a winner, and few Americans loved to win as much as Senator Henry Cabot Lodge. Prominent in the affairs of the Republican party, ardent in his support of American commercial expansionism, and the scion of two distinguished New England families, Lodge identified the spirit of victory as the energizing force in the nation's destiny. He believed that athletic victories physically manifested this spirit. At a dinner during commencement week in June 1896, he recalled for his fellow alumni at Harvard his own enthusiasm for rowing and baseball and his pride of accomplishment in winning. He and his classmates of '71 had excelled in the sports and athletics that formed a wholly new realm of social enterprise and a new kind of education. "The time given to athletic contests," Lodge reminisced, "and the injuries incurred on the playing field are part of the price which the English-speaking race has paid for being world-conquerors."[1] Winning at Harvard was a prelude to winning a world.

Hardly an average citizen, Lodge nonetheless exemplified an influential segment of American society that was trained to adopt a role of leadership in the nation's political affairs and in its foreign relations. Numerous political leaders, particularly those emerging from the genteel tradition, and a growing cadre of Army and Navy officers were captivated by the psychology of victory; and they linked sport to a general program for renewing their society and reordering world affairs. They included the likes of Lodge and Theodore Roosevelt, secretaries of war such as Elihu Root, Army Chief of Staff Leonard Wood, and

28

Shown here in 1896, when he spoke at the Harvard commencement, Senator Henry Cabot Lodge exemplified those national leaders who advocated sport as a key to a masterful national character. Such public figures lent respectability to sport and claimed for it a role in achieving national objectives. Photo by C. Chickering of Boston. By permission of the Library of Congress, Biographical Files.

Rear Admiral R.D. Evans who commanded the North Atlantic Fleet — men who placed great emphasis on personal commitment as the cornerstone of public achievement. As these politicians and officers made their public pronouncements and sometimes pursued practical policies to promote sport and organized physical education, they came to form a highly visible and reputable constituency strengthening sport's grasp at institutional permanence and importance. Although some of these leaders specifically sought to alter the character of middle- and working-class Americans by changing their sporting behavior, their impact may have been even greater in lending the dignity of their offices to sports such as football and boxing that had once been the realm of children and ruffians. Thus, they helped to change the climate in which sport could emerge to prominence, even while they made some specific contribution by advocating sports of their own choosing.

Lodge captured the mood of many who shared his background and interests, or aspired to them, and advanced their particular version of an underlying community of ideas which they shared with various other constituencies of sport. For one thing, the widespread determination to create a scientifically rational and efficient society became a precondition for experimenting with sport to shape American institutions, particularly in light of the ambivalent legacy of Darwinian thought. Seen one way, the concept of "natural selection" contributed to the idea of progress by suggesting that physical and intellectual gains were possible; seen differently, it also showed that the same mechanisms could lead to the decline and extinction of species. Will and sacrifice were imperative, but so was adaptability. Nothing could be achieved without personal commitment, yet the individual will could not negate heredity. To some extent, anatomy was destiny, at least in the particular case of each human life; yet each man or woman had a unique duty to develop fully the scope of this biological fate. At the same time, the growing effort to condition behavior allowed some latitude for change. The rational and efficient society, then, coupled the predisposition toward order with the necessity for change, making change the end product of behavioral conditioning and thus allying it to the survivability of an evolving order. Within this frame-

30

work, sport was to be taken as a guarantor of the existing order of society, even as it was expected to generate moral qualities whose kind or intensity might alter that order in the future. Although much of what Lodge and other American leaders said about the importance of physical exercise was anticipated by the Muscular Christians such as Thomas Wentworth Higginson and Thomas Hughes, the greater credence given to such comments during the last decade of the nineteenth century distinguished them from the claims made earlier. The fact that health reformers, nutritionists, and Muscular Christians were fewer and more scattered than later in the century had opened them to charges of eccentricity and faddism. By the end of the century, however, practical behavior in the world and remedies for its improvement played against a different level and range of philosophical assumptions. The sense of oddity then dropped from the increasingly ritualized homilies linking sport and social achievement. The rise of philosophical pragmatism and its incorporation into daily conduct challenged the separation between thought and fact, between an object of study and the means for its examination. It was an age that placed special emphasis on "physical learning"— not so much learning about the body, although that was increasingly attempted, but actually learning by means of it. The genteel tradition in America had never shown quite the disdain for the body and the world that sometimes appeared among evangelical and even moderate contemporaries. But in the late decades of the nineteenth century, the more positive and tolerant attitude toward the body among the heirs of the genteel tradition was paralleled by a shift in thinking among other Americans. Reflecting an underlying shift of philosophy, mortification of the flesh in service of faith yielded to training and conditioning the body in pursuit of victory.[2]

THE DEPENDENCE OF CHARACTER ON EXPERIENCE

The commitment of genteel politicians and military officers to the importance of sport depended upon their usually unconscious but often manifest ideology of experience — an intense belief in the intrinsic worth of experience itself, an advocacy of ideals that promised a chance of practical attainment, an insistence that moral force must show itself in social action. In sum, physical actions were taken to have social effects and moral impact; and social and moral aspiration were seen to have meaning only through physical expressions. In this way, the development of a vigorous personality capable of leadership at home and abroad proceeded from the nineteenth-century genteel tradition, extending the premises for cultivating the gentleman into the means for producing statesmen and warriors. The American gentry's disposition to see manners as the building blocks of genteel character reflected, on a philosophical level, an inclination to see experience as the antecedent to theory. Although one might have a sense of the goal toward which one aspired in the fabrication of the gentleman, the goal itself was only the distillation of innumerable deeds and gestures carried out over a period of many years. The commitment to act in detail according to a lengthy code did not automatically require either prior belief in, or understanding of, the principles from which the code itself derived. More likely, those principles would be summaries of experience undertaken along the lines of little-questioned traditions — general projections from the vast data-base of the particular. As the man became the gentleman by acting like one, so did he become a leader and a winner by doing the same; and it became the more important to seek out arenas in which leading and winning could be experienced with regularity.[3]

For Henry Cabot Lodge, whose speech to the alumni at Harvard in 1896 was a specific example of this general mentality, the role of athletic competition in shaping character was practical and not metaphorical. Sport did not imitate other experiences that yielded values which the society favored; it actually produced them by means that occasionally resembled activities other than athletics, although the resemblance was only incidental. Training and competition in sport were taken to create a pattern of conduct and to shape a habit of success; and the conscious pursuit of sport had the effect of producing an unconscious but deep commitment to victory. This process worked not through a ritualistic appeal to sentiment but by the practical governance of behavior, introducing physical order and discipline into the actual experience of young men fated to serve their country as leaders. For the "spirit of victory" was only another expression for a concrete phenomenon. As Lodge said: "It is but another phrase for what the philosopher dealing with nations calls social efficiency. It is the spirit which subordinates the individual to the group, and which enables that group, whether it be a college or a nation, to achieve great results and attain to high ideals."[4] By equating the spirit of victory with social efficiency, Lodge made clear that he expected sport to pattern conduct and mold action rather than merely to affect mood or attitude. After all, the spirit of victory existed only as its own expression in social action. "Attaining to high ideals" meant actualizing them as programs and policies in the material world. High ideals, in sum, expressed themselves as great deeds and had no actual existence apart from them.

This approach, which permeated Lodge's thinking, virtually necessitated scrutiny of all behavior and public display, since maximum social efficiency was practically equated with the accumulation of moral strengths, achieved through a physical process of conditioning. In this sense, moral power was rooted in physical, material experience; and it was both concrete and specific. Therefore, when Lodge praised baseball, football, and rowing as generators of moral force and social efficiency, he meant that these sports actually developed the predictable and customary behavior needed to act as a national or world leader. Only in a casual sense would the Senator have said that sport was a training for war, or a preparation for responsibilities in the world. Such a statement would have focused on an alleged similarity between sport and war (something that a twentieth-century football coach was far more likely to do than a nineteenth-century politician, and largely as metaphor). Instead, the key was that sport produced moral qualities within the character of the athlete that could be applied to virtually any later social enterprise. To compare sport and war was to engage in a rhetorical exercise; but to speak of the moral effect of sport within the character of the individual athlete was to claim a behavioral molding of real human beings. In favoring baseball, football, and rowing, Lodge hoped to inculcate specifically the quality of teamwork or, as he put it, a "capacity for acting together" which was precisely the heart of social efficiency and the reason why the English-speaking people were "the conquering race of modern times."[5]

It was to Henry Cabot Lodge, his friend and political confidant, that Theodore Roosevelt dedicated *American Ideals*, a collection of essays first published in 1897 in which Roosevelt argued similarly for the inseparability of ideals and action. Any right interest in politics compelled a man to act, according to Roosevelt, "undeterred by the blood and the sweat." His biographers and commentators observed this quality in Roosevelt during his own time. Speaking of Roosevelt's youth, Hermann Hagedorn wrote in 1918: "While he was developing the muscles of his spirit, Theodore Roosevelt was with no less persistence developing the muscles of his body." Hagedorn's emphasis that Roosevelt was not a natural athlete underscored the reciprocal relationship and value of will and action, and he linked physical strength and moral force in this biography, which was intended to serve as a model for American boys to emulate. The French commentator and traveler Felix Klein, who met Roosevelt after he became President, perceived this same concern for practical achievement: ". . . . he has always the same end in view; and whether it is through the emulation of heroic examples, or by actual deeds, or the beauty of moral ideas, his purpose ever is to elevate and stimulate to higher effort the souls of his fellow-citizens. The theory of 'art for art's sake' does not seem to him worthy of discussion." Indeed, for Roosevelt, nothing was to be pursued for its own sake but only in the context of the general social good. If the man of affairs employed his ability wrongly, he became "noxious." If he were doctrinaire, he would become "useless." Roosevelt even suggested an equation of efficiency with moral status when he asserted that "the doer is *better* than the critic and that the man who strives stands far above the man who stands aloof . . ." (emphasis added). Drawing on his own early experiences and offering a simile "from the football field" to enjoin his readers, Roosevelt proclaimed: ". . . success can only come to the player who 'hits the line hard.'"[6]

Since they considered values something concrete, residing in the person and body of the individual, Roosevelt and others like him believed that those values could serve as an autonomous force in many areas of endeavor; but, precisely because they considered morals to be definite and specific, they did not carelessly assume that the practical efforts of pursuing sport could substitute for the expedient preparation for any other activity, such as war or political crusades. Rather ironically, it was the great power that they saw in sport for shaping morals (which was effectively the same as behavior) that kept them from equating sport with other enterprises. Thus, Roosevelt distinguished between training for sport and the expertise needed to carry out military duties, business activities, or political responsibilities. In "The American Boy," he wrote: "We can not expect the best work from soldiers who have carried to an unhealthy extreme the sports and pastimes which would be healthy if indulged in with moderation, and have neglected to learn as they should the business of their profession." By his failure to use the words *athletics* or *competition*, the Rough Rider hinted that the merely playful quality of the diversions would more likely incline the young person to a habit of frivolity than to the spirit of victory. In his capacity as part of a military machine, "A soldier needs to know how to shoot and take cover and shift for himself — not to box or play foot-ball." Efficiently supervised athletic contests could instill in the soldier a winning spirit, but the Army still had to show him how to handle a weapon. Such remarks might seem strange coming from Roosevelt, given the man's reputation as a promoter of athletics and sport. Yet the distinction he made was a crucial one — sport gave one qualities of character and not transferable skills, further undermining the notion of easily equating sport with other activities. The superiority of sport over war in the shaping of character lay in the fact that it was less likely to kill the participant; but sport had no advantage in preparing one for the practical aspects of war, business, or politics, and Roosevelt knew it.[7]

Genteel leaders such as Roosevelt shared a significant body of feeling, thought, and temperament with important experts in physical education; and, to some degree, it is reasonable to infer that they drew upon some of the opinions of the physical educators. Although not the only center of study in the new "sciences of the body," Harvard University gave great attention to sport and athletics and pioneered supervisory structures for

their management. It gave academic status to physical education, attracted the outstanding physical educator Dudley A.
Sargent, poured financial resources into well-equipped gymnasiums, supported a new architectural concept in the design of
stadiums, and approved of sport for the mass of the students.
All of this occurred while Roosevelt, Lodge, Francis A. Walker,
Augustus Hemenway and others were enrolled at Harvard and
during their years as alumni when they actively promoted the
development of physical training and sport at their alma mater.
Sargent personally worked with Roosevelt and Hemenway in
planning the college's program; and, in any event, they demonstrated a remarkable symmetry of viewpoint. This similarity
of perspective strengthened and justified the efforts of these two
separate constituencies of sport — genteel leaders and physical
educators. The likes of Roosevelt and Lodge reaped the benefit
of association with professional expertise in an area outside their
own realm of close study; and the physical educators gained
added credibility and status by their new familiarity with members of old, established families.[8]

Although never fully integrated into the world of the gentility as social equals (something which neither side would have
intended), the physical educators had, in many cases, become
adjuncts of the upper class's system of education. Their doctrines conformed only partly to the beliefs of a Roosevelt or
a Lodge; but their practices were sufficiently similar to provide
little cause for open disagreement. Seeing man as a "community of atoms and cells," Dudley Sargent appealed for the balanced development of all muscles because "partial, one-sided,
or excessive" development "will surely lead to disease and death."
Both in his emphasis on the human being as part of an organis-
mic society and in his belief in moderation, Sargent paralleled
the views of the traditional gentry whose sensibilities tended
to be repelled by extremes of boosterism or narrow and one-
sided activity. Sargent believed that human health and organic
growth were correlated to specific physical activities, not meta-
phorically but practically, much in the manner that Roosevelt
believed physical action actually shaped practical morals. According to Sargent, the wealthiest merchant would likely have
a disordered liver (apparently, from sitting too much); shoe-

makers became round-shouldered; printers had diarrhea; bakers developed rheumatism. Physical educators such as Sargent thus reinforced the view that exercise could affect the health of the individual and that specific activities had discrete effects. On the other hand, their passion was greatest when considering the salutary impact of sport and exercises upon the fitness of the body; and they tended to trail off into generality when claiming that this heightened fitness enhanced the common social good.[9]

The more professionally accomplished and distinguished the physical educator, the more likely he was to focus on the physical effects of sport and athletics, which were at least measurable. Focusing on the inherent desirability of health and balanced development, they were thus far more likely than the Roosevelts and Lodges to enthuse over dumbbells, Indian clubs, and highly specialized "corrective gymnastics"— which many people found excruciatingly boring; by contrast, Roosevelt appears to have concentrated most on sports which had a social component. Sargent believed that a young man must choose sports according to his deficiencies and practice them, not until perfect in his performance, but until he was balanced and complete as an organism. If sluggish, he should play baseball to develop alertness. To the timid, football would give courage and daring. The undisciplined benefited from Swedish gymnastics, military tactics (which was usually included as a branch of physical training and exercise), and calisthenic drills. Distance running and mountain climbing bestowed endurance. The "whole man" did not participate in all sports; and, for Sargent, he did not even have to participate in a single team sport. But he profited from using activities chosen carefully to fill in the rounds of his muscle and the chinks of his personality. Beyond this fulfillment of the individual, Sargent lapsed toward metaphor. Roosevelt, on the other hand, found this achievement of personal strength and well-being only an intermediate step; and he refused to let the individual fall into inutility or narcissism. In "The American Boy," he wrote that sport should never be pursued for its own sake but for the character that it would impart, enabling the youth to do "work that counts . . . ." Physical strength assumed social value when its possessor enjoyed the "lift toward lofty things," because physical vigor and manliness not only shaped but constituted, "to a certain extent, his character." Athletics thus not only taught, "pluck, endurance, and physical address" but, more important, actualized them in the person of the player who must then make use of them for the benefit of his society. Thus, while physical educators tended to subordinate sport to fitness, Roosevelt tended to subordinate both to the general social good.[10]

Physical educators who were not as well known as Sargent, and some professionals and academics from other fields, tended to share the genteel emphasis on the social pertinence of physical training and sport. Certainly, these specialists in physical education, psychology, social work, and other areas had a material interest in the promotion of organized play, sport, and the management of social behavior — even as the regeneration of social energy among the Roosevelts and the Lodges had a basis in their social and economic background. But the difference between the claims they made for sport and exercise appears to have been rooted also in the degree of their sophistication in physical education as a professional discipline and in whether they cared more about the establishment of physical education as a scientific study than about the practical social applications of the training they supervised. Thus, one of the clearest expressions of the linkage between physical exercise and morals came from the distinguished psychologist G. Stanley Hall, who was interested in the relationship of physiology and neurology to willpower but far less in physical education as such. For the *Proceedings of the American Association for the Advancement of Physical Education*, he wrote in 1894: "You cannot have a firm will without firm muscles; and there is nothing so dangerous for morals as to have the gap between knowing what is right and proper and healthy and the doing of it, yawn; and it always yawns if the muscles get weak." For this influential psychologist, as for Roosevelt and Lodge, moral deficiency was the manifestation of physical weakness and stagnation.[11]

Physical educators of the American *turner* movement, who carried on the tradition of German and "Swedish" gymnastics, also claimed social value for sport and exercise that exceeded the more temperate comments of Sargent. Significantly, their motivations included the encouragement of social cohesiveness, the preservation of German culture and language, and the inculcation of a sense of hierarchy and authority. In short, social goals were judged as significant as physical fitness, and perhaps more so — a view that Sargent would have had trouble endorsing with enthusiasm. In the April 1900 issue of the turners' *Mind and Body*, B.F. Boller all but equated work and play, arguing that the "overflowing, joyous, radiant life of the child" shaped the adult who would do his work "with the zeal and energy of earnest, joyous play . . . ." As for Roosevelt, so for Boller, the play and games of early life were intended to shape the character of the young person so that properly formed moral behavior could be applied reliably throughout the duties of later life. In this sense, play did not prepare one for work — in the same sense that sport did not exactly prepare one for war. Instead, play and sport formed a character better suited than otherwise to undertake the varied and specific tasks of later life; and they yielded a "symmetry and harmony of the intellectual and moral forces," so that "bodily exercise is at once a means as well as an end of mental and moral training."[12]

Although the evidence is far from conclusive, the physical educators who made the most facile claims for sport and play as sources of social benefit seem to have traced their origins to the earlier tradition of exercise and bodily training in America, as with the turners who first came to America in substantial numbers in 1848 when they left Germany under a cloud of political suspicion. They held their first national festival in 1851, gained considerable notoriety by 1855 for their strong endorsement of abolition of slavery, and numbered an estimated ten thousand members by the beginning of the Civil War. Despite its European origins, then, the turner movement must also be regarded as an antebellum phenomenon; and, in this light, its chronological coincidence with the rise of Muscular Christianity in America suggests how the turner movement might later produce spokesmen whose prescriptions for American society would have at least some symmetry with the proposals made by the heirs of Thomas Wentworth Higginson. To a considerable extent, Dudley Sargent shied away from casual and usually unfounded assertions about the relationship of heredity to performance in sport, of race to willpower, and a host of issues that roused the curiosity of many turners, psychologists, and politicians — again, largely out of an apparent concern that he would impeach the integrity of his infant discipline. Those who made use of Sargent's findings in order to set out strategies for social control or renewal did so largely by exceeding his purposes and eluding the tunnel vision of his particular version of science.

Partly because of their belief that body, soul, and will were inextricably bound together, a Roosevelt or a Boller never quite had to offer a fully logical or exact explanation of how change occurred in an individual's personality and character or how the accumulated changes within individuals altered the nature of society. If the discussion of various aspects of character was no more than an analytical exercise to them, then they could, in effect, dismiss it without resolution. Thus, for example, another turner and physical educator, Theodore Hough, claimed that well-being was a trinity of distinct but indivisible aspects: heredity, environment, and activity. But to Hough, the interplay of environment and activity (the latter conditioned by will, and being conditioned by it in turn) gave an existential actuality to the mere potential determined by heredity. Even environment stood less as an external force working its effects uncontrollably upon each human being than as an assortment of areas and problems in which the actions of each person would achieve "the best physical, mental, and moral results"— a triad of adjectives that appears to have corresponded with the trinity of aspects in human development. Within this trinitarian physiology, the perfection of moral purpose was equated with exercise of the human organism. In speaking of any specific human body, Hough provided a model: "A growing nerve-cell which never sends an impulse over its axon cannot become an efficient nerve-cell. A growing pancreas which never secretes pancreatic juice cannot grow into a perfect gland." Quite literally, practice could make perfect. So, too, negligence could produce inferiority. Hough asserted that "within certain limits the efficiency of an adult cell is proportional to the amount of activity it has had during development . . . ." It was never clear where the effect of each influence reached its limits; and, to this extent, the whole trinitarian "psychophysiology" became a matter of faith rather than science. Central to that faith was the necessity of action as the basis of character.[13]

For the proponents of the genteel tradition and those whose work was used to support them, physical activity coexisted with spiritual or moral activity in a symbiosis that could not be undone and the timing of whose development ought not to be trifled with. In such a framework, sport was not play, and could not be play, unless those engaging in it held an equally light view of spirit and morals. Sports were not "deadly serious" but vitally so, for they afforded the young American with the medium for the perfection of body and spirit as a unitary being — a discrete, purposeful, correctly coded cell in the social organism.

EXPERIENCE AS PERIL AND PROMISE

The belief that character depended upon experience carried perils and promise at the same time. If character depended upon actions, then it could be warped or ruined if it were molded through the wrong experience. Social commentators from the old-line families of the genteel tradition expressed concern — sometimes even fear and despair — over the country's future, doubting that its people would respond effectively to the demands of the nation's duties at home and abroad. Even those genteel politicians who showed more optimism agreed that the situation was fraught with danger, seeing eternal sacrifice and commitment as the price of survival and dominance. Military officers and theorists shared the sense that America faced a critical moment which could turn into tragedy or triumph, according to the behavior of the public and its leaders.[14] These observers helped to describe an aura of urgency to control Americans' experience; and, among an audience of comparable background and interests, they shared their interest in a strenuous and rugged approach to life, in sport and athletics, and in a disciplined code of behavior which they thought would save the country from degeneration.

The language with which military theorists spoke of the need for national unity to guarantee success in war paralleled that which many physical educators used to describe the quest for victory in sport; and they shared a common concern to prevent excessive civilization from corroding the militant, dynamic, primitive impulses of the people. In this respect, when Major General J.P. Story stated bluntly that "The nature of man makes war inevitable," he was not indulging in war-lust but expressing a considered opinion about a residue of "primitive savagery" within man which was the raw energy from which societies were shaped. Although reformers sought to imbue the Army and Navy with a taste for bureaucratic order and scientific management, the services attained their greatest place in the hearts of the nation's leaders because they expressed the militant spirit, which military analyst Homer Lea called the "ultimate consummation of the nation's existence." Militant force had supreme value as the "primordial element" governing the formative process of a nation, and all activities that cultivated this primordial force shared its high esteem. Simplicity, discipline, subordination, physical commitment (or "address") — these qualities loomed as most crucial if the society was to be preserved. In the civilian world, sport served purposes parallel to that served by actual military experience; and military officers and theorists were enthusiastic about both. Each cultivated primitive combativeness.[15]

In *The Valor of Ignorance* (1909), Homer Lea called upon his countrymen to develop discipline and to accept austerity as paths toward primordial vitality. Sometimes eccentric and occasionally brilliant, Lea had been barred by his hunched stature from service in the U.S. Army, which he had deeply desired, though he was compensated somewhat by his designation as a General in the Chinese Army. Such quirks notwithstanding, he was well regarded by General Story; and Lieutenant General Adna R. Chaffee, the former Chief of Staff of the Army, wrote an introduction to Lea's book expressing hearty approval. Lea derided commercialism and its twin, opulence, as "a protoplasmic gormandization and retching that vanishes utterly when the element that sustains it is no more." National health depended on a sober economic nutrition, and the primitive vigor of any national endeavor required the strengthening of the individual human cells. Lea feared the tendency of nations to become "intangibly complex," and, when that tangible simplicity was lost, nations decomposed and values that were once national degenerated into a miscellany of mere particulars.[16]

Fear and resignation ran through the pages of Brooks Adams's *The Law of Civilization and Decay* (1896), which predicted the decline and final ruin of the United States on the basis of its growing taste for luxury. An heir of one of the most distinguished American families, the descendant of two presidents, and a friend and associate of Theodore Roosevelt, Adams believed that actions constituted character and that the tone of America's morals was weakening under the influence of what he called "economic man." Adams thus expressed in the civilian world the same dilemma that Lea outlined for military theorists, but he did so with little hope that the future could be saved. According to Adams, wealth—which he equated with "stored energy"—became the controlling force in society whenever a race passed the peak of its primitive vitality. The result of economic and military victories, wealth also embodied the spirit of individual and national greed. But it was fear, rather than greed, that inspired and accomplished the creation of the nation in the first place through emotional and martial vigor. Peoples thus oscillated between barbarism and civilization; and human societies, which Adams called "forms of animal life," passed from being primitive, martial organisms to being elaborate, cultivated economic ones. The rapid increase in "the velocity of the social movement" of a nation, which corresponded roughly to the pace of its economic growth and accumulation of wealth, ultimately produced a crisis in which "the waste of energetic material is so great that the martial and imaginative stocks fail to reproduce themselves . . ." and the society fell to the usurer and the peasant—a fate as ugly to the gentility as to the military. Extreme interest in economic competition and a personal devotion to wealth thus damaged the social organism, and they presumably contributed to "race decline" by changing the physical circumstances in which heredity worked its way into moral behavior. To make matters worse, Adams saw little evidence that conscious thought had ever molded "the fate of men" and assserted that "at the moment of action the human being almost invariably obeys an instinct, like an animal. . . ." Although Brooks Adams did not think it could be achieved, the one chance for a society's survival was to turn a thoughtfully chosen course of action into an instinct.[17]

An ingenious historian, faculty member at Harvard, and president of the American Historical Association, Henry Adams complemented the thinking of his brother Brooks. In *The Degradation of the Democratic Dogma,* which Brooks released in 1919, Henry criticized especially the presumption of upward evolution and progress that some of Darwin's popularizers promoted. Sharpening his sense of danger was his denial of the indestructibility of energy. Observing that entropy "tends toward a maximum," he remarked: ". . . to the vulgar and ignorant historian it meant only that the ash-heap was constantly increasing in size. . . ." Not only was society in organic flux, but the energy of the natural organism naturally inclined toward depletion and extinction. This reading of the current scientific findings led Henry Adams to share his brother's pessimism for the future of American civilization, although with sharper intellectual barbs and less legalistic rigor than Brooks displayed.[18]

In *The Forum* of January 1897, Theodore Roosevelt sought to counter the "melancholy" prospect that Brooks Adams had described, exposing what he thought was "a devious furrow" in the new ground plowed by *The Law of Civilization and Decay.* Roosevelt argued that new and more efficient forms of activity could replace the primitive patterns that had guaranteed survival in earlier times; and they could do so more profitably. The old religious instinct that Adams had paired with martial ardor still remained strong in America, according to Roosevelt, but as "practical morality" rather than "emotional religion." Roosevelt was pleased to agree with Adams that the militance of the savage had passed, except "in the slums of great cities"; and he insisted that "a martial type infinitely more efficient" had been developed in the armed forces. So, too, in industry he identified challenges that called forth "more hardihood, manliness, and courage" than any in the past. Clearly, Roosevelt assumed that conscious thought and planning could be used to turn the raw energy of human action into sustained social power. Forethought and willpower could be used to set out beneficial patterns of behavior that would prevent "the waste of energetic material" which Brooks Adams thought would doom the country.[19]

Seen from one vantage, there was a significant common element in the thinking of Lea, the Adams brothers, and Roosevelt — a similarity in tone. They shared a contempt for mere wealth and a revulsion from mere consumption. All of them valued the concept of service, the role of sacrifice of personal interest for the public good, and the effectiveness of discipline and restraint in forming personal character. These were survivals of the code of gentility, tinged with expectations that varied from one man to the next. The difference that emerged among them centered in the varying levels of their confidence in their countrymen; and, to a considerable extent, it was an act of faith for Roosevelt to speak of Americans' "virile, manly qualities" and to deny that they would ever "sink into a nation of mere hucksters." They would support the national honor, he said; and, "while more gentle and honest than before," they would remain "certainly more efficient as fighters."[20]

If Americans could make struggle within their society more rational and efficient, then the degeneration of the race need never occur. "There must be a certain amount of competition," Roosevelt wrote in 1895 in a commentary on Kidd's *Social Evolution* for *The North American Review*, ". . . but it is equally undoubted that if this competition becomes too severe the race goes down and not up." In terms that echoed his prescriptions for Harvard's athletic program, he urged sympathy for those who faltered in competition, arguing that gradual familiarity with moderate stress would raise them to a greater strength and social utility. Roosevelt's sense of fairness led him to oppose inequitable competition in athletics as much as in business. Indeed, the hostility of the gentry and the military to commercialism in sport was an extension of their objection to the damaging effects of "economic man." The reforms which Roosevelt sought throughout society — in politics, in business, in athletics — aimed at preserving the competitive and questing spirit by giving it fair terms on which to run the race.[21]

What Roosevelt recommended for society in general he insisted upon for sport in particular; for the assurance of rational, regulated competition in athletics gave security to society's institutions by preventing its potential leaders from becoming deranged. Control and rational intervention were the remedies for the urgency of the moment and would enable Americans to interrupt Brooks Adams's law while enjoying the fruits of civilization. Sporting activities wedded consciousness to the primitive and linked thought to action. Descent into decay resulted from unconsciousness of the peril and from sloth, but people such as Roosevelt sought to breed them out of their systems. Thus would they resolve the ambivalence of change in favor of the promise of victory and dominance. Making this happen, however, called not for theory but for actions.

THE PRACTICE OF SPORT AND THE HABIT OF VICTORY

In the actual practice of sport, Americans from the genteel tradition and the military services sought out the experience of victory, seeking to make the qualities needed to attain it a matter of habit and instinct. For these people, sport was a way of learning about themselves, a way of enlarging their abilities, and a means of commitment to public enterprise. Many were attracted by the doctrine of physical educators such as turner Theodore Hough, who asserted, in May 1900: "The leaders in life's activities are almost without exception men of strong physical constitution; a large percentage of the failures are men of weak constitution. . . ." Much in line with this view, Theodore Roosevelt used an energetic test for his principal appointees to military service, linking physical fitness to the capacity for leadership. As proof of military proficiency and patriotic zeal, a candidate for promotion had to keep up with the robust President on one of his "hikes" in the varied and often rugged terrain of Washington's Rock Creek Park. Roosevelt inclined to associate quick wit with quick limbs, and so he attributed much of the disorder of the Cuban campaign in the Spanish-American War to the physical enormity and mental indolence of General William R. Shafter, who had to be hoisted onto his long-suffering horse.[22]

Although Roosevelt's strenuous life invited voguish press coverage and faddish imitation, it also stood as a model of sport's efficacy in molding a man for an active and creative life in the business of the nation. Through determined training, Roosevelt broke the restraints of childhood asthma and defective vision. He was an enthusiastic boxer at Harvard and won his own piece of the West as a cowboy. Self-evidently successful in public affairs, Roosevelt remained an indefatigable sportsman, although an indifferent athlete; and the confusion of sport and policy making persisted. Unlike many men of breeding, Roosevelt showed no disdain for wrestling with professionals while he was Governor of New York. He also continued to practice his college sport of boxing until 1904, when he suffered a serious blow to his left eye that eventually resulted in loss of vision. Members of his staff and political associates joined him at tennis, and they formed an unofficial "Tennis Cabinet." While President, Roosevelt took time off to recreate himself in Yellowstone Park, simultaneously promoting the conservation program that he had developed in concert with Tennis Cabinet member Gifford Pinchot. His excursions in the American West, which entered national legend during the years of his Presidency, were followed closely by his African safari. His purposeful enthusiasm and practical accomplishments seemed to testify to the effectiveness of the practices that he preached.[23]

Roosevelt's breadth of interests permitted him to move freely among many different sectors of the society. His personal confidence and inquiring mind thus enabled him to endow each arena that he entered with a degree of respectability, and each field practically reinforced the others. Roosevelt's participation in the events surrounding the National Rifle Tournament at Sea Girt, New Jersey, in 1905 drew attention to the interplay of sport and military preparedness. The rifle competition itself was paramilitary, and the competitors represented the armed forces as well as civilian clubs. The President also took time out to make a descent in a primitive submarine called *The Plunger*, which magazine writers called one of the "diversified phases of sport." Yet with equal ease the President left the bustle of Washington for the stimulating wilderness of Yellowstone.[24] Each act provided personal fulfillment, leading toward full realization of his personal potential. Yet each also had social or political effect.

By accepting the honorary presidency of the 1904 Olympic Games at St. Louis, Roosevelt lent some of the prestige of his elective office to the fledgling competitions. He became the butt of good-natured humor because of his long history of commitment to the strenuous life. But it was always worth a little kidding to promote a worthy cause. On April 9, 1904, the editors of *The Illustrated Sporting News* observed:

> It may be taken for granted that Mr. Roosevelt would rather be a contestant than an honorary ornament of this great carnival of sport, if he were a few years younger and a few pounds lighter. The program is amazingly varied and extensive, yet it is even now to be regretted that the Olympic Games do not include "bronco-busting" from scratch, chasing the mountain lion against the watch, and long distance sprinting over high hurdles up the slope of a specially constructed San Juan Hill. The exhibition of such seductive pastimes as these might cause the Honorary President to fidget uneasily on his Olympic throne, and to this list might be added vaulting ambition, and an obstacle race for the White House Trophy, trial heats to be run on the indoor track of Convention Hall. [25]

The practical goals of Roosevelt's reelection and of his advancement of sport dovetailed as he and his daughter Alice awarded medals during the hot and humid Missouri summer. Athletic virtue and political reward were unknowing twins.

The press coverage of the Roosevelt phenomenon extended to the President's kin, and the articles about his family implied that physically conditioned traits could be passed on from one generation to the next. The medium for the transfer — environment or heredity — was not specified. "Theodore Roosevelt, Jr.," *The Illustrated Outdoor News* noted on September 1, 1906, "the strenuous son of the strenuous President, is already making his mark in sports, although still a freshman at Harvard." Young Roosevelt played end for his school's freshman football team and participated in "several of the big games" of the 1905 season. Politely, the editors chose not to specify his physical dimensions, observing only that he was "not so big as his father was while in college." Full of enthusiasm for sports, the boy followed his father's edicts and example. "He was badly used up" in one game, said the editors, "but pluckily stuck it out." [26] Manly discipline and self-sacrifice had become family traits.

The same article reported the activities of cousin Theodore Roosevelt Pell, cousin Andre Roosevelt, and nephew G.E. Roosevelt. A "crack athlete" at Columbia, Pell was a "clever all-around athlete" who played tennis of championship caliber, sharing the indoor doubles title for 1905. As added proof that he was a fit cousin for the President, the editors specified his height of 6 feet 2 inches and weight of over 180 pounds. Roughly the same size, cousin Andre represented the Missouri Athletic Club in the 1906 National Swimming Championship held at the New York Athletic Club. Widely traveled, Andre played rugby during his stay in England; and the editors noted that he "later represented France in some international football games at the World's Fair."[27] He also fenced and played water polo.

Young G.E. Roosevelt had a body good enough to justify mention of his 6 feet 1½ inches and his 173 pounds, and the statistics stood as a clinical demonstration that the Roosevelt name was physically alive and well. He won the New England Interscholastic Championship in the high jump for St. Mark's School in the spring of 1905, and he went on to Harvard where he was "a crack high jumper and a good baseball player." All of these Roosevelts prided themselves modestly on their achievements, and none felt squeamish about public athletic display. Although their various competitions took place, for the most part, in socially distinguished circumstances, the family performed in the open. By their actions, and by the photographic reproduction of their exertions, the many Roosevelts proved the vitality of American life and the efficacy of the nation's sports.

Occasional excess in the press coverage of the sporting ventures of prominent Americans and their relatives almost conceals the fact that their athletic commitment was authentic and long-standing. A close associate of President Roosevelt and the Army's Chief of Staff under William Howard Taft, General Leonard Wood exemplified the man in public life who had integrated sport into his very being years before the metamorphosis occasioned any journalistic notice. Unlike many American officers, Wood loved the rough life of the Southwest during the campaign against Geronimo; and he delighted in horseback riding and "hiking." After the submission of the Apache, Wood and his boss General Nelson A. Miles (later Chief of Staff under Theodore Roosevelt) engaged in boxing matches. Soon he cultivated an interest in football. While stationed at the Presidio of Monterey, Wood joined the team of the San Francisco Olym-

Although William Howard Taft, an avid golfer, never reaped the political advantage as a sportsman that accrued to Theodore Roosevelt, his endorsement made sport seem up-to-date, like the telephone with which Taft also liked to be photographed. He is shown here in a 1908 photograph by Waldon Fawsett of Washington, D.C. By permission of the Library of Congress (LC-USZ62-10306).

pic Club, enjoying victory over the University of California in his first game on October 29, 1892. With missionary zeal, he proselytized for his new athletic faith after his assignment at Fort McPherson, Georgia, in 1893. To compensate for the boredom of what he called a "dull, stupid post," Wood assembled a football team at Georgia Tech in Atlanta and became its coach and star player. As governor of Cuba's Santiago Province and later as military governor of the whole island, he learned the national sport of jai alai. In the 1900s, he developed interest and skill in fencing, and he took long and vigorous walks. Clearly, sport and rough experience were not concessions to fashion or paths to Presidential favor but a chosen way of life.[28]

Rough and energetic, Wood had no sympathy for friendly persuasion. As World War I passed through its second month, the General gave it qualified endorsement in words that echoed Lodge's and Roosevelt's. "I would not speak of the war in Europe as a reversion to barbarism," he wrote to a friend, "as it really represents the highest development of organized effort, and a most superb sacrifice for the purpose of national integrity and policy."[29] Pacifists enraged him by their neglect of the law of "survival of the fittest," and he dismissed Oswald Garrison Villard as "an emasculated traitor." For speaking against the war, Luther Burbank occasioned pointed wit: "Isn't he the man who developed the spineless cactus?"[30]

It was not only outstanding individuals such as Roosevelt and Wood who were affected by the passion for sport, along with their leading subordinates. It was the system itself, which was touched by confidence in the worth of rough and strenuous experience. Notable was the commitment of the Army and the Navy, and by the latter part of the nineteenth century both services had accepted sport as part of their training programs. The War Department officially recognized gymnastic exercise and sport as a reasonable means of training soldiers during the 1880s; and, especially thereafter, Army personnel found ways in which sport and gymnastic exercise could be seen to promote military preparedness. During the 1880s, the secretaries of war concluded that physical training conducted in advance of specific, pertinent military drill would make the latter easier and more efficient. Although officials in Washington were reluc-

Shown here in 1917, General Leonard Wood, who attended Harvard Medical School before his rise to Army Chief of Staff, ardently pursued such sports as boxing and football, introducing the latter at Georgia Tech. He typified the emerging leadership of the Army which saw sport as an adjunct to military training. By permission of the Library of Congress (LC-USZ62-17481).

tant to designate funds for use in sport and physical education, they affirmed that such activities had military value and should be promoted in ways that did not increase the Army's budget. In the 1890s, Army officers wrote numerous articles, seeking to meet these specifications, although sometimes casting a cynical glance at the niggardliness of the War Department. In 1890, for example, Lieutenant C.D. Parkhurst began a series of essays on "The Practical Education of the Soldier" for the *Journal of the Military Service Institution of the United States* which asserted that physical training should precede all specifically military activities with the exception of battle itself. Exercise in the gymnasium, according to Parkhurst, would bring the soldier to "quick and unthinking obedience to orders." After that, the recruit would be easily transformed into a real soldier. This would occur, in Parkhurst's opinion, largely because men showed great enthusiasm for engaging in sports and exercises in their after-duty hours. What mattered most, however, was that the character and attitude of the recruit would have been altered by sport and exercise so that he would then be a more suitable candidate for true soldiering.[31]

In March 1891, Captain Morris C. Foote of the 9th Infantry continued the campaign to use organized gymnastics and sport in the pages of the *Journal of the Military Service Institution of the United States*, even as he successfully waged it on post. Foote told his brother officers of the virtues of these activities, claiming that they reduced the rate of desertion (a serious military problem at the end of the century) and asserting that the exceptional skill of some few military gymnasts would captivate the attention of the average soldiers and discourage their otherwise strong tendency to leave post. In turn, apart from the benefit in lessening the likelihood of desertion, sport would strengthen the muscles and make it easier for the soldiers to handle their rifles and drill more effectively.[32]

Criticism of exercise and sport within the Army was virtually absent, although some Army officers did criticize their superiors for not providing funds adequate to the task of raising the physical fitness of their units. Colonel J.J. Coppinger of the 23rd Infantry asserted that exercises in the gymnasium were among the very few reliable forms of training in areas

Adapting sport to military purposes, the Army produced such hybrids as mounted wrestling, in which the soldier's stamina is tested along with his balance and control of his mount. Such sports were contested on base and between different stations. Shown here is the championship team of the 7th Cavalry, ca. 1910–16. Courtesy of the U.S. Army Cavalry Museum.

Troopers of the 4th Cavalry, probably C Troop, enjoy a boxing match at Fort Riley, Kansas, ca. 1910. Between 1880 and 1910, various sports were introduced as suitable parts of the soldier's duty-day, especially when the soldier was in training and when the sports were either obviously combative or else played in teams. Courtesy of the U.S. Army Cavalry Museum.

touched by severe cold or blistering heat. Major John Brooke of the Medical Department praised exercise conducted in a well-supervised gymnasium as an extraordinarily efficient means of securing both muscular development and a proper attitude. It was not mere strength that one sought, according to Brooke, but "unerring grip and lightning-like rapidity" so that one preferred a "Belvedere Apollo" to a "Farnese Hercules." Litheness and quickness were deemed more worthwhile than bulk and force. Parkhurst added more to the discussion, as did Captain Samuel Miles of the 5th Artillery who saw exercise and particularly sport as a viable means of increasing the military proficiency of his men. An officer in the 9th Infantry, Lieutenant Charles R. Noyes even claimed that the Army should boost foot racing, boxing, rowing, lawn tennis, baseball, and football. "The last-named game" he wrote, "is eminently suited . . . to develop what is called 'team action,' that is, united aggressive effort under control of a leader or commander. In this respect it is instructive from a military point of view." From the 10th Infantry, Lieutenant W.C. Wren added the observation that the Spartans and the Romans had long ago shown their belief in a link between athletic training and military proficiency and asserted that the Americans should follow their lead.[33]

Rather like their professional counterparts in physical education, military officers came to emphasize skill and balanced development over brute strength and further explored the possible moral advantages of team sports. In 1892, Lieutenant Colonel A.A. Woodhull, an Army surgeon, used the James J. Corbett–John L. Sullivan fight to prove that speed and agility were the superior qualities to be developed through physical training; and his appraisal of boxing echoed the belief that primitive force must be made efficient by intelligence. Showing a similar taste for the marriage of physical and moral power, Major John Brooke specifically suggested that the Army should follow the lead of physical educators in the colleges so as to adopt the most effective means of instilling bearing and great proficiency in the soldiers.[34]

By 1897, the notion that athletics and gymnastic exercise was a desirable part of the Army's training program was well accepted, although debate continued over budgetary shortages

Like many other units, the 6th Battalion Field Artillery at Fort Riley, Kansas engaged in baseball enthusiastically, partly to relieve the tedium of station in remote areas and also to develop unit spirit. Some officers also saw sport as a prophylactic against indiscipline and immorality. Courtesy of the U.S. Army Cavalry Museum.

In 1909, the "athletic team," which competed in track and field, posed with the pennant of the 7th Cavalry at Fort Riley, Kansas. The spiked shoes, introduced at Mott Haven in New York some 20 years earlier, had now become standard — a symbol of the application of modern coaching to sport. Note the mascot in the second row. Courtesy of the U.S. Army Cavalry Museum.

58

and the need for practical help from Washington. The degree of commitment to physical training and sport was signified by some of the makeshift measures proposed by officers in the field, who sought ways of preventing financial constraints from choking out the program. For example, Lieutenant A.B. Donworth of the 14th Infantry urged that officers use reasonable substitutes for regular barbells, such as iron rods; and he promoted gymnastics as universally virtuous in their effect. Donworth showed how deep the interest in gymnastics and sport had become in the Army when he even integrated them into military theory. Precisely because theorists specified that future wars would be brief, Donworth argued that physical training and sport would assume ever greater importance in keeping the soldiers fit and combative during the long and boring periods between battles. Most important, it was clear that officers and men not only thought about sport and gymnastics but practiced them; and physical fitness through sport and gymnastics came to be taken as a military duty which generated socially favored values in each athlete.[35]

In the Navy as well, officers recognized the value of athletics in developing mental and physical alertness, and there was some active encouragement for seamen to engage in combative games. Rear Admiral Robley D. Evans, a hero of the Spanish-American War and Commander in Chief of the Navy's North Atlantic Fleet, promoted teams in baseball, football, track and field, boxing, and fencing and ordered that these sports be considered "part of their drill." In this way, athletics literally became a military duty. In addition to raising morale, Admiral Evans expected sports to provide his men with opportunities to develop the specific attributes that the Navy needed. "That the athlete has muscles, nerves, eyes and brain which unconsciously work in unison, is axiomatic," he observed, adding that "it is just such qualities as these the officers and men of the United States Navy must have if we are to continue to uphold its proud traditions."[36] The regeneration of the Navy as a fighting body so that it would discharge its duties with stable and traditional efficiency would issue, in part, from conditioning through sport.

Military veterans sometimes worked to spread their gospel of sport and combative exercise in civilian society; and, despite

Under command of Admiral Robley Dunglison Evans, the U.S. North Atlantic Squadron included team sports and combative exercises as part of their duty-day. Sport had become a recognized naval or military obligation. Evans is shown aboard ship in 1905, in the latter part of his distinguished career. By permission of the Library of Congress (LC-USZ62-19793).

the occasional dissimilarity of their social and economic dispositions from those of the people they sought to influence, the military men had some notable successes. To some extent, the traditional inclusion of military drill among the branches of physical education lent credence to the officers' entry into the civilian sphere; but it is also true that some distinguished military men lent their own eminence to sport and athletics. Thus, throughout the late nineteenth century, General George Albert Wingate promoted military training in the public schools of New York City, coupling it to the more palatable pursuits of sport. By the first years of the twentieth century, various independent groups in the metropolitan area formed the New York Public School Athletic League, which brought Wingate's efforts to fulfillment. With 100,000 members, the League claimed to be the "largest athletic body in the world." The editors of *The Illustrated Sporting News*, giving their blessing to the organization on December 5, 1903, observed that its military and athletic programs were to be kept in fruitful balance. In addition to "musket swinging," the League planned to support running, jumping, putting the shot, discus throwing, basketball, fencing, and a wide range of other activities. Yet "the patriotic idea will not be in the least minimized," the editors noted. For the additional activities would generally benefit the military hardihood of the young people. The editors praised drill as "a very excellent exercise," but they confessed that the students — like soldiers themselves — showed more interest in games and sports. The League's transformation of Wingate's military training program would win it more recruits because "the various forms of athletics indulged in are more attractive . . ." than drill alone. Through their athletics, the students would thus get an early start in acquiring combative virtues; and the influence of the military, which was itself much affected by genteel values, would intermix with civilian leadership.[37]

Those who challenged the military's influence in society and questioned sport's capacity to prepare Americans for war and leadership often had more in common with Roosevelt or Lodge than they knew. The prominent editor E.L. Godkin, for example, who was a persistent critic of excessive zeal in the pursuit of sport, railed against those who "regarded football as a good

Like boxing aboard ship, playing baseball when in port was considered a military duty, as well as a boost to morale. This team from the U.S.S. *Washington* was under the overall command of Admiral Robley Evans, known in New York sporting circles for his positive views on the military value of sport. By permission of the Library of Congress, George Grantham Bain Collection (Lot 10786).

62

preparation for service on the battlefield." Writing in *The Nation* in 1894, he anticipated much of Homer Lea's critique when he accused sport's promoters of having a false "Homeric" vision of war in which combatants "'clinch' and 'slug' each other as they roll over in the mud, each trying to stab the other with a spear, or hold him down till another man on the same side can break his back with a club . . . ." The editor's dismal view of football and his progressive belief in a rationally managed society inspired his grisly rhetoric; and he outlined less the inutility of sport than the corrupt, barbaric, and inefficient nature of football as then practiced. As Lodge called for athletics as a means to attain to high ideals, Godkin urged the development in youth of "capacity for high resolve, noble aims." In this pronouncement, he differed little from Roosevelt who, in "Manhood and Statehood," insisted that physical strength must be molded by the "lift toward lofty things." In fact, Godkin echoed criticisms that were stated by some of sport's strongest enthusiasts when he opposed rampant individualism, unbridled commercialism, and inefficiency within athletics. Evidently unaware of this deep commonality of their views, Godkin concluded his challenge of sport with praise for the military values of "heroic spirit, a capacity to meet death and wounds calmly, and to see them all around him without flinching."[38] Roosevelt could hardly have waxed more eloquent. What distinguished Godkin from Lodge, or even William James, was Godkin's focus on the faults within the practice of athletics. Instead, Lodge and James were willing to regulate sport's effect on society in order to preserve it as a force in the shaping of morals.

The imaginative and prominent psychologist William James voiced the hope that physical activity could develop the moral qualities that Godkin and Roosevelt both desired without either the abomination of commercialism, which Godkin had mentioned, or the horrors of inefficient war, which he had not. In proposing "a substitute for war's disciplinary function," James echoed the reverie over the effects of the Civil War; but he insisted that militarism was not an end in itself. Rather, James insisted that several different courses could be equally effective in developing the same qualities of character in Americans. He advocated an "army enlisted against Nature" in which conscripted youth would use conservation programs as if they were military campaigns and national forests as if they were moral battlegrounds. In this way, "The military ideals of hardihood and discipline would be wrought into the growing fibre of the people . . . ." So, too, organized team sport provided an effective way to develop "the manliness to which the military mind so faithfully clings," and he extolled "intrepidity, contempt of softness, surrender of private interest, [and] obedience to command" as the "rock upon which states are built."[39]

James declined to endorse the "bestial side of military service" —which, ironically, most military officers disliked as well— and disapproved of the randomness and contingency that almost inevitably prevailed during a conflict. Obligatory participation in sport or in conservation would ingrain the virtuous hardihood that military experience was also believed to inculcate, but it would do so with superior efficiency. Carefully regulated and disciplined physical effort, far from subduing and suppressing action, would free the individual to thrive within the organism of the society, displaying "every sort of energy and endurance, of courage and capacity for handling life's evils."[40] Man could thus conquer without wanton destruction—and be tested without being destroyed.

It is worthy of mention how similar these views were to those of Theodore Roosevelt, who emoted over the "infinite woe and suffering" of the Civil War for having created "nobler capacities for what is great and good." But, when the whole truth was told, he preferred the finite and restrained suffering of sport as sufficient to bring Americans to a combative spirit. Although he considered Americans "the richer for each grim campaign, for each hard-fought battle" of the Civil War, he also resisted the mere violence of football played to extremes. In this regard, sport—like war—must be conducted with moderation, balance, and control. The socially efficient training of the young man could not include the arbitrary, disorderly surrender to primitive bloodlust. Rather, the primitive instinct was to drive the engine of social efficiency.[41]

As American involvement in World War I neared, the enthusiasm of sportsmen for America's military preparedness movement and the lusty service of many of them in the armed forces undercut the pacifists and seemed to validate the maxims of men such as Lodge and Roosevelt. For example, General Leonard Wood endorsed the Plattsburgh military training camp program and became its heroic patron. The campaign to give citizens military training won the support of Hamilton Fish and Crawford Blagden, two of the most famous All-American linemen in the recent history of Harvard. Yet another supporter of the training camp movement was Benjamin H. Dibblee, a San Francisco banker who had captained Harvard's football team in 1899.[42] Promoters of the military training camp program advertised in the sports pages of the *New York Times*, looking in particular for Southern volunteers endowed with the militant spirit and a sense of discipline. Despite its Northeastern origins, the Plattsburgh movement sought to become national in scope, and its leaders sought trainees through sports such as football that extended into all regions of America.

The response of the comfortable classes to the prospect of war vindicated Roosevelt's claims that they could regenerate themselves. Brooks Adams had concluded, partly from his analysis of medieval society, that the "mercantile type" transmuted physical force into money. This financial alchemy poisoned individual strength and deadened personal courage. For Adams, the payment of money for military service replaced the principle of personal obligation, and artificial cash nexus substituted for natural relationships in the societal family. Time and again through *The Law of Civilization and Decay*, Adams railed at the destructive effects of separating man from immediate and simple experience. That which generated wealth corrupted the individual, without whose integrity the continuation of the society was doomed.[43] Yet the Plattsburghers and others who supported a strong American armed force showed that the athletic veterans born in what Roosevelt called the "best elements of the race" had avoided degeneracy. Immediate in their experience of the material world, they also proved instant in their display of the militant spirit.

On the eve of the United States' entry into World War I, when the nation would have the opportunity to plumb the depths of its instinct for victory, physical educator Raymond G. Gettell of Amherst College rehearsed the value of sport in society.

Gettell summarized the specific merits of football in terms that recalled Lodge's equation of spirit with social efficiency. Not only did the game afford the chance for "physical combat" and satisfy the "primitive lust for battle." It also "satisfies the higher and distinctly civilized interest in organization, cooperation, and the skilled interrelation of individual effort directed to a common purpose. It typifies the highest achievement in its unusual emphasis on discipline and obedience, on the subordination of the individual to authority and law."[44] Primordial vigor surged through the structure of the rational society, as blood through the veins of the athlete. All performing special tasks to the fullness of their predetermined demands, the members of the team created an actual living entity. Like the team, the organism of the state would pulse and throb to the consistent rhythm of birth, development, and extinction of its individual human cells — ever primitive, ever civilized, a scientific miracle of victorious animal power and social efficiency.

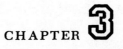

Winning and the Regulated Life — The New Experts in Physical Culture

"DID you ever try to reason out why it is necessary for athletes to go into training?" asked nutritionist and physical culturist Horace Fletcher in 1903. Fletcher disapproved of crash programs for the athletes, demanding a balanced and scientific program of nutrition and exercise that would make extreme expedients unnecessary. In this emphasis on thoughtful and efficient management of the body, Fletcher exemplified the new expert in the various aspects of physical culture who had been transforming the world of American sport since the latter decades of the nineteenth century. They emphasized scientific principles and applied them to produce efficient results.[1]

Although they functioned as a common constituent group favoring sport, the physical educators and the coaches differed in one cardinal respect that went far to explain their disagreements on many subsidiary issues. The physical educators identified sport as a means to strengthen and renew health, which they hoped to see realized in the balanced fitness of all Americans. They protested any measure that risked the welfare of the individual merely for the sake of athletic victory; and they often sided against the coaches, along with athletic directors who aided them, by criticizing their training techniques, their influence in colleges and society, and their apparently compulsive thirst for winning. Coaches and trainers were inclined to waste little time in debating such charges, concentrating instead on shaping a winning team. Their concerns tended toward the tactical and the practical, and relatively few of them voiced opinions on how sport fit into the broader goals of the society. Although the behavior of coaches varied from one individual to the next, they were not basically in the business of improving the physical or moral health of their charges but rather of producing sport and sporting events. Personally and often emotionally committed to winning, the coaches nonetheless dealt with sport as an end in itself—indeed, as a thing in itself. Victory came to exist apart from the players whose work created it; and the vocabulary of coaches and trainers—as in referring to athletes as "material"—suggested the priority of an athletic competition over the human beings taking part in it. For the one group, sport was one means of forming fit human beings; for the other, human beings were the raw components for creating a sporting event and an athletic victory.

For all the difference in perspective among the new experts in the applied "sciences of the body," however, they shared a significant common ground. All prided themselves on their own expertise, seeing their work as a kind of practical and popular science. They shared an appreciation of rational and systematic training and, even in their sharpest internal disagreements, challenged specific methods or programs but not the underlying premise of expert management. Coaches, trainers, nutritionists, physical educators, physical culturists—all in their various ways sought to subject sport to rational analysis, to systematize its performance, and to mold it to rational purpose. By doing so, they made sport more compatible with the "progressive" tide in American culture.

PHYSICAL EDUCATORS AS ADVOCATES OF SPORT

Physical educators, whether men or women, generally recognized that athletics had swept to an important role in the colleges without their influence and, to be sure, without their control. If earlier educators had helped to create a climate in which the practice of sport was permitted, they had nonetheless failed to exert their professional influence in determining just how it would be practiced. By the late decades of the nineteenth century, all articulate proponents of the new, scientific approach to physical education resented what they regarded as excessive competition and deplored the consequent injury to less capable players. Yet these same experts believed that sport was not intrinsically damaging to the individual, nor to the college's general educational mission. They included sport within many of their own regimens for physical improvement of the average student and for the restoration of adults already engaged in the hectic life of the business world. If rationally controlled and applied, sport could be a benefit.

As Director of Harvard's Hemenway Gymnasium and head of the school's program in physical culture, Dudley Sargent was among the most visible of the late nineteenth-century physical educators, and his analysis of sport's impacts exemplified the sentiments of his colleagues:

> In consequence of the popular enthusiasm and the wide public interest in athletics, a large number of young men upon entering college are filled with the ambition to become athletes and get on university athletic teams. In many cases the zeal of these young men is greatly in excess of their abilities, and in their efforts to get into university form and keep pace with the stars, they often do themselves injury. In football especially a great deal of raw material is used as a temporary battering-ram, or made to furnish a wall of temporary resistance to develop the defensive or attacking power of the more stalwart rushers. The coaches cannot afford to use their time and energy in developing men, for their business is to develop football players; so they are anxious to weed out the weak ones, that they may give their undivided attention to the most promising candidates.

Thus the male physical educator did not form a part of a simple homosocial world that included everyone concerned with physical culture. Unlike the coach, who might actually benefit from the short-term use of the less accomplished player but who could not "waste" time on the player's improvement, Sargent considered it an obligation "to protect the weak and feeble from their own folly and rashness." This was more than paternalism; it was the expert's quest for the regulated, rational life.[2]

For decades, Sargent campaigned for a comprehensive program of exercise and health care that would be a cornerstone in the lives of his charges. In 1880, he instituted an annual strength test for Harvard students, in which participants gained points for their performance in numerous and varied events. Sargent kept the schedule of events diversified so that no single

Eminent among 19th-century physical educators, Dudley Allen Sargent made Harvard's Hemenway Gymnasium a focus for the professional study of exercise and advocated "corrective gymnastics" as a means to symmetrical bodily development. For Sargent the proper goal of sport was the promotion of health and well-being. Photo undated. By permission of the Library of Congress, Biographical Files.

physical type would have advantage over others, thus seeking to preserve the fairness in gentlemanly competition which the genteel overseers of Harvard deeply favored. The results of the strength tests were later published in the *Harvard Graduates' Magazine,* which kept an eye on how the "fifty strong men of Harvard" compared with those of preceding years. Although the alumni thus seemed intrigued by the possibility of progress in the development of the students, Sargent was equally interested in providing opportunities for all students to participate irrespective of their athletic skills and training. The strength test, after all, employed an indefinitely rising criterion of health and fitness and did not depend on the restricted and absolute pursuit of victory in a game.[3]

Sargent's emphasis on the need to mold the bodies and the living patterns of all students led him to pioneer in the field of "corrective gymnastics," in which specialized exercises were developed to meet the particular muscular deficiencies of students. His programs at the Hemenway Gymnasium hinged largely on this concept; and influential alumni even proposed making such gymnastics a general requirement, despite Harvard's commitment to the elective system in its academic program. Sargent favored sport at Hemenway, but only as an adjunct of the general improvement of a student's health. Undue concentration on a single sport, such as was common for the competitive varsity athlete, offended Sargent, who believed that this malpractice led to bodily imbalance and deformity. Despite his reputation and the considerable esteem he enjoyed at Harvard, Sargent remained skeptical about the balance of interests among students, faculty, and administrators. He noted critically: "Under the influence of the present tendency the college is not so well adapted for developing athletic qualities as it is for exhibiting them"; and he urged that schools and colleges accept the responsibility of promoting the physical development of the population as a whole, not merely the stars.[4]

Physical educators related the findings of physiologists to their own general concern for health in attempting to set standards for the training and athletic performance of their college charges. Studies of the "mechanical performance" of the body were frequent, and chemists such as W.O. Atwater analyzed the dietary

71

habits of athletes and their possible link to performance. For the physical educator, however, such work aimed not simply at athletic conquests but at the development of the "whole person" in a balanced way. Sargent cautioned against "partial, one-sided, or excessive" exercise as "surely [tending] to disease and death." Although too much specialization led to death, it did so only in the extreme. In this sense, what Sargent objected to most strenuously in athletics was not specialization itself but the degree to which it was pursued and the purposes to which it was subordinated. He deplored the sacrifice of the individual to a mere game in which the attainment of victory had assumed unrealistic importance. "The grand aim in all sports and athletic exercises," he insisted, "should be to make them supplement, so far as possible, the deficiencies in one's life work or occupation. . . . Where the muscles are soft and flabby from disuse, they should be strengthened by the use of dumb-bells, Indian clubs, or chest-weights; and so on through the wide range of developing and recreative exercises, which are admirably calculated to strengthen and improve the weak points in one's organism." Excessive zeal made sport irrational and destructive; and so training and practice, as well as competition, had to be "brought down to a rational basis."[5] It was an injunction from science as well as from common sense.

The physical educators shared the intense commitment to the principles of professional responsibility that coaches had, but they dissented sharply in their view of the function of athletics. R. Tait McKenzie, a nationally known expert in physical education and a professor at the University of Pennsylvania, explained in 1905 the purpose of his own academic department and his perception of the proper place of athletics: "The mere making of athletes was the last thing in the world for which this department was founded. A strong, healthy, symmetrical body for the mass of our students had been our primary object, with athletics as a secondary matter. We have recognized from the start, however, that the natural way for a boy to take exercise is through athletic contests, and this method has accordingly been encouraged."[6] McKenzie thus discriminated not only between his position and the coach's, but also between that of the physical educator and that of the moral reformer. His virtual obsession with "symnetry of the whole figure" and his insistence upon instituting regular exercise schedules for all students at his university showed his inclination toward standardization in human performance, albeit at a high level of efficiency. His selectivity in using exercises and sports to develop those muscles that his students had previously neglected carried into physical education the revulsion against disorder and excess.

For his part, McKenzie placed less emphasis on the spiritual effects of athletics and sport upon students than a genteel politician or moral leader would have, though more than most coaches did. Instead, consistent with the tone of professional and scientific neutrality so much admired by experts in the Progressive era, he gave attention to organic improvements, forecasting greater "efficiency of their heart and lungs." Despite disagreements with coaches, then, the physical educator gave a valued role to sport—to aid in the scientifically efficient upgrading of the body. Thus, although they deplored athletics as widely practiced as a matter of fact, the physical educators gave support to the notion that sport was a worthwhile enterprise as a matter of theory. It was not sport that was regrettable but rather their inability to dominate it and to control its expression in athletics.

THE WINNING WAYS OF THE COACH

The open secret of the coach's success in rising to popular esteem and prominence in athletics lay in his sharp and nearly exclusive focus on victory, even if he was tasteful enough to avoid public adoption of a "win at all costs" doctrine. Not everyone was single-minded about the need to win. The heirs of American gentility, for example, often perceived victory as more attainable when it was not pursued for its own sake but only as a side effect of the quest for character. So, too, subscribing to a code of behavior that required him to take no pleasure in causing pain to others, the gentleman could hardly sympathize with the rising passion of athletic enthusiasts to rub their opponents' noses in the dirt in a "zero-sum" game. Yet the moral impact and persuasiveness of this segment of American society had diminished substantially by the late nineteenth century; and even Theodore Roosevelt, who campaigned as hard as any-

73

one else against flamboyance in the conduct of sport, was often turned into a symbol of energetic excess — and was admired for it. Moreover, Roosevelt obviously preferred not to lose; and the code which lay under the distinction he was able to make in his own mind between victory and defeat was usually lost on others. Instead of emphasizing the processes that molded a winning character, a great many Americans readily subordinated these means to the end of victory; and they formed a constituency to whom the coach had a growing appeal.

Unlike the physical educators, the coaches and trainers emerged as a basically new professional group during the late decades of the nineteenth century; and their appearance coincident with the rise of sport suggests that coaches and trainers drew their values from this new and increasingly autonomous force rather than from physical education or some other institution. The very word *coach* appears not to have been associated with games and athletic competition in the years before the Civil War. B.H. Hall, in *A Collection of College Words and Customs* (1856), considered it primarily an English term referring most often to a private tutor and cited only applications of the term to academic pursuits and to manners in polite society.[7] Within a decade after the Civil War, however, coaches who regarded sport as a scientific study had already attained some recognition in various of the older schools of the Northeast and in a number of well-sponsored private athletic clubs. The extension of any form of academic status to the coaches was largely a means by which a college's faculty or administration could claim some control over the athletic behavior of the students and athletic management in general. For this reason, although they found a niche in the schools, coaches did not act as teachers in the conventional sense. They offered little or no physical benefit to the average student or to the spectator, and no assurance of happiness or longevity even to the few individuals who composed their teams. They also prudently left the defense of athletics as a molder of character to others, who attempted to reconcile the coach's emphasis on practical, goal-oriented development of the bodies of athletes with the traditionalist respectable classes' vision of sport as an agent in the formation of character. Moral renewal was not the business of

74

the athletic coach — winning was; and, increasingly, the belief spread that the coach provided the indispensable difference between victory and defeat through the application of his special skills.

Interest in a particular coach and the detailed study of his techniques originated in an attractive win-loss record. If successful, a coach might be analyzed as much as he himself studied his players, as commentators sought the sources of victory. Such was the case with Cornell's highly touted crew coach Charles E. Courtney, who often insisted — with no great modesty — that he started with "material" no better than most coaches had but that he got more out of his athletes. Praising Courtney as a sensitive observer of human nature and individual psychology, sportswriter Sol Metzger enumerated the other special qualities that accounted for his string of victories with the Cornell crews. The recital included the qualities typical of the progressive expert, although Metzger's own concern was to share the secrets of success and not the details of social analysis:

> [Courtney] makes a *scientific* study of the sport, is *unbiased* in the selection of his crews, which give him the support and confidence of the entire college; can rig a boat better than anyone, and admits that there is a lot more to be learned about handling a sweep. There is a *businesslike air* about Courtney when he is doing his work that one cannot help but admire. . . .
>
> In coaching his crew he uses perfect judgment in correcting faults or in praising a piece of good work, and he is a *strict disciplinarian* all the time.[8] (Emphasis added)

The concentration on the pursuit of victory encouraged coaches to experiment and to innovate. In 1906, British commentator Theodore A. Cook observed in the *Fortnightly* that numerous rowing styles had developed in America. Cook thought the state of affairs was needlessly confusing and tended toward inefficiency, and he noted critically, and with perhaps a touch of cynicism, that "owing to their system each professional coach desires to justify the special income paid him by producing a special theory." The American coach and commentator Walter Camp took issue less with Cook's description of America's athletic system than with the implication that this diversity of styles

Shown here late in his career, Charles E. Courtney earned fame as oarsman in the late 19th century, and later as coach of winning crews at Cornell and Harvard. He typified the new coach who transformed the practice of sport into a profession, emphasizing victory for its own sake even more than as a vehicle for social regeneration or control. By permission of the Library of Congress, Biographical Files.

yielded confusion rather than progress. At times, though, eccentric training clearly proved counterproductive. In advance of the Intercollegiate Regatta in rowing in 1906, the University of Wisconsin's crew "had some unfortunate and disastrous experiences . . . ," evidently due to a change in responsibilities among the school's athletic personnel. "It has leaked out, the past few days," Sol Metzger recorded, "that the trouble has been caused because O'Dea has not of late years been anything but the rowing coach, another man acting as trainer, whose ideas about training a crew for a race were odd, in that he gave the men but little work, some days not permitting them to get out." Metzger insisted upon the need for regular training to "get a crew together" and to correct specific faults. Failure to attain a properly high level of conditioning and skill was the coach's fault, even as victory was to his credit.[9]

The changes in football rules for 1906 gave a major opportunity for coaches to experiment and to seek new paths toward athletic glory. Edward R. Bushnell reported a sharp increase in secret practices during the season with "astute coaches preferring to have their trick plays employed first against their rivals in actual games."[10] Coaches whom a genteel American of a decade or two past might have called sneaky were praised as "ingenious" for inventing new plays and formations which, in effect, kept shifting the practical rules of the game until all of the ambiguities were clarified. Clever coaches became prominent ones, and Amos Alonzo Stagg typified the football expert whose comments on athletics won considerable public notice. Along with some exceptional trainers such as Yale's Johnny Mack, they were assuming something akin to celebrity status.

Referee Nathan B. Stauffer certified the importance of the coach in shaping a team's chance for victory. He expected great things to occur at the Carlisle Indian School after George Woodruff was appointed to run its football program in 1905. Stauffer said that Woodruff had built "a modern a-date-ahead system" at the University of Pennsylvania, where he "ultimately conceived phenomenal plays" that raised the Quakers to "a pinnacle of fame." Sympathetically, the referee recorded Woodruff's desire to teach the Indians a brand of football with "more brains and less brawn," nor did he disregard the coach's expectation that they would become a powerful team. One expert could make all the difference in the battles on the gridiron, and Coach Woodruff now presided over Carlisle's "Council of War." Similarly, the centrality of the football coach to the prospects for victory led Harvard's boosters to call in 1904 and 1905 for their old coach W.T. Reid to rescue them from mediocrity. For his return as an advisor, writer Edward R. Bushnell affirmed, Harvard "should be devoutly thankful."[11]

The move to accept professional coaches hastened as the desire for victories intensified. Reporting on the capture of the Western Athletic Conference's baseball championship by the University of Michigan in 1906, George Downey took note that, "As a first step, the graduate coaching system was abandoned and in its stead a competent professional [former major league player Lew McAllister] was installed." In "foot and track," in which Michigan's successes had assumed near inevitability, the paid expert had already won the day; and the Wolverines maintained a mixed system in which paid professionals and unpaid graduate [alumni] coaches coexisted, with the former rising to control the sports that the university targeted for future championships.[12]

Commenting on "Harvard's Athletes for 1904," Ralph D. Paine derided the conservatives who had delayed the school's adoption of professional coaching in rowing. At long last, though, the administrators were opening a new athletic era. "The graduate [alumni] coaching plan was thrown overboard," Paine observed, "amid wails of distress from the conservatives, who preferred to be whipped from now until kingdom come with the aid of gentleman-graduate-amateur-coaches rather than to defeat Yale with the assistance of imported talent whose ability to 'deliver the goods,' had been proven." Suggesting the extent to which alumni were themselves beginning to contribute to the emphasis on competition, the desire for victory over archrival Yale had intensified greatly, with Harvard having bested the Elis only twice since 1885 (in 1891 and 1899), with the dubious assistance of "fifty-seven varieties of home talent in the coaching line." Social status did not matter any more to Harvard's rowing fans, either in the choice of coach or of candidates for the crew. On recommendation from Cornell's Charles Courtney (whom Paine referred to as a scientist), Harvard selected Courtney's Assistant Coach Colson, who didn't care "one tinker's damn whether the candidate for a seat in the boat was born in or around Boston, in Painted Post or Medicine Hat; whether his name is known back to his great-grandfather in Beacon Street, or whether he is working his way through college, dragging after him the vulgar handle of John Jenkins Smith." Colson was hired to coach, and to win; and his scientific expertise, which held the promise of victory, crushed his conservative opposition. "[He] knows exactly what he wants," Paine said approvingly, "and as a result, both of his ability as a scientific master of rowing principles and his knack of handling men to the best advantage, he is doing wonders with his material."[13]

Futilely, F.S. Lang, chairman of the Board of Stewards of the Intercollegiate Rowing Association, dissented from the concentration on winning. He encouraged opposition to the increasing professionalization of the coaching and training duties in his sport. To bolster his views, he challenged even the growing sense that championship performances required the paid expert: "Columbia has had its greatest success under graduate coaching and under a system intended to develop individual intelligence in the boat. Between 1886 and 1897 there occurred a period of abject dependence upon a coach which added nothing to our available coaching material; but in the later years we have endeavored to build anew, and for a revival and continuance of the old spirit I plead."[14] But Lang perceived rightly that the amateur spirit which he sought to preserve and defend was of the "old school," and its future depended greatly on the kind of demands that would be made by students and alumni in the "better" schools. Experience suggested, however, that the cause was passing beyond recovery.

Even within the colleges of the "better classes," ambivalence reigned. At the University of Pennsylvania, for example, Edward R. Bushnell reported "an athletic revival such as it never knew before." The trainers in track and rowing, Mike Murphy and Ellis Ward, enjoyed squads of about 135 men each. Yet, at the same time, Pennsylvania dropped its professional coach from baseball altogether. Bushnell offered no explanation but only surprise: "If the history of college championship nines counts for anything the experiment is likely to be a costly one. The professional baseball coach can teach his players more in a week than an amateur collegian in a month, so wide is the gulf fixed between amateur and professional ball." But the de-emphasis of baseball that the elimination of the professional coach represented may well have represented less an experiment in training techniques than a belief that baseball was more suited to "the boys of people in poor or moderate curcumstances. . . ."[15]

Philadelphia Nationals outfielder Roy A. Thomas, who had coached the University of Pennsylvania team and also the boys at the reputable Hill School of Pottstown, Pennsylvania, encouraged a focus on winning, underscoring the need to train diligently at specific parts of the game — preparation that a professional coach, such as Thomas himself, could best facilitate. "[College boys] think that the fielding they do in the regular practice is sufficient; but it is not. It is necessary to work every spare moment at fielding in order to perfect a player in this department. These chaps think they can do justice to their work by giving just so much time and no more." Such niggardliness of commitment also accounted for the deficiencies in coaching among many of the college teams. Thomas considered it inconceivable that a few alumni, each of whom had limited time to devote and whose ideas would differ in various respects, could ever match the crack professional coach. Working at cross-purposes and at half-speed, the graduates would falter before the onslaught of the full-time expert. Yale's success in the 1905 baseball season Thomas regarded as due to William Lush who was a standout batter and baserunner for Cleveland; and he predicted rising fortunes for Holy Cross, Bates, Maine, and Bowdoin, who had all hired professional baseball players as coaches.[16]

Similarly, when Princeton decided to make a major effort to achieve success in track and field, its first step in seeking a championship was to hire Al Copeland of the New York Athletic Club to serve as coach. Underscoring the crucial function of the expert in molding the team into a victorious unit, columnist Bushnell observed that the college's old trainer, Jim Robinson, had been in poor health, which kept him from fulfilling Princeton's hopes for a winning team.[17]

The growing emphasis on competition in the world of collegiate sport sometimes permitted candor about the importance of victory. By 1905, authors Crowther and Rule recognized competition as the "only incentive to any undergraduate sport." Sport had become goal-oriented, and the medium for its attainment was the race. Crowther and Ruhl observed: ". . . we do not row much for pleasure in our colleges — it is all to beat someone, and a sport without an end can never prosper." James A. Ten Eyck, world famous oarsman and coach of Syracuse's 1904 intercollegiate champion crews, clarified the difference in emphasis and perspective that the coach brought to sport:

> Who is it that gets "a hand" from the layman at the finish line? No thought is given to the losers, it is all for the victors, and no small boys are dead anxious to tote grips and satchels for losers, but hang close to the heels of their heroes. It is human nature, and things will not change until perhaps that far-off millenium is reached. The spirit which permeates the men in charge and the men participating, is to win by "all honorable means." There is no getting behind the fact that races are entered to be won. The men who make the crew do not endure the long months of training or subject themselves to the discipline of crew life just for the fun of the thing.

For the coach, the goal at the end of careful training was not a "symmetrical body," which appealed to the physical educator, but the greatest of all manifestations of social efficiency in sport — victory.[18]

THE CULT OF TRAINING

To his great good fortune, the coach was not alone in his devotion to athletic success, nor was he the only expert committed to achieving it. The athletic trainer supported him in his efforts, shared the same focus on victory, and emerged from a comparable moment in the history of sport. Significantly, the trainers did not develop as an offshoot of medicine, which would have seemed a logical place for them to have come from, but as an adjunct of sport itself and especially of the athletic programs of the colleges and clubs. Along with the coaches, trainers formed a group that was particularly the creature of sport and athletics, which they in turn perpetuated with their increasingly professionalized skills. When other observers expressed concern over excessive training, the professionals responsible for insuring the effective performance of athletes cared instead about whether the training had been appropriate and sufficient. Yet, by concentrating on careful evaluation of the basis for effective performance, trainers often came surprisingly close to the more moderate views of some of their own critics. As Henry D. Sheldon noted in 1901, improper training often "overshot its own mark," putting a stale and tired team on the field. Even the pursuit of victory thus might lead toward the adoption of a training program that was reasonable and avoided the signs of mere compulsive behavior. On the other hand, trainers who attained popular note usually did so in conjunction with their efforts to support the work of coaches and their teams, and not because they had made a special contribution to the improvement of health.[19]

The specific use of the word *trainer* to apply to sport was largely an innovation of the nineteenth century. Although scattered references appear from earlier periods, the most common usages came in areas other than sport, as with respect to a militia "trainband." The word's gradual introduction into sport reflected the change in the temperament of players, who not only sought victory more systematically and diligently than in earlier times but were also conditioned to seek it as the proof of their dedication to training itself. Moreover, the concept of training, as it developed during the nineteenth century, extended out of the orbit of college or club sports and into the society more generally, although it did so in a climate that sport had helped to dispose more favorably toward the notion of personal fitness. Thus, the training of an athletic team played against a more popularized interest in training among nonathletes, exathletes, and frustrated athletes. Indeed, by some time in the early twentieth century, the application of the term "training" to matters other than sport seemed to be a metaphor drawn from athletics; and the change in linguistic usage provides a clue to the acceptance of this particular form of expertise.[20]

The promotion of numerous systems and plans for the improvement of health and bodily condition strongly indicates the ascent of expertise in training to considerable public acceptance. Physical culturists who developed their own systems often mar-

keted them for use in the home and recommended them universally for the population. Most important, they were normally
neither art nor magic, but system and science. A transitional
figure of tremendous impact was Eugene Sandow, who had made
a name for himself as a wrestler and strongman in England
before pursuing the same activities in America. Relying on the
appeal of his own exceptionally well-developed body, Sandow
sought names to add to his list for promotional mailings by offering in return an 8½ x 11 picture of himself in a classical
pose, relying on the intimation of paganism to shield him from
criticism. Exploiting the commercial success he had gained by
using his body in public display, Sandow persisted in showing
physical culture as an art. But even he admitted the need for
reasonable and balanced training; and he promoted the systematic use of barbells and dumbbells after he attracted an audience's attention with such sensationalism as a staged fight
with a tamed lion. Despite the fact that he was a largely theatrical figure, Sandow added to the belief in rational training of
the body.[21]

Understandably, physical culturists whose temperament
tended toward professionalism rather than theater gave clearer
emphasis to science and system. In the *Saturday Evening Post*
of October 10, 1903, for example, Dudley A. Sargent provided
a plan of seven exercises of "Home Gymnastics for the Business
Man," hoping to increase the practice of rational training and
moderate living which he encouraged among his students at
Harvard. Significantly, Sargent wore long trousers and a long-
sleeved shirt for the photographs taken to illustrate certain stages
of the exercises, thus avoiding what Thorstein Veblen ridiculed
as mere "flesh worship." Also, Sargent offered his plan to the
businessman as a practical part of the latter's career, creating
the fitness needed to endure the struggles of competition. Those
who neglected physical conditioning "drop out of the contest
and give up the race." According to Sargent, the only qualities
required to undertake the program were courage and persistence. No art. No photograph of Sandow. No magic. For each
injunction he gave the reader, Sargent provided a justification
based on simple observations from physiology that would soon
become the core of popular hygiene.[22]

Comparable emphasis on scientific precepts and on commitment to a systematic program marked the promotion of the "Stone Method," popularized through the Stone School of Physical Culture in Chicago. Frederick W. Stone, its instructor, formerly served as athletic director of Columbia College and of the Knickerbocker Club of New York. He also held the position of athletic director of the Chicago Athletic Association, presiding over its daily classes. He held the record in the 100-yard dash until 1902 (clocked at 9.8 seconds) and pronounced himself "a physically perfect man at 52 years of age." Although no one could accuse Stone of modesty, he was no charlatan. Requiring ten minutes a day, his simple program was described as a "system of concentrated exertion," in which Stone's expertise would enable students to gain rapidly the same benefit that otherwise required two hours of work with apparatus. Expressing the Progressive physical culturist's appreciation of order and science, Stone emphasized that his exercises were rational and moderate, "taught by an instructor who is thoroughly versed in physiology."[23]

Stone also claimed to be the only instructor providing specialized attention to the training needs of women and children, a boast that Prudence Barnard, the Directress of the Grecian School of Physical Culture, would surely have disputed. Barnard's "school" was a mail-order house operating out of Chicago — one of a number offering their services to the specialized but growing market of people seeking physical self-improvement. Apparently, Barnard provided her customers with charts specifying what their various measurements ought to have been when compared to a uniform standard scaled according to height. From her assurance that she demanded no special apparatus or unpleasant dieting, one may infer that she recommended concentrated and task-specific exercises of a kind that would meet the approval of responsible physical culturists.[24]

Machines not only have uses within systems — often, they actually embody systems themselves. Thus, the appearance of mechanisms which were supposed to increase health or fitness was a factor in the rise of popular bodily training, although an ambivalent one. Not all machines that were marketed were epitomes of dispassionate expertise. Some inventors, with more nerve than scientific knowledge, claimed to offer mechanical cure-alls, comparable to the special potions which purported to relieve gout, rheumatism, obesity, morphine addiction, and cancer. One such device, promoted at the turn of the century in the 1903 Sears, Roebuck & Co. catalogue, was the "Heidelberg Electric Belt," offered at $18 and touted as a wonderful source of relief from nervous disorders and from "weaknesses peculiar to men." Going beyond the promise of cures of the liver and kidneys, the guarantee of a triumph over sexual impotence suggests that sensory pleasure was being marketed as a health aid. "Every wearing brings current in contact with the [male] organ," an advertisement ran; "every wearing means that part of the organ is traversed through and through with strengthening, healing current; means a liveliness imparted, a vigor induced, a tone returned, a joy restored that thousands of dollars' worth of medicine and doctors' prescriptions would never give."[25] This was hardly what Dudley Sargent, or even Frederick Stone, had in mind by "training."

Yet there were other devices that were aimed more seriously at physical conditioning. In some devices, the electric current served as a stimulant to exercise and a reward for it, as with the Fortis Electric Exerciser, produced by the Badger Brass Company of Kenosha, Wisconsin. The Fortis Exerciser was a simple pulley-and-weight machine wired with a mild, battery-powered current. It offered a "stimulating, bracing, healthful and harmless combination of ELECTRICITY With Physical Exercise"; and it was supposed to combat headache, nervous exhaustion, insomnia, rheumatism, neuralgia, and other ailments for which some doctors specified electrical treatment. The exercise itself may have afforded some relief from the tension-born ailments that the Fortis device sought to conquer, but the Badger Brass Company clearly expected a greater consumer response to the extraneous electrical current. "Its Effect is Magical," the advertisement continued, impeaching its pretensions to science. The pulleys and weights may have been worthy enough machines, but they were marketed under something of a commercial ruse.[26]

By contrast, the Whitely Exerciser Company of Chicago, which produced a machine almost identical to the Fortis device except that it omitted the electrical wiring and battery, appealed boldly and directly to the consumer's interest in the body with its assurance of "Health, Strength, Grace, Form." Far from being magical, the Whitely machine presumably deserved attention as "the STANDARD exerciser of the World," with a claim that the company had received over 500,000 testimonials praising the merits of the device. In its straightforward acceptance of the body as a proper object of cultivation and its pride in standardization and the wide approval its product enjoyed, the Whitely Exerciser Company marked itself off from the merest hucksters and shared in the progressive spirit of the sincere physical culturists.[27]

"Mail-order" physical culturists who aspired to act as trainers to the masses may have been taking advantage of the more positive attitude toward the body of which the rise of sport was a part. But colleges and clubs took a more direct approach, aiming to upgrade sporting performance by hiring expert trainers to handle the practical conditioning of their athletes. These were the sort of men who trained with tools rather than gimmicks. When they identified a physical need, they often developed machines to meet it. They shared their lineage, in this respect, with the expert coaches and trainers who had developed the rowing shell, which revolutionized the sport. It was perhaps appropriate, if teams were metaphorical machines, that the athletes should be trained with the aid of real ones. Increasingly, the invention of specific training devices reflected the selective knowledge of the experts. In the November 11, 1905, issue of *The Illustrated Outdoor News*, an article by Princeton's football coach William H. Edwards featured a photograph of "The Michigan Charging Machine," a primitive blocking-sled. Although more refined by 1917, the apparatus (now referred to as a "bucking" machine) remained novel enough for mention in *The Book of Modern Marvels*, edited by Waldemar Kaempffert. The editor noted approvingly that the machine substantially reduced the time required to train young players in the basics, allowing still more time to be devoted to finer points. Similarly, tackling dummies were developed; and, by 1917, they seemed to be the most widely used "mechanical contrivance" for training in football.[28]

Nor was the introduction of mechanical training devices re-

This crew, practicing at Columbia University in 1910, had front- and side-view mirrors by which to check their body-position and form — a hint at how the motion-studies of Muybridge and Eakins prompted coaches and trainers to provide athletes with visual images against which to check performance. By permission of the Library of Congress, George Grantham Bain Collection (LC-B2-963-11).

stricted to football. Enterprising inventors provided baseball coaches with devices for the more effective and selective training of pitchers. One such device was the "automatic umpire" with a target the size of a strike zone and batters in silhouette — right-handed or left-handed at the discretion of the coach. Another machine used dummies rather than a plain geometric target and a batter in silhouette. Here the umpire's chest protector defined the strike zone. Both inventions had become popular with some serious baseball players; but the automatic pitching machine — known as "the mechanical batting instructor" — had become the most common by World War I. So, too, by the turn of the century, rowing machines had been brought to an appreciable level of perfection, and their use became standard.[29] Machines gave coaches and trainers the ability to control variables, testing a pitcher against the constant standard of a target rather than against the variable skills of a batter. Similarly, a batter who practiced with the aid of a "mechanical batting instructor" expected steady pitching; and this presumably served as a more scientific means of training and testing his skill than pitting him against a live player whose own skill would have become another confusing variable. The machines suggested an element of standardization within the training process.

No mechanical device could substitute for human intervention, and the trainers knew it, along with the coaches whom they supported. Indeed, for these experts, machines were symbols of their own quasi science and proofs that they merited esteem and deserved the authority they exercised over their charges. The trainers and the coaches might use mechanical devices, but it was they who molded mere men into athletic machines. Trainers were sometimes specifically given the credit for the otherwise surprising improvement of athletes, such as John Stone of Mercersburg, Pennsylvania. The son of a former governor of Pennsylvania, Stone's faster time as a two-mile runner during 1906 "reflects great credit on the new trainer," one writer noted. Other athletes supposedly improved because of weight-training conducted under expert supervision. But whatever the specific sport or training technique, the role of the expert was affirmed.[30]

Proper training, which would make young men function effectively as part of the team, promised higher levels of performance and lower levels of injury. Cornell rowing coach Courtney wrote in 1905: "In training the men, I always look on them as well-regulated and delicate steam engines," except that they had brains on the inside. Courtney observed that the challenge was to work hard to get the machines into outstanding condition without damaging them or leaving them in poor shape when their use was at an end. Methodical preparation would make the difference. Syracuse University's football coach C.P. Hutchins suggested that even the rate of injuries would decline if all schools hired professional coaches and trainers. With some frustration, he expressed doubt that football fans appreciated all the effort behind what they were seeing, asserting that "not one spectator in a hundred outside of college men has the slightest conception of the processes involved in preparing a college football team for the season." Hutchins attempted to explain the benefits of methodical care:

Aside from the technique of play, scientific exactness is exercised in maintaining a perfect balance between physical fitness and work [practice] (a process known as "conditioning"), every possible circumstance is anticipated and players are persistently instructed how to meet plays in such a way that liability to injury is reduced to a minimum. In colleges where this training is intelligent and skillful, fatalities and even serious injuries are rare.

The Illustrated Sporting News expressed a similar view on December 5, 1903, observing that "grave mishaps are reported only among young and untrained players."[31]

The emphasis on competition had enhanced the importance of training systems and devices, and observers believed that they were yielding more effective performance in sport with athletes depending increasingly on their expert advisers. By the early part of the twentieth century, commentators considered it unreasonable to compete without having trained intensively for specific events, usually under professional supervision. Describing the outdoor swimming season of 1906, L. deB. Handley cited the marked improvement of performances by Americans in distance events occasioned by the "systematic manner in which promoters of swimming are forcing things ahead." Handley's acceptance of this systematic manner encouraged his defense of a swimmer, the New York Athletic Club's C.M. Daniels, who had "refused to enter events he had been unable to train for." What an earlier day might have considered pluck, Daniels would have dismissed as foolishness.[32]

Daniels similarly demanded complete mastery of any one stroke before the competitor moved on to other elements of training and certainly before entering a meet. "Practice slowly," he said, "with a coach over you, until you are satisfied that your stroke is correct in every way, then go ahead and compete." The champion swimmer attested to the value of careful study of human motion when he described how American athletes had emerged to world-class performance by the time of the 1904 international competitions. In 1903, a group of "practical and intelligent swimmers" had assembled at the New York Athletic Club, pored over all news concerning technique and strokes from all available sources, experimented on the basis of their study, and set out a body of swimming doctrine that pulled the Americans to victory.[33]

In 1906, trainer Charles W. Green of the Boston Americans asserted that a "first-class trainer" was "undoubtedly a part of a first-class outfit nowadays, and to be without one is as grave a mistake as can be committed." Unlike the manager whose attentions Green believed would be too divided to permit expert and effective scrutiny of the needs of all players, the trainer would reduce injuries and increase efficiency of performance by coordinating exercise programs; and he would exert control over the athletes' diet, their hours of rest, and their personal hygiene. Green also inferred that his recommendations for baseball players in particular applied to competitors in other sports as well. He expostulated: "Imagine a lot of athletes [track and field competitors] never practising starts and trusting to win any race in which they entered without preparation at all!" Green's observation that practicing starts and sprints would improve a team's overall performance supplied new testimony to the case against the presumptions of the natural athlete and raw talent. New York pitcher Albert Orth attested to the need for "constant practice" as the only way of gaining perfect command. He considered this the secret of Cy Young's manifest success. "He is a glutton for work," Orth said, "and can work twice a week, and more, too." Similarly, an effective curve ball resulted not from luck but simply as a matter of practice. From another vantage, J. Parmly Paret underscored the value of systematic training when, in coverage of the national tennis championships in 1906, he dismissed the defeat of former singles champion Beals Wright as totally predictable, citing the "hopelessness of trying to play championship tennis at Newport without proper preparation and training."[34]

Training thus developed into a network of cults and subcults, in which various prominent figures established competing programs for the development of athletes and those swept up in the concern for the body during the institutional emergence of sport. Notwithstanding the fact that some trainers had no advance preparation in their chosen field and no form of certification, they sought to carve out a professional niche for themselves; and, in the process, they both capitalized on and strengthened the growing interest in more effective performance in sport. In this sense, as creatures of sport and creators of athletes, they were dependent upon the institutional success of sport for their own professional success. But even when trainers and physical culturists competed within the same market or for the same reservoir of popular esteem, they strengthened the sense that sport and athletics were important pursuits.

FOOD FOR SPORT

In the late decades of the nineteenth century, nutrition emerged as yet another area of concern — in some quarters, as an applied aspect of chemistry; in others, as a means toward increased health; and for still others, as an aid in achieving higher levels of sporting and athletic performance. Because of this diversity in origin and interest, nutritionists were not automatically the subordinates of coaches and the firm hands controlling the public display of collegiate and professional sport. One wing among the nutritionists traced its heritage back to the good instincts of Sylvester Graham, whose primary concern was health as a basis for social reform. Those who aspired to wear the mantle of chemistry were also seeking the legitimacy of science and professionalism. Yet there were others whose concentration on sport and athletics led them to subordinate nutrition to the enterprise they loved most of all.

The application of nutrition to sport depended upon the fact that coaches came to realize that there was a connection between diet and athletic performance and upon the fact that there were some specialists who had attempted to show that such a connection existed. The nutritionists did not necessarily care about sport, whatever use might be made of their work; but they were deeply committed to the same sort of reasonable and restrained style of life that was coming to be a hallmark of the professionally coached and trained athlete. For example, Horace Fletcher, an early leader in this new field, urged that readers of his *A.B.–Z. of Our Own Nutrition* commit themselves to "rationally economic alimentation," the value of which he claimed to have been confirmed by work and endurance measurements. His charts and tables testified to his conviction that nutrition deserved experimental study, and he strongly suggested that human performance depended on a carefully regulated diet "thoroughly masticated." "May we not assume," he wrote, "that beings who have learned to breed and train horses to race with human intelligence, and to run, trot, or pace a mile in less than two minutes, may also train themselves to have the proportional relative speed, endurance, and longevity that has been attained by race horses through man's care . . . ?" Fletcher cited the work of the Russian experimental physiologist Ivan Pavlov, the French physiologist Blondlot, the British physiologist Sir Michael Foster, Director Russell H. Chittenden of the Sheffield Scientific School at Yale, and many others; and he synthesized their findings into a coherent series of recommendations to the reader. He specifically charged athletes to maintain a proper diet at all times so that extreme, "crash" dieting to overcome "false conditions which they have brought upon themselves" would be unnecessary. Instead, the athlete would remain in perfect condition all the time. Perfection was pretending to be normality.[35]

An ardent advocate of natural foods and the publisher of *Physical Culture Magazine*, Bernarr MacFadden (who was also a devoted follower of Horace Fletcher) later commented on the

Among the "new experts" in physiology was nutritionist Horace D. Fletcher, who developed schedules for achieving health by improving diet. They saw the body as a material process, undergoing endless change, but believed that careful regulation could impose predictability in behavior and performance. By permission of the Library of Congress, Biographical Files.

turn of the century, when he had joined the campaign against drugs, adulterants, and nutritional imbalance. In the preface to his *Physical Culture Cook Book* (1924), he recalled:

> When *Physical Culture* was started twenty-five years ago it entered a world in which many foolish and artificial conceptions of life were prevalent. These ideas were a mixture of old superstitions and half-baked conceptions of new-born science. . . .
>
> With the exceptions of a few athletes and artists, people cared little for the appearance of the body and tried in every way to hide its existence, and preserve their ignorance of its forms and functions.

MacFadden admitted that his own knowledge of nutrition had been limited when he first took up the cause, but he had also had faith that science would tell what constituted proper diet. In the absence of scientific knowledge, he taught reliance on natural tastes and flavors instead of artificial ones. MacFadden praised the establishment of standards for proper daily intake of food, and he greeted warmly the arrival of Federal interest and the continuing battle against the adulteration of foods.[36]

The work of such specialists aided in the specification of food intake for athletes. But there had been regimens of varying quality for some time. The term "training table" seems not to have appeared until the turn of the century, suggesting that the scientific preparation of special food for athletes was uncommon much before then. Mitford Mathews finds references in Waldron Post's *Harvard Stories* (1893) and George Ade's *People You Know* (1903), sufficiently casual in tone to justify the inference that the institution of the training table had been established in at least a few schools for a number of years.[37] For the most part, however, the lag between their existence in the schools and their mention in print is not likely to have been excessive.

By the time the expert came to have broad impact on American sport, however, nutrition did not escape his interest. In describing how big league baseball teams prepared for competition, Allen Sangree wrote in 1904 of the intense interest that his correspondents had in diet. In fact, he believed this to be the most common question about training. As liberal as professional baseball coaches could be in this matter, so were the college coaches and trainers in other sports restrictive and, at times, eccentric: "When the football season begins you will see columns in the sporting pages as to what the Yale captain allows his men for breakfast, dinner and supper. Harvard's captain decides that a bottle of ale per day is just what his eleven needs; Princeton boys are gorged on mutton chops; Cornell must have plenty of vegetables." But Sangree did not ridicule this striving toward system in diet. He disapproved only of the excessive paternalism that he considered the bane of managing college teams. He shared the view of many professional coaches that "an ambitious athlete . . . is wise enough to look after his physical welfare without coaching."[38] Expertise was in order, but it was the athlete's duty to gain knowledge of his own dietary needs. The college athletes soon gave reason to credit Sangree's opinion.

The "mutiny" of the Cornell crew of 1904 signified the acceptance by college athletes of the principles of planned nutrition and of the athletic training table. The sixteen young men on the varsity squad had complained about their food for months. But the climax of their protest came after a twelve-mile practice in cold winds that could "breed a ravenous appetite in a dyspeptic." According to one reporter, "they wanted slabs of beef inches thick, mashed potatoes brought on in tubs, loaves of bread heaped mountain high, and when these were gone, more bread, beef, and potatoes. Instead of these satisfying and muscle-building staples, the oarsmen were offered the properties of a dainty afternoon tea, with an entrée, and a charlotte russe." After they had "swept the table as a Kansas grasshopper army skins a wheat field bare," the oarsmen stormed out on strike swearing not to return until the university's Athletic Association insured a training table suited to strong men doing hard work. Without proper food, the magazine editorialized, victory was impossible. Coach Courtney agreed that he could not turn out winning crews unless they were well fed. Yet there was a happy moral to this otherwise distressing story. The students had shown their acceptance of rational, proper diet as essential to success in sport. With proud approval, *The Illustrated Sporting News* elaborated upon the students' enthusiasm for straightforward nutrition uncomplicated by the frivolities of foreign cuisines:

95

There used to be much talk about the "Spartan" sacrifice of the college oarsmen, and the hardships he was willing to undergo for glory, subjecting himself cheerfully to rigid monotony of diet. The Cornell strike shows that the young men who train for crews know what is best for them, that they are as anxious to keep in splendid physical condition as their coach is to have them so, and that of choice they prefer the simple, nutritious foods in place of the pies, pastries and flummeries of the cuisine they are popularly supposed to be pining for during their months of training.[39]

Training schedules varied, but they represented careful thought and an attempt at science even when they made extraordinary demands. For example, Jasper Goodwin's remarks about permitting his oarsmen at Columbia to train indoors until a break in "cold, damp and disagreeable weather" may have sounded "a bit soft and ladylike to some"; but Goodwin defended his decision by arguing that overtraining was counterproductive. "I do not think that heroic methods do a crew any good," he added. *The Illustrated Sporting News* of March 5, 1904, thought he might have a point:

Twenty years ago college athletes were put through a course of sports that sound foolish and cruel to-day. There were long and killing runs before breakfast, with a diet mostly of raw beef and oatmeal. Only twelve years ago the Yale oarsmen in the trying heat of the final training at New London were given a limited allowance of water and suffered from feverish and irritating thirst. It may be that in football and rowing methods of training not all the unreasonable traditions have yet been eliminated.[40]

Breeding unreasonable and unscientific practices out of training also appealed to S. Crowther and A. Ruhl, whose commentary on the history of American rowing appeared in 1905. Crowther and Ruhl also thought that the excesses of the Yale crew typified the old regime:

The training of Wilbur Bacon's crew at Yale is an example of the old way. That crew rose each morning at six, and then, in heavy flannels, ran from three to five miles on empty stomachs; in the forenoon they would row from four to six miles and do the same distances in the afternoon, and these rows were not easy paddles, but hard, stiff trials mostly on time. They ate under done beef and mutton, with the blood running from it, with now and then a few potatoes or rice, but no other vegetable, and drank weak tea in small quantities.

Since the taking of water was apt to put back the weight that had been lost through perspiration, the men were given only what they positively could not do without, and the best trainer was he who could train without water. The absolute limit was one glass for breakfast, two for dinner, and one for supper, and they had none between meals. The agony of such a course when men were rowing in the hot sun and perspiring freely can be imagined, and it was further increased by the prohibition of baths; some coaches would not permit their men to bathe for three weeks or more before a race. The results of this system are well given by Mr. Blaikie (a former Harvard oarsman), who says: "No wonder that with such a lack of variety of nutrition, sore boils broke out on them until we heard of one man who had seventy-three." [41]

However misguided Bacon's training regimen was, it is crucial that he had one. Although error based on custom or quackery riddled his program, the training of his athletes followed a system, and in this Bacon's efforts prefigured the more sophisticated and medically sounder programs that burgeoned at the turn of the century. One is tempted to quip that the trials and sufferings of his crews aimed not at ensuring their morality but at proving their mortality. But it is more truthful to admit that they aimed to enhance athletic performance; and the dedicated submission of the oarsmen to a torturous water discipline, inelegant personal habit, and restricted diet reflected the obedience to authority that surfaced boldly after the Civil War. It also, of course, implied the acceptance of authoritative and expert wisdom whose most bizarre demands were not to be questioned.

THE SELF-DEFEATING CRITIQUE OF COMPETITIVENESS

The rise of coaches, trainers, and nutritionists as experts in managing sporting performance nonetheless raised objections from some who believed that decorum and traditional values were laid waste by the athletic mania and who considered the emphasis on competitiveness to be individually and socially destructive. Although approval of the new experts of the body was widespread, such critics as did arise were usually well placed and articulate. Yet their critique of competitiveness and excess — and of the experts with whom they associated these aspects of sport — ultimately stumbled on its own logic. The critics often railed at the unreasonableness of spending large sums for the sake of a winning team, yet they approved of the rationality and order that were the heart of the team and of its relationship to the coach. Accepting authority as a principle, they objected to the diminution of their own authority in guiding behavior; and they even called upon experts of their own from the field of physical education to bolster their dissent from the coaches and trainers. Often rooted in the tradition of American gentility, such critics opposed the way in which the common practice of athletics was affecting society, yet they acknowledged that some social link was probably inevitable. Thus, although their position was internally coherent, it ran the risk of ambiguity in its confrontation with competing views; and it even allowed for the importance of sport and properly managed athletics.

Vocal among those who feared that the rising tide of professional experts would demoralize and debauch the young, E.L. Godkin inveighed against the "athletic craze." In *The Nation* of December 7, 1893, he reported disparagingly that Yale had "spent last year about $47,000 on athletics, and the team went to Springfield the other day with three drawing room cars and fifty men as substitutes, doctors, trainers, rubbers, and cooks." Although these facts suggested a remarkable degree of specialization of function within Yale's program, Godkin preferred to focus on the problem of inordinate attention to the players and excessive spending for the competition.[42]

The headmasters of reputable Northeastern schools resented the impact that the athletic movement was having on the standards and attitudes of their students, seeing the particular professional focus of coaches and their staffs as a major source of the difficulty. William Beach Olmsted, Headmaster of the Pomfret School (Connecticut), blamed the coaching system for "the teaching of the necessity of winning at any cost," and added pointedly: "To the same system may properly be traced the degeneracy of athletics from sane sport to insane and real business." Alfred E. Stearns, Headmaster of Phillips Academy (An-dover), pointed to the "unnatural and abnormal position" of athletics in the schools and called for reform. Stearns considered extravagant expenditure to be vicious and demoralizing, suggesting his intellectual kinship with the Brooks Adams of *The Law of Civilization and Decay;* yet he believed that sport should be retained for its "inherent goodness" as long as it could be conducted on what he called a "normal basis." The acceptance of sport as a fundamentally worthy enterprise, however, made their case hinge on the definition of what was normal; and the criteria of normality were evolving at a considerable pace. The headmaster's view, for example, suggested a preference to avoid change and a failure to seek progress. While the headmaster could only wish for the fulfillment of each student as a gentleman according to a substantially fixed code, the coach could at least seem to be an agent of progress, measured in the growing statistics of athletic victories.[43]

Although some critics of athleticism attacked college administrators and faculties as powerless to govern sport, the situation had developed less from inability than from disinclination. Until late in the nineteenth century, college authorities believed that they should have no official role in sport and athletics. Even those who were favorably disposed toward Thomas Wentworth Higginson's calls to Muscular Christianity usually saw the cultivation of bodily health as a personal and largely private matter. In 1860, the Reverend F.D. Huntington, Preacher to the University and Plummer Professor of Christian Morals in Harvard College, advocated parental guidance of the child's sport and games while he was at home and "judicious self-regulation" for the young collegian. Speaking to the Massachusetts House of Representatives, Huntington acknowledged that a scholar's success, happiness, and utility depended on his physical condition; but he did not anticipate that bodily training and health guidance should become the business of the college. In short, even if one's physical condition had some social consequence, it was a personal and not a corporate responsibility.[44]

In 1894, E.L. Godkin reiterated the view that undue emphasis on the team, the coach, and athletics would undermine the prospects for the health of the student body at large, Extravagance in athletics, he asserted, "has begot and is spreading the fallacy that if you are not a member of a team, and have no coach, it is not worth while doing anything to keep up your bodily vigor." Would it not be absurd, he mused, if such erroneous views propounded by some advocates of professional coaches and trainers disqualified the nation's young men from "the competition which is the law of life?"[45] Godkin's argument lost some of its force when analyzed carefully, since coaches, for example, did not discourage average students from seeking physical fitness. They simply were not his problem; and, to confuse the matter further, there were physical educators eager to take up the slack. Thus, Godkin's criticisms drew from the older school of the Reverend Mr. Huntington without quite adapting the traditional concerns to the actual circumstances of the 1890s. For other critics of excessive athleticism, even the physical fitness of the individual required the exertions of a group to create circumstances favorable to it. Even more, some realized that, whatever their personal preferences, college presidents and faculties had to extend a hand in controlling athletics or else an absorbing aspect of student life would elude their influence.

The essence of reform of the athletic system lay in providing centralization and continuity to administrative control. In the past, sport had generally been handled by free associations of students and sometimes additional supporters of a team, who elected their own officers. The managers of these teams, "who possessed the substance of authority, were commonly selected by either the athletic teams or captains." This self-regulation yielded to what Henry D. Sheldon called, in 1901, "a more powerful, stable, and representative body" consisting of faculty, alumni, and student members serving as a central governing body. The specific organization of a controlling committee varied from college to college; Sheldon asserted that, by the turn of the century, "a reasonable degree of uniformity had been reached in the regulation of sport . . . ." Eligibility rules were specified, and there were efforts to standardize the rules of intercollegiate games, procedures for choosing the teams' managers and captains, and matters of finance. The growing belief that education must be conceived as an orderly and well-regulated experience for the student culminated in internal pressure for order and regulation of collegiate sport. If each aspect of the student's life was related to all others, the educational objectives of the college would logically be hostage to the athletic pursuits of its students unless the faculty and administrators also sought influence over athletics. Thus, President Charles W. Eliot of Harvard, whose intellectual abilities were sometimes attributed to his own youthful exercises by promoters of sport, approved of official bodies within the colleges to govern sport so as to end what he called "wanton exaggeration" of its importance. Overemphasis on athletics converted the student into "a powerful animal, and [dulled] for the time being his intellectual parts." Eliot would not tolerate the vagaries of the old system. [46]

For the educator who valued the traditional liberal arts, the assertion of control over sport was a defensive measure. But for the new class of physical educators, such as E.M. Hartwell, sport and physical education emerged as intrinsically worthy and hence crying out for the attention of rational, scientific, well-trained experts. In his statement "On Physical Education," published in the *Report of the United States Commissioner of Education* (1897–1898), Hartwell evinced a disdain for the excessive spirit of rivalry and "undue prominence of athletics"; yet his reasons seemed to grow more from his specific professional interests than from Eliot's concerns. Hartwell appeared as irritated by the specific phenomenon of peer influence and the imitation of senior players by junior members of the team as he was by the general corruption of sport; and he generalized that the "best interests of rational and effectual physical training have suffered much in this country. . . ." [47] By the latter part of the nineteenth century, these two quite separate influences — the college administrators and the progressive physical educators — fed into the stream of reform in collegiate athletics. But the instruments that both recommended for control over sport — management, standardization of rules, and the institutionalizing of the administration of athletics — could prove ambivalent. For they originated in the same spirit of efficiency that had supported the rise of the coaches.

In fine, what distinguished the physical educators, trainers, and coaches of the turn of the century from the relatively few professionals of the 1860s and 1870s was the fact that the body of scientifically verified information was far greater. Hunch had yielded to experiment; guess had become datum. In all, the experimental accumulation of reliable data about numerous sporting activities had made possible a fundamental change in the role and in the image of the sport expert. For without the existence of a body of scientifically tested knowledge, he could not have been regarded as an expert in the first place. Behind all the particulars of the emergence of the expert, however, lay the equation of athletic supremacy with triumphant social efficiency. Dazzling but erratic performance lost much of its appeal, and greatness in the athlete became associated with predictability, methodical and analytical preparation, and standardization of performance — albeit on a high level.

The experts in physical culture increasingly viewed themselves as a professional group, or even as separate professional groups. Taken as a general discipline of the body-sciences, they might have aspired to govern the world of sport, at least in the schools and colleges. Yet the inability of each to extend dominance over comparably strong competing groups left it dominion over no more than an island within the whole world of sport. When they distinguished among subgroups dealing with different aspects of bodily training, they further divided the realm; and their competition among themselves for the control of what was left of sport and athletics weakened the chance for a true alliance of professionals to oppose designs on sport that might arise in other quarters. As Robert Wiebe has suggested, the new specialists who formed professional organizations and associations desired "to remake the world upon their private models."[48] But the diversity of private models harbored by advocates of the new body-sciences all but precluded any practically effective alliance. On the other hand, this very multiplicity of interests allowed sport to become a multiform phenomenon, even within the colleges, and to draw strength from the differing groups, whose one common belief was that the athlete's achievement depended less on the character of the man than on the managerial science of the new experts who regulated his life.

CHAPTER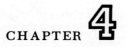

Sporting Life as Consumption, Fashion, and Display — The Pastimes of the Rich

IT has been argued that the newly emerging class of extravagantly rich Americans whose wealth was rooted in industrial capitalism came to challenge the role of social leadership and political power of the traditional American gentility. Later historians have questioned the degree of antipathy between old and new wealth.[1] But in sport, quantities of money meant the ability to govern the games that could be played. Although ultrarich Americans did not dictate institutionalized sport among other classes, they made possible the emergence of certain sports that required large outlays of money for facilities and their maintenance. Most important in the interplay of varying attitudes about sport in the early twentieth century, the ultra-rich — the Vanderbilts, the Harrimans, and others — embodied an alternative sensibility about sport.[2] They conducted it as a mode of consumption and as a fashion; and what regeneration they were likely to experience through sport flowed from its social outlets. That the remnant of the gentility, such as Roosevelt and Lodge, might have harbored such sentiments at an unconscious level is possible; but that they could have pursued them deliberately is nearly inconceivable. In this difference lay the curious contribution of the ultra-rich toward attitudes about sport.

It is debatable whether America's sporting life was ever truly democratic, and the question itself hinges largely on matters of definition; but it is certain that democracy of nearly any description had no place in the world of the very rich. Using their sports as badges of social status, the ultra-rich generally confined themselves to pursuits whose cost put them out of reach

103

of ordinary Americans. Yachting, polo, fox-hunting, tennis, and golf — these were the characteristic sports of the American rich. Indeed, their penchant to use sport as a means of establishing social exclusiveness and prestige showed itself not only in the activities that they favored but in their departure from various sports that they could not control. Baseball, for example, had been strongly favored by the New York Knickerbockers, widely considered the earliest baseball club and composed of players from the economically advantaged class. Despite baseball's subsequent reputation as a sport of the American masses, it thus found early encouragement among the rich. As the control of baseball came to be concentrated largely in the hands of middling men of commerce, however, the interest that the rich and socially distinguished showed in the sport fell off sharply. Although it was not necessary for them to avoid all contact with baseball or those who played it, it did seem important to mark out some other sports as their distinctive realm.

In this passion for exclusiveness, the very rich, who sought means of certifying their worth, often made the criticisms of Thorstein Veblen seem a miracle of understatement. In the words of Price Collier, they were "a widely advertised, though fortunately small, class, diligent in making themselves conspicuous, who, having been recently poor, are trying to appear anciently rich." In a 1911 volume predicting their passing, Frederick Townsend Martin called them the "idle rich." He thought it a pity and a disgrace that high society in the United States had come to be confused with a small minority who had grafted their quest for outrageous display onto the more conservative system that had preceded them. Martin derided the very rich as imitators of the gauche and vulgar excesses of the underworld, which they merely brought to new levels of extravagance. Expense was the only standard by which to judge their activities; and it was a criterion that Martin deplored as bad sense and bad taste. Moreover, it was a criterion that differed fundamentally from the standards of duty and dedication to the public interest which held such deep appeal for middle- and upper-middle-class Americans. Yet the new ultra-rich were accorded a peculiar publicity; and, while excluding those of an inferior economic class from the scenes of their sport, they nonetheless assumed a certain paradoxical visibility, through which they became the embodiment of the quest for pleasure and self-gratification.[3]

Simultaneously a source of personal amusement and a component of an exclusionary social system, the sports of the very rich industrial magnates and financiers were thus special in kind, special in place, and special in function. The characteristic sportive activities of the rich took place in distinctive environments shaped for their pursuit — whether a country club or even a whole compound such as at Newport, Rhode Island. Sport further served as a device for governing their etiquette and signifying their status. Ironically, the rich found their own way of giving meaning to Grantland Rice's maxim that what mattered was "how you played the game"; and social manners frequently predominated over athletic prowess in determining who really won or lost. Yet, for this reason, sport itself seemed all the more real, as it was tied to the very core of one's social goals and aspirations. Sport thus gained an added constituency that perceived it to have value, fastening on it as a nonproductive amusement and an instrument of display.

THE EXCLUSIONARY SPORTS OF THE RICH

By the very sporting ventures they chose, the American rich set patterns of behavior that distinguished them from the masses and even from much of the respectable middle class. Infected with a desire to set fashion and keep pace with its mercurial changes, the wealthy elite often opted for the customs of the British upper classes — a phenomenon that showed itself in the sudden vogue of tennis and golf and invited satire in the rise of fox-hunting. A key means of distinguishing fashionable sport from common amusement was the price tag. Those requiring expensive and well-maintained facilities had a special appeal for the rich, who affected a lack of interest in the cost of their undertakings while glorying in their ability to pay it. It was the attitude of J. Pierpont Morgan who, when asked how much it cost to maintain his yacht, replied that anyone who had to ask could not afford one. Thus, the difference in dollars segregated the very rich from the majority of Americans, even if temperament might not always have done so. Indeed, it was less a division of the sheep from the goats than a segregation of the sheep from the wolves — an economically predatory group that now feigned purity and breeding and rode to hounds.

Armed with the money to realize virtually any whim, the new rich sometimes experimented with frivolous variations on established sports, at the same time revealing a fascination with mechanical and other novelties that added to the pace of fashion and drawing strength from a somewhat perverse appropriation of the idea of progress. In 1906, for example, the machine made a bumpy and bizarre entrance into the garden of the well-to-do when a Professor J.F. Draughon of Nashville, Tennessee, became an ardent exponent of "Fox Hunting in an Automobile"; and word of his exploits circulated among the curious. Uniting two oddities — one old and the other new — Draughon's short-lived fad suggested, at the level of ideas, a somewhat egoistic desire to amplify personal control over the natural components in sport. This same tendency showed itself in the growing vogue of defying the seasons by traveling to a climate more hospitable to one's favorite sports. Midwinter horse racing in New Orleans gained a following scattered around the country, and midwinter golf tournaments at Pinehurst and elsewhere lured devotees of the links and of country club life. Thus, either modifications of a sport or the gathering at a distant venue might lend social distinction to one's pursuits; and they did so in a way that placed maximum importance on the pleasuring of the individual sportsman taken as a consumer, albeit a wealthy one, and on gratification as a suitable goal in his life.[4]

Reports of costly sporting endeavors mingled with social notices and advertisements for expensive consumer items in the pages of magazines catering to the country club set and to elements within the middle class. *The Illustrated Sporting News* exemplified this tendency in its lavish issue for Christmas 1906. Included were articles devoted to "Hunting Big Game in Africa," "Automobile Touring in the Rocky Mountains," and "The Phantom Fox." To illustrate an article on fishing, the editors chose a man who could hardly be considered an angler of average social status or personal influence — William Loeb, Jr., the personal secretary to President Theodore Roosevelt. Adding to the impression that sport was a part of fashion and distinction (and hence a fusion of services and commodities to be consumed), advertisements for champagne, luxurious automobiles, banks, and stockbrokers were freely interspersed among announcements of kennels specializing in Dalmatians, Pomeranians, and English and French bulldogs.[5] To someone imbued with the values of the traditional gentility, all of this seemed a dissipation that threatened to become the serpent in the private Eden of the rich. Among the very wealthy, however, it signified the dominance of material things and pleasurable experiences over philosophical sentiment.

Americans who enjoyed wealth and cultivated social distinctions, rather predictably, shied away from various more popular sports that pretended to egalitarianism and suited the means of the more modest consumer. Baseball and cycling thus appealed less to the rich than to others, largely because of the broad interest that the "middling sort" and the working class showed in them. Moreover, the rich demonstrated less commitment to the disciplined development of their abilities in such sports, partly because of their tendency to move restlessly from one diversion to another and also due to their greater sense of sport as leisure. Professional baseball player Roy A. Thomas, who coached at the fashionable Hill School in Pottstown, Pennsylvania, complained that boys born to the upper class pursued too many sports and had little interest in the "national game." By contrast, boys from modest and average backgrounds played the game compulsively, devoted all their play hours to it. "They study it," Thomas added, "look at it from all of its phases, and they naturally become adept at it." For his part, Thomas preferred the schoolboys to the scions of the wealthy, whose lack of enthusiasm for his game suggested their social distance.[6] Yet one must temper Thomas's criticism with a recognition that, as a professional, he carried the spirit and the code of work into his pursuit of a game; and, while the rich surely allowed sport and games a role in their lives, they were no more likely to confuse sport with work than to carry the precepts of play into the world of business and finance.

The rich sportsmen came to compose something of a nationwide network, their customs setting them off as a group from lesser economic classes despite the differences they often had among themselves. Yet the wealthy shied away from that national inclusiveness which cut across social class, ethnic origin, and economic condition and which the likes of Lodge and Roosevelt claimed to want. In *America's National Game*, published in 1911, Albert Spalding asserted: "The genius of our institutions is democratic; Base Ball is a democratic game." Notwithstanding the disingenuity of their coming from a corporate magnate of considerable means, such remarks marked baseball off from the political sympathies and social instincts of the rich, for whom sharing in popular sport would have been a rank eccentricity. In the afterglow of Roosevelt's presidency, Spalding sought to use the mantle of democratic egalitarianism to cover social and economic differences. "The son of a President of the United States," he insisted, "would as soon play ball with Patsy Flannigan as with Lawrence Lionel Livingstone, provided only that Patsy could put up the right article. Whether Patsy's dad was a banker or a boiler-maker," he added, "would never enter the mind of the White House lad."[7] Spalding glossed over the fact that Patsy's chances of playing with a Roosevelt greatly increased if he attended Groton and Harvard; but his overoptimistic, perhaps even self-deceptive, assertion of a classless cosmopolitanism in the great American pastime epitomized what the Vanderbilts and their kind were in the process of avoiding.

Cycling, too, had become virtually a national mania in America by the turn of the century; but the upper classes did not take it up as a regular feature of their sporting regimen. According to Elizabeth Barney, an acute observer of sporting behavior, cycling was "the amusement *par excellence* of the people"; and, in this case, she meant the great middle classes, including smaller shopkeepers, tradesmen, mechanics, and clerks. She conceded that it would be "absurd" to deny that some few members of the upper class had taken up the wheel. But only a small number would thus risk seeming to consort with their presumptive inferiors. So unfashionable did this middle-class participation make cycling that, according to Barney, those few women of the upper stratum who deigned to cycle at all were "not apt to use their wheels in public." The implication was that they would ride within the privacy of their estates. So, too, wealthy women disdained the new "rational costume," such as the bloomers that advocates of dress reform promoted, and thus cycling became more difficult for a very practical reason. The rich showed reluctance, then, to join in "the cycling set," as Barney called them, since the group was not very discriminating and since it was both too large and too established for the wealthier sort to take over its control.[8]

Although many advocates of pure amateurism from varying economic backgrounds were concerned to avoid excessive attention from journalists and sports fans lest it lead to commercialism and subversion of gentlemanly values, the desire for privacy harbored among the rich was another matter entirely. The seclusion of the country club, for example, halted not the corruption of American life but the dilution of upper-class society. Yet, while seeking privacy at one level, the rich invited public attention at another, partly because their exclusionary measures provoked idle curiosity and also because the magnificence of their display could hardly have escaped notice under nearly any circumstances. The first American country club, Brookline, opened in 1882 as a center for Boston's elite in polo, racing, and the hunt. Soon it added golf links, making available to its aristocratic membership yet another sport whose expense barred it from the common citizen. The Newport Country Club, spearheaded by sugar magnate Theodore A. Havemeyer, attracted founding members from the moneyed class such as Cornelius Vanderbilt, Perry Belmont, and John Jacob Astor. Similarly, men of wealth took the spotlight when they joined in 1908 to promote tournament play through the National Golf Links of America; and the roster of promoters included the fashionable names of William K. Vanderbilt, Harry Payne Whitney, J. Borden Harriman, Elbert H. Gary, W.D. Sloane, and Henry Clay Frick.[9] The amateurism preserved by such a group was not much more than a test of wealth or, at best, a yielding of governance of the sport to the wealthy. Less publicized separate competitions were staged among the club "pros," who were more talented but socially beyond the pale. Thus, the structure of the tournament system as well as the identity of the players served the rich in their quest for exclusiveness.

Sportsmen in the socially elite classes did not usually identify themselves as exclusionary and undemocratic. Yet their periodic claims that sports which they favored were open to all Americans form something of a farce in the literature of sports promotion at the turn of the century. For the word "popular" did not really include all Americans when it was used by a member of the upper economic class. The yachtsman Duncan Curry, for example, showed no irony when he wrote of "Yachting as a Sport for the People" in a 1904 article. Curry dismissed as erroneous the widespread belief that yachting belonged exclusively to "kings and millionaires." He freely conceded that the grand steam-yachts such as the *Valiant* cost $1 million and that the syndicate owning the America's Cup contender *Reliance* spent half a million dollars to beat the *Shamrock III.* Ignoring the difference between catfish and caviar, Curry asserted: "Nowadays, when a man can buy a good, serviceable sailing dory for from $35 to $50, or purchase a small power launch from $175 to $250, there is no reason for him to envy a Vanderbilt or an Iselin. . . ." In fact, not only could most of "the people" not afford a yacht comparable to Henry Walter's 224-foot *Narada;* they could not have spent $175 or even $35. In 1890, the average daily wage of the urban industrial worker came to only $1.69. The poorest classes averaged a mere $150 income for the year, and the average family income in the United States was only $500. Per capita income in 1900 reached only $236; and, in 1910, only 4 percent of the population of working families earned more than $2,000, the line that analysts said divided "families enjoying at least modest comfort from families that can scarcely be called well to do."[10]

Curry's assertion of the almost universal accessibility of yachting foundered on his own interpretation of class, status, and exclusivity. As a frame of reference, he used not the national population but the New York Yacht Club and the Royal Yacht Squadron. In their earlier years, Curry admitted, these societies had discouraged the building of small boats by refusing to register craft under certain tonnages. He may have thought the New York club more democratic than the Royal Squadron for having based its restrictions on the indiscriminate standard of wealth, while even so prosperous a businessman as Sir Thomas Lipton was barred from the Royal Squadron for lack of aristocratic pedigree and involvement in mere trade. But the inclusiveness of the sport, if not among the New Yorkers, purport-edly showed itself when other clubs "sprang up in response to a demand by people of limited means who were fond of water" but lacked the uncommon wealth of the Vanderbilts. Like *popular, limited* had meaning only in context; and Curry's sense of economic modesty formed in the shadow of millionaires. The average industrial worker would have been sufficiently awed by the $1,400 price tag of a Herreshoff & Gardner raceabout and quite uncomprehending of Curry's buoyant conclusion: ". . . there is really no excuse for any one who seriously thinks of going into yachting being stopped by the expense, for it is a sport that is open to practically everyone."[11] What Curry meant was everyone of the better sort.

The new clubs to which Curry referred included the Corinthian clubs, whose genesis belied the simple democracy that the yachtsman imagined in his comfortable world. Influential members of the major yacht clubs observed with deep concern the rising importance of the "sandbaggers," shallow-draft vessels of broad beam that were often owned by men of no social distinction and even by the denizens of taverns in harbor towns. Emerging in the years before the Civil War, the "sandbagger" phenomenon represented a challenge to the integrity of the gentility or the "old stock" in America, since young men who came from good families but lacked money could sail with persons of lesser birth on one of these strange, unstable craft. Even more, it challenged the ability of the superrich to regulate the behavior of young offspring of the gentility and thus to strengthen their claims to legitimacy in social leadership. The Corinthian clubs provided for shared ownership of boats, and even for common ownership that allowed men wellborn socially, but of lesser economic means, to confine their social life to people of their own sort. No longer would they be inclined to consort with longshoremen in a waterfront saloon. Curry's history of the development of yachting, then, failed to note that the "people of limited means" for whom the new clubs provided access to boating did not include the preponderance of Americans and certainly not the working class.

Among wealthy women, the same bias against workers and the common middle class appeared as among men. Anne

O'Hagan's "Athletic Girl," described in *Munsey's Magazine* for August, 1901, had little truck with the common working woman. Even for O'Hagan, some gymnasiums seemed to set unreasonably steep and exclusionary fees. "There is one gymnasium," she reported, "with pillowed couches about the room, soft, lovely lights, and walls that rest weary eyes; where a crisp capped maid brings the exerciser a cup of milk during her rest upon the divan, where her boots are laced or buttoned by deft fingers other than her own." These amenities cost her a hundred dollars a year. Other clubs whose appointments were "less Sybaritic" charged membership dues on the order of forty dollars per year. O'Hagan rather blithely noted that, "if one has the distinction of being a working woman," ten dollars would suffice to obtain gymnastic instruction. Although O'Hagan found ten dollars an inconsiderable amount of money, the working girl for whom this represented a week's pay may have thought differently.[12] Among many Americans, bodily exercise was still essentially a private matter; and the inaccessibility of gymnasiums on economic grounds meant the exclusion of large numbers of Americans from the kinds of activities that took place there. Only the gradual provision of facilities through public funding and private voluntary action would remedy this deficiency, and that movement was still only in its early stages in the last decades of the nineteenth century. As a result, glib pronouncements about the availability of gymnasiums with pillowed couches and well-trained maids said "Let them eat cake" to people who struggled for bread.

Elizabeth C. Barney provided readers of the *Fortnightly Review* of August 1894 further evidence of the social myopia of the upper classes, as well as insensitivity to the economic pressures that the working classes faced. In "The American Sportswoman," Barney claimed that tennis had become "a favourite with rich and poor," observing that New York's Central Park included tennis courts where anyone could play for a fee and ignoring the issue of relative levels of disposable income. Her judgment that riding "follows hard upon tennis in popular favour" also exposed her economic and social bias, for even she admitted that hundreds of girls could afford to ride only infrequently. Barney's audience and the object of her concern was the wellborn element of society that considered riding in New York City *de rigueur* and used the term with no hint of parody. The thread of fashion tied together the patchwork of Barney's vision of women's sport; and she spoke of tennis clubs as "fashionable institutions," certified riding as part of "the usual round of social events," and praised the social events attendant upon fox-hunting as "among the *debutantes'* most cherished aspirations." Only in this context did Elizabeth Barney escape self-conscious irony when she pronounced tennis a sport that "all can play without cost."[13] *All* was a term that excluded the humbler classes.

Women of upper-class instincts and means thus tended to isolate themselves from the preponderance of Americans of their sex. Welcoming greater interest in sports and games, they nonetheless used it — perhaps unconsciously — in ways that only sharpened their distinctiveness from men and from working women. Females did exchange muscular for "nervous" strength, and their conscious cultivation of bodily health through sport gave evidence of a "delight in action" that brought them into step with the American male. But they remained three paces behind in the variety of sports available, in their control, and in public sentiment concerning their purpose. No longer a "pallid hot-house flower"—which the working woman had never had a chance to be in the first place — the American sportswoman indulged with most enthusiasm and greatest approval in sports such as tennis, riding, boating, and walking.

Suggestive of the importance of class distinction, the desirability of tennis for women evidently stemmed from its social effects as much as from its hygienic benefits. According to Elizabeth C. Barney, writing in the August 1894 *Fortnightly Review,* the enjoyment of tennis revolved around the "social intercourse" at the club house. The game strengthened and unified the community by drawing together the young people who played and the matrons who watched, while talking over "servants and babies on the club piazzas." Barney praised tennis, therefore, as a "strong, centralising influence," asserting that "the girl who does not play tennis feels that she has missed something out of her life."[14] This sporting scene served as a common ground upon which women could develop social values, much as the sporting options open to men enabled them to realize their own ideals; but the codes for women differed from those of the men. For Elizabeth Barney and others of her station, tennis served to organize polite society and to put a healthy flush in its cheeks.

The flow of fashion which illuminated the wealthy woman's sporting habits extended into the physical trappings that surrounded them, such as clothing styles and accessories. In a society that prized conspicuous consumption and wasteful dress, the realm of sport had the advantage of adding a whole new set of activities for which special costumes could be devised and socially mandated. Moreover, the criteria of taste and acceptability could be changed from season to season. In 1904, Marion Burton indicated the need for careful judgment so as to conform to prevailing norms. She warned against the "promiscuous wearing of handsome jeweled rings when arrayed in sporting apparel," observing that only "'mannish' rings of seal or Roman gold" were suitable for the woman on the links or courts. Other columnists simply played sport as another area in which the twins fashion and waste could be developed. "Originality of design and diversity of style are so marked in the newest spring apparel," one article read, "that a well-groomed sportswoman, who does not wish to come a sartorial cropper, must needs exercise a nicety of discrimination and a keen sense of the eternal fitness of things in the selection of her outing garments." The author went on to provide the latest advice: whips were "in" and riding crops most assuredly "out"; the pleated front had made a strong comeback; and the ankle-length tennis outfit would be all the rage.[15] Such commentators promoted the wasteful and unproductive behavior that Thorstein Veblen termed conspicuous consumption, emphasizing the value of certain sports — often marginal sports, one might add, such as croquet and fencing — in enhancing the worth of woman as an object of pecuniary display.

The conduct of sports themselves became an object of fashion, and social grace competed — successfully — against athletic ability in the design and management of tournaments. In woman's events as in men's, strict control was exerted over admission to play in ostensibly national events. Elizabeth Barney, for example, reported that upper-class women were able to contrib-

At the Essex Country Club in Orange, New Jersey, the men supervise the Metropolitan Golf Tournament of 1908, while the women observe or read the newspaper. Although identified on the plate as spectators, several of the women are dressed to play, including the seated woman wearing gloves at left of center. By permission of the Library of Congress, George Grantham Bain Collection (LC-B2-2065-1).

115

ute "beautiful form" to the mixed doubles matches in tennis that did so much to enliven weekends at the country club; and they carried the same spirit over into tournament play. The *crème de la crème*, Barney noted, made their way, in 1894, to the Ladies' National Championship at the Philadelphia Country Club, which ranked with "the foremost in tone and social standing, and every thing that it does is in the best of style." The tournament operated on rules that ensured protection of the women competitors from contact with their social inferiors. Matches were determined by invitation only, in a way that openly violated the supposedly democratic quality of modern sport, and only those of "assured social position" would think to submit their names for screening.[16]

Much of the "sports" coverage designed to appeal to rich women readers confirmed the view that social pedigree interested them more than athletic achievement. In the regular column "The Sportswoman" in the February 6, 1904, issue of *The Illustrated Sporting News*, word was published of the establishment of the York Athletic Club, composed exclusively of women, with membership limited to 500. Aimed primarily at "women of athletic tastes," it would also provide "accommodations for those who may wish to join simply for the sake of the social privileges afforded." The club's Committee on Organization included women from well-known and well-placed families, such as Mrs. J.J. Astor, Mrs. J. Borden Harriman, Miss A.T. Morgan, Mrs. William G. Rockefeller, Mrs. Harry Payne Whitney, Mrs. Robert Sturgis, and Mrs. Walter Damrosch. To be sure, Irish need not apply.[17] The same issue carried a story about "The Only Pack of Hounds Hunted by Women," a theme pursued the following year by Richard Strong in "Great Britain's Famous Women of the Hunt." Strong insisted that the modern sportswoman took chances equal with men; but he apparently had only a limited equality in mind. For example, "The modern woman not only controls her own fishing-kit, but unhesitatingly gaffs her own salmon." Yet gaffing a salmon hardly constituted equality. Strong himself added a hint that discrimination lay heavily in assigning sports according to sex, and he specifically cited "a few little courtesies of the field which the stronger still show to the weaker sex."[18] It was the sheerest fantasy to suggest that many of the better sort of Americans could compete, whether in sport or in society, with the "women masters of hounds": Miss Isa McClintock of the Tynan and Armagh Harriers; Mrs. T.H.R. Hughes, Master of the Neuadd-Fawr Foxhounds; Master Edith Somerville of the West Carberry Hunt; and Mrs. H.P. Wardell of the Hawkstone Otter Hounds. Perhaps the highest marriage of society and genteel sport received notice in "Dogs of High Degree and Their Titled Mistresses," which provided women with rare and superfluous models. Queen Alexandra of England was featured with her Chinese spaniel, Little Billie, and the Princess Beatrice posed with her pugs "President Faure," "Dumas," and "King of Siam."[19]

The enthusiastic and influential physical educator Dudley A. Sargent observed, in an article published in 1901, that fashion actually accounted for the rise and fall of many sports themselves, rather than merely the costumes for their pursuit. Archery and fencing, for example, would be pursued as "fads and be rushed for a few seasons, and then become obsolete." Obedient to society's edicts, the *beau monde* took up even serious sports as "the proper thing" and dropped them with equal unintelligence when style changed, substituting social caprice for scientific assessment of their hygienic value. Sargent did not confine his analysis to women, although they were more likely to succumb to the specific voguish sports he mentioned. He feared that the serious sports which could bring great physical benefits would fall before fashion just as marginal activities did, blurring the difference between the substantial and the trivial.[20] The physical educators — whether male or female — wished to avoid turning sport into a secular religion to which scientific hygiene would be sacrificed. But the social elites, who shared the educators' revulsion toward excessive competitiveness, remained deaf to their protests against frivolity. For many socially luxurious sportsmen and sportswomen, moderation was a polite term for laziness, as the real, social competition was played with relentless zeal. An educator such as Dudley Sargent might choose his sports for hygienic reasons, but the rich selected theirs against the criterion of social esteem and fashion.

SPECIAL PLACES FOR SPECIAL SPORTSMEN

Although there was a strong current in America toward sharing certain sports which were national in sweep and were usually conducted in public places, the new rich bucked the trend and created a more specialized environment for sports. The country club was their most repeated form, and lavish clubhouses designed by leading architectural firms served as centers of social interchange as well as focal points of golf and tennis. Since social aims permeated country club life, one cannot see this institution as unambiguous proof of the rise of athletic sport to respectability; but the relative place of sport in the social world, as compared to the place of business in it, suggests something else. Separated and distinct from work, sport had become an autonomous focal point in the life of the rich. Unlike middle-class Americans who claimed that sport ingrained in players those qualities that empowered them to do life's work, the rich favored sport for its inutility. Their country clubs, then, became symbols of a quite different, pleasure-oriented ethic, which was to make a major contribution to the American notion of leisure.

The physical segregation of sporting activities in a special place for their pursuit, which was an intrinsic feature of the country club, had equivocal implications. On the one hand, it suggested the isolation of play, as ritualized in the games at the club, from work. On the other hand, it made a comprehensive and interactive, if separated, system out of the activities which were conducted there. The gathering of several sports under a single administration at a central facility constituted a limited form of "horizontal integration," as if a corporate structure had been applied to sportive behavior.[21] In short, the sporting life of the rich thus assumed an institutional shape, one which affirmed the viability of sport as an autonomous enterprise and one whose very comprehensiveness helped to provide foundation for the belief that a man might even pursue sport as a calling and an independent source of meaning in one's life.

The fact of physical segregation of the sporting rich and, certainly, its degree were substantial departures from the traditional pattern in the use of resorts. One of the key features of the earlier American resorts, notably the spas and baths that were to be found in many of the original states, was that they were accessible to patrons of no more than ordinary means. Foreign travelers were astonished to find great diversity in the social and economic background of the clientele at the watering places. In theory, such accessibility illustrated both democracy and gentility — democracy in that no rigid social system barred a potential paying customer, and gentility in that the grace of the social interchange was presumed to flow from the gentlemanly decency of visitors and not from lavish facilities and some variant of a caste system. The spas thus showed signs, in corporate terms, of both vertical and horizontal integration; for they included Americans and foreigners of varying economic and social levels, even as they sought to offer a range of amusements and entertainments.[22]

Moreover, earlier resorts were more likely to be diverse in their social roles, as well as in their clientele. For the men operating the great hotels, it was a business venture, as it might well be for those seeking to monopolize public transportation to the facilities. For the natives, there were service-related jobs. The promotion of gambling at various of the resorts added a related but separate industry. So, then, the focus of the earlier American vacation-places was somewhat diffuse. By the end of the century, however, when the ultra-rich established their compound at Newport, Rhode Island, these characteristics were all but eradicated. The wealthy families did not rely on public hotels but on their own "cottages" of as many as seventy rooms; and they maintained permanent staffs to tend the grounds and keep the houses in order, supplemented by a company of personal servants during the brief summer season. As a result, many of the business features that had appeared in the earlier resorts were absent at Newport. Gambling went private, and even the admission of spectators to competitions in sports such as tennis was restricted on social grounds. Although the aim was to create an isolated playground for the rich in which social distinction exceeded athletic ability in the pursuit of diversion, the effect was also to lay the groundwork for the concept of the "destination resort," which, while complex in its economic base, was devoted to nothing but the pursuit of pleasure. Newport lent itself, in effect, to the horizontal integration of the high rung of the leisure class, but it also helped in defining the terms of leisure as it was soon to be pursued by Americans of lesser means.

A comparison of Newport with its forerunner in fashion, Saratoga Springs, New York, makes the distinction in the type of resort somewhat sharper. The reputation of Saratoga Springs as a sporting resort originated around the time of the Civil War; and, despite early associations with men of wealth and social prominence, the town soon became more significant for its links to racing and to the emergence of intercollegiate sport than for its catering to the rich. After decades as a popular watering place, the New York resort moved into the business of sport in 1863, when John Morissey opened its first horse-track. Born in Ireland, Morissey came to America in 1834 at the age of three. He later worked as a bouncer in a brothel, entered politics as a ward heeler, was an American heavyweight champion under the London Prize Ring Rules, and emerged as the boss of New York City's lucrative gambling houses. In all, his record invited wicked curiosity but discouraged the close friendship of the social elite. Nonetheless, eager for acceptance among the more reputable classes, Morissey evidently hoped to curry their favor by catering to their desire for amusement. He built lavish facilities at Saratoga which pampered his guests while adding to his own wealth; but he soon identified a restiveness among the patrons, who seemed to crave more elaborate, exciting, and active entertainments. He succeeded in enlisting the advice of the prominent New York stockbroker William R. Travers, whose ideas contributed much to the quality of the early racing seasons.

Whatever the motives of Travers, who was to become a leading figure in the social life of Newport, Morissey's interests in sport grew principally from his growing need to keep Saratoga a commercial success; and even his desire for social acceptance could not possibly be fulfilled unless he continued to attract the rich and wellborn as guests. Moreover, Morissey—as well as other hotel-keepers at Saratoga—did not make the same nice distinctions that some of his guests did; and so he was willing to hazard supporting attractions that might ultimately alienate the self-flattering superrich. Thus, when James Gordon Bennett, publisher of the *New York Herald* and an ardent sports fan, proposed Saratoga as the site of the annual regatta of the newly established Rowing Association of American Colleges in 1874, the hotel operators responded enthusiastically. Yet, by identifying themselves with the generality of college men, by encouraging average citizens in the region to come out to view the events, and by permitting an unseemly amount of betting on amateur events, the proprietors actually made Saratoga ineligible to serve as the true capital of America's wealthy elite. That role fell to Newport, Rhode Island, where sport was by no means the servant of commerce.[23]

The enclosure and definition of space, whether public or private, give it cultural and even ceremonial meaning.[24] In the late nineteenth century, this process exemplified the passion for discipline and order in life that pervaded middle-class society; and it enhanced the sense of importance shown toward the activities pursued within it. With the establishment of the grand compound of the rich at Newport, there came upon the American scene such a defined and enclosed space that was devoted exclusively to leisure; and, although sport was not the only entertainment or amusement pursued within its confines, it occupied a major place and thus became integrated into the concept of leisure itself. Although this latter phenomenon prevailed only within a rarified community at the time, namely the very rich, it lent credence to an interpretation of the worth and respectability of sport that was quite different from what was encouraged by the middle class and the remnant of the gentility. In such a view, sport no longer needed to be a "healthful amusement" that readied one for work; it could become an end in itself, to be sought only as a means of diversion and pleasure.

The concentration of summer houses for the rich at Newport came largely during the last third of the nineteenth century, although it continued much later. In a process that began in 1859, Newport emerged as the summer social center of the "great American families," who had previously been scattered about in resorts of their own choosing. The gravitation toward Newport suggested a certain nationalization, or centralization, of America's rich upper crust; and this, in turn, was to lend itself to a standardization of behavior and amusements among the wealthy. As early as the Civil War years, fashion-setting men of leisure, led by Ward McAllister whose picnics and outings on the coastal beaches became famous, began to move to the attractive bluffs and hills near the old colonial town. Even then, it was a refuge from the world and its troubles, or, somewhat more exactly, a world unto itself with its own cares and concerns. In a sense, even the absorption into the social rounds that became a staple of Newport's image and self-image furthered the sense of insulation from the practical affairs of business and politics, sharpening the sense of protective enclosure.[25]

In at least one regard, the life of the rich at Newport shared in the temperament often seen among other Americans. The summer colony was said to be characterized by a "restlessness" that showed itself in the constant round of parties, yachting trips, rides, social visits, and sporting events.[26] Although the wealthy might choose somewhat different ways of expressing it, a love of action and events predominated. Simply being in Newport was not quite enough. One also needed to be doing things there. This interest in a social life that included activity helped to make the elite of Newport a more eligible model for imitation by those of far lesser means and saved them from complete irrelevance.

Nonetheless, the annual renewal of social ties at Newport itself became a kind of competition, in which sporting events and social occasions became devices for the definition and measurement of status, as had not been the case before, except perhaps in the colonial Tidewater. This relationship applied within the social elite and also between wealthy society as a whole and the rest of America. In the great bulk of cases, the actual performance of athletic feats was less important than the grace and style with which people performed them; and instances in which competitive excellence was prized — notably in yachting — themselves hinged partly on the purchase of expensive, specially designed vessels and on the maintenance of a substantial crew and staff. Even in yachting, however, a social note obtained; and extravagant expenditures conspired with contempt for "new money" to govern participation in competition on the waters off Newport. The dedicated British yachtsman Sir Thomas Lipton was snubbed widely at Newport since he had made his money in trade, and much too recently at that.[27] At least a generation or two was needed to separate the glamour of wealth from the tawdriness of its sources; and so the names of Oliver Belmont, Pierre Lorillard, Cornelius Vanderbilt, and E.J. Berwind loomed high over that of a mere British baronet. As rigid as they could be with outsiders, so were the sportsmen of Newport competitive among themselves, always seeking to put forward the best image and the most stylish display as a substitute for pedigree and as a proof of wealth.[28]

The tendency of the rich at Newport to use sport as part of a whole system of leisure showed itself in their disdain for games that needed no more than an open field and a ball. Instead, they lavished their attention on pastimes that demanded much time, special facilities, expensive equipment, and, sometimes, extensive travel. Although the enthusiasm for yachting, lawn tennis, fox-hunting, and the like was often genuine, so was their social role. As J.P. Morgan put it succinctly, "You can do business with anyone, but you can go sailing only with a gentleman."[29] The devotion of resources to sport and other aspects of leisure thus became more than an emblem of wealth, although it was assuredly that; it also became a means of delineating leisure as an institution whose complexity invited members of the wealthiest classes to pursue it as if it were life's very purpose.

This kernel of difference helps to account for the interest of the American rich in the sporting life of the British upper class. It has been suggested that American sport was largely an imitative extension of British sport. Around the nation as a whole, the claim is rather exaggerated; but among the very rich the imitation ascended toward parody. The wealthy Americans aped what they thought to be the sporting traditions of the British upper class in an effort to stay in international fashion and to act convincingly as an American aristocracy by re-creating the behavior of a confessedly leisured society. Although the imitation often stumbled on bad taste, it encouraged the setting of spatial and temporal boundaries for the life of leisure. Polo ponies were kept in lavish stables, sleeping on monogrammed linen sheets. (Oliver Belmont housed his ponies on the lower level of his own house because he could not bear to treat them as if they were not members of the family.) Pink-coated riders pur-

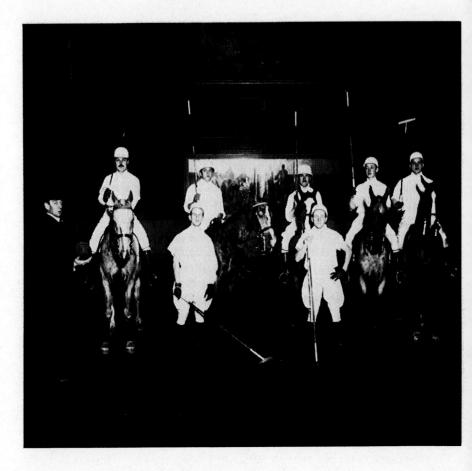

This portrait of the polo team at Durland's, New York, in 1908 reinforces the fact that clubs were often restricted by wealth which, in turn, was meant to suggest social standing. George Grantham Bain Collection, Library of Congress (LC-B2-311-1).

sued the fox across the fields of disgruntled Rhode Island farmers, who eventually banded together to put an end to the trampling of the crops. Comparing them to plants, Maud Elliott called such sports "exotics"; and their impertinence to American life was taken as a virtue, for it gave the promise of endlessly pursued social distinction.[30]

From another vantage, however, even the "exotic" sports that gradually withered on American soil helped to set the boundaries of leisure as an idea; and they affected the sense that rich and ordinary Americans as well would have of the less flamboyant sports which the wealthy managed to control. The passion for things British, for example, encouraged the rich to show interest in lawn tennis, although the game's survival also depended on its suitability to the needs of the American rich. First brought to New York by Mary Outerbridge after a vacation in Bermuda, where she had observed the game played by British officers, tennis soon became a fixture of Newport's summer season. Partly because it brought the well-dressed spectators together at the Casino, Tennis Week—the informal name for the National Lawn Tennis Tournament—emerged as the most estimable sporting event of the season. The very choice of a grass surface gave it an air of greater style, since it required much more careful and costly maintenance than hard-packed clay. Players in the tournament, which was initiated in 1881, came from the ranks of social fashion; and professionals were unheard of. Clad in knickers, blazers, and caps, they competed in a mild game, paced by "the genteel pat of the ball against languid strings."[31] Richard D. "Dicky" Sears, who won the first championship match and held the title for eight consecutive years, came from a reputable Boston family; and he held a certain charm for the spectators who gathered behind ropes on campstools, watching him play with his tongue lapping out of his mouth somewhat like a napping dog's. Not until 1890 was a grandstand installed, nor were invitations to compete allowed by the Casino's board of governors to players outside the Newport social set until the turn of the century. As with the rest of Newport's summer activities, tennis was as much a matter of style as one of athletics.

Yet one should not miss the fact that this sense of sport—this definition of sport in terms of style, manners, and expression — allowed it a certain space as an autonomous variable and a separately observable force within the life of the rich. Special costume, special facilities, special identity among the players, special limits among spectators — all became a part of the landscape of sport as an independent branch of leisure. In the process of seeking to use sport to define themselves as a special aristocratic class, the American rich thus also did much to confirm the institutional status of sport itself, as an enterprise with facilities, rules, demands, and, above all, purposes of its own.

THE SPECIAL ROLE OF SPORT FOR THE ULTRA-RICH

Although the ultra-rich pursued sport as a fashion, it was still something that could be a calling. In this regard, they veered sharply from the gentility who, as Stow Persons has noted, tended to disdain fashion and regard it, in Emerson's phrase, as "virtue gone to seed." Although the thought that "fashionable society was a caricature of the gentry" may have been declining, traditionalists such as Roosevelt found little to approve in the antics of the ultra-rich. Roosevelt never condoned the use of sport for purely personal purposes, arguing that it was a means through which one prepared for societal tasks. Yet, among the very rich, ever more elaborate trappings were forged in service of selfish goals, seeking to use material splendor as proof of personal importance. At the same time, however, the likes of Roosevelt also objected to the implications of the physical separation of the very rich from the great majority of Americans. They were hiving themselves off, apart from the national stream; and they risked firming up a class structure that would threaten national unity. Hence, the very process of physical exclusion that showed itself in the growth of country clubs and in the development of the wealthy colony at Newport ran afoul of the gentility and the middle class, even as it made the undiluted pursuit of a sporting life a more credible and creditable option among the rich themselves. It has been suggested that the instinct of the traditional gentility was to "dignify a humble occupation by a noble purpose."[32] For the very rich, however, the dignity of sport inhered in the lavishness of circumstance and in the impertinence of its pursuit. Truly, the ultra-rich were pioneers of

126

sport as a leisure activity which required no justification. Precisely this, which so alienated and disgusted the traditional gentility because it seemed to debase sport by subordinating it to motives that were trivial because they were merely personal, constituted the major contribution of the turn-of-the-century rich to the development of twentieth-century attitudes toward sport.

If not uniquely, at least specially, the ultra-rich came to their sport partly from the vantage of excess "spare" time. Although the mere existence of "nonwork" time did not require that sport be used to fill it, "nonwork" did have the potential to become an individual and a social problem if it surpassed a certain magnitude and extensiveness. Admittedly, it is significant that nonwork time was appearing during the nineteenth century; and, especially with the alienation of labor from the household and removal from the farms increasing, the very fact of identifiable nonwork time became easier to recognize. On the other hand, the magnitude of nonwork and its pervasiveness in the society must not be exaggerated. For the industrial worker who saw little of the light of day, such "spare" time was hardly a problem requiring a managed solution through sport or anything else. So, too, the dissipation of energies in unsupervised play loomed as a problem only with the reduction of child labor and similar measures. In short, despite the fears of middle-class managers and upper-class industrialists, excessive indulgence in uncontrolled leisure was more a fancied than a real problem among vast numbers of Americans in the late decades of the nineteenth century.

Among the very rich, however, the problem was much more tangible and convincing. Because of its reliance on fashion and its imitation of supposedly British patterns, this small, influential economic stratum wished to seem above and beyond work of virtually any sort; and, in fairness, the rich often showed a genuine desire for a change of pace. J. Pierpont Morgan showed symptoms of this tendency toward leisure when he noted that, although he could do twelve months' work in nine months, he could not do twelve months' work in twelve. A certain restlessness overtook him, and he would be off to Egypt supervising the excavations for the Metropolitan Museum of Art or out on his 302-foot yacht, *Corsair III.*[33] In an age that equated activity with life itself, it seemed senseless and unacceptable to fall into total indolence or passivity. It was in this context of the general need for the sensation of action and the specific need for the impression of economic inutility that the very rich helped to create the American sense of leisure. Contrary to Marx's sense that it was simply uncommitted spare time or rest, the wealthy American capitalist made leisure a rather exhausting round of organized amusements and consumer activities. Transcending or even just ignoring the traditionalists' focus on duty and service, the ultra-rich thus developed a sense of leisure and leisure time that was permeated by activities and suffused with an underlying conviction of the primacy of experience. It was insufficient to have free time, unless you showed it.

Nor was leisure convincing without material expression. Even as the common sense of what constituted the sports hero came to center on the primacy of deeds over virtues, so did the more general sense of a hero of culture center on action over character. In at least one of their guises, the rich thus did much to create the concept of the "sportsman." The very rich could establish influence — other than their manifest economic power — only by accumulating objects and by establishing a record of elitist activities. The absence of usefulness in sport was more than charming, then; for it made sport a superb instrument for the creation of leisure. Ironically, the wealthy Americans' emphasis on the intertwined goals of self-gratification, identity, relief from the tedium of a stultifying structured life, and expressive display resembled the supposed preferences of the laboring class more closely than those of the economic and social middle. In this way, the very rich helped to advance notions about sport and its role in purposeless leisure which would simultaneously compete with the middle class's concentration on the work-ethic and service and encourage the working class to see sport as a part of the American Dream. Like the very rich, the workers could prove their achievement of leisure only by expressing this fact through action, as deeds increasingly assumed greater eloquence than words in the formulation of American ideas. Sport had become a fixture among the idle rich; and Americans who cherished a belief in upward material mobility were prone to follow the reigning models of the culture.

It is not necessary to repeat the criticisms that the gentility, the military, and various elements of the middle class aimed at the rich because of their emphasis on luxury; but it is useful to appreciate that the rich, in their pursuit of luxury and leisure, implicitly asserted that there was such a thing as surplus. In David Potter's term, abundance appeared, even if still more an image than a reality; and the diversity and inefficiency of America's sports system owed much to the fact that a gradually growing surplus encouraged complexity and tolerated waste. In modern times, the new industrial and financial rich were the first to sense this fact and to exploit it. Thus, despite the rarified atmosphere of wealth in which they lived, the rich tended to anticipate trends that would extend throughout America in the twentieth century with progresssively less reference to economic level. Sport became one of several important means for consuming surplus and for persuading Americans that they were indeed sharing in the nation's abundance. [34]

Since the ultra-rich on the one hand and the middle-class and the gentility on the other each considered themselves the guardians of amateurism, an analysis of their respective concerns in this matter helps to clarify their differing understandings of the role and impact of sport and so also to cast light on the conceptual contribution that was developing among the rich. As has been noted earlier, the great captains of industrial wealth, rather paradoxically, did not generally apply the precepts and values of industrial life to their sport. As a consequence, they adopted a relatively narrow and simple test of amateur status. Did the athlete live on money acquired in direct payment for his performance in a sport, whether in competition or as a professional instructor? This simple construction focused on the distinction between work and leisure as it applied in the individual case, and it associated amateurism with the idea of leisure. To their periodic embarrassment, the middle class and the gentility had much more complex notions with far more confusing implications.

Fearful of the supposedly corrupting effect of luxury on character, the respectable middle class and the gentility identified excessive concentration on sport as a form of luxury in itself, thus opposing themselves to the concept of the sportsman as it was emerging among the very rich. Though important to the whole man, sport remained only a part for the likes of Theodore Roosevelt or Dudley Sargent; and the exaggeration of sport thus threatened basic social values. Roosevelt said bluntly that the one-tracked athlete "becomes a bore, if nothing else." Writing in 1901, the perceptive historian and analyst of the athletic movement Henry D. Sheldon decried the fact that spectators and the press had debased sport by giving it more than its appropriate attention. As a result, undue interest in winning had been encouraged; and, with it, team captains and managers developed a cycle of lavish outfitting of players, special foods for them, the hiring of coaches, and the thorough distortion of the college experience for many athletes. Since some players were training four or five hours each day, Sheldon observed, they soon became unsuited to "anything more than nominal participation in the intellectual life of the college."[35]

At Harvard, the effort to stamp out professionalism centered on overseeing the membership on teams to ensure that only students in good standing were permitted to play and on resisting the hiring of coaches paid only for their training of athletes. Yet, in its 1897 report, Harvard's Committee on Physical Training, Athletic Sports, and Sanitary Condition of Buildings— which included Augustus Hemenway, Theodore Roosevelt, and Charles Francis Adams, Jr., among its members—acknowledged that players were provided all athletic equipment and clothing, received better food than other students without additional cost, and generally were accorded special treatment. On the other hand, the Committee urged that spectators, especially at football games, "be limited so far as possible to college men, and that the games be played only on college grounds," all with the aim of discouraging an unbalanced view of the place of athletics in one's life. In order to undercut a natural "tendency to extravagance," the Committee urged that no surplus of funds be allowed to accumulate, recommending that gate receipts in excess of operating expenses be channeled into the maintenance of athletic grounds and buildings.[36]

It is not lacking in irony, however, that Harvard alumni simultaneously pursued victory as a goal of ever greater desirability and importance. Undercutting the genteel critique of the rich, some 500 alumni gathered at Sanders Theater on January 26, 1898, to establish a new Graduate Athletic Association that would include members from all major segments of the university community and would give centralized governance to the athletic programs.[37] Regardless of the reasons for which they focused on the value of victory, the Graduate Athletic Association accorded institutional sanction to a more comprehensive and, arguably, excessive emphasis on sport. In the process, both the Association and the Hemenway Committee came perilously close to the practical policies of the ultra-rich — bar those who made their living through athletics, develop lavish facilities, and reinvest money into the physical plant of the sports programs. Even middle-class and genteel proponents of reform in collegiate athletics unknowingly flirted with the creed of the rich, as when E.L. Godkin protested Yale's playing a football game in New York City. Writing in 1893, Godkin warned that the choice of this venue made the "gambling fraternity and the prostitutes" among the most prominent of those in attendance and turned the event into "a spectacle for the multitudes." In one sense, such criticism aligned itself with the growing effort of college faculties and administrators to exert control over their students' sport; but it also showed similarity to the spirit of exclusiveness that characterized the sport of the rich.[38]

In its actual operations, the collegiate system was riddled much more with equivocation on the matter of amateurism, contamination by outsiders, and the role of sport than was the sporting behavior of the very rich. After all the noble pronouncements and the committee work, only financial sleight of hand permitted Harvard alumni to continue to think of themselves as guardians of the amateur spirit during the 1903–1904 collegiate sporting season. In one of the more imaginative examples of specious reasoning, they decided that their rowing coach F.D. Colson, who had been brought from Cornell for the season in order to share his winning ways, was "not technically to receive any remuneration for his services as a coach." But the Athletic Committee also said that it must "make good to him any loss of income incurred by the temporary surrender of his work at

Cornell, as well as any extra expense involved in the trip" to the Boston area. The members of the Committee insisted that this arrangement was consistent with amateurism on the grounds that it gave Colson no official gain over his previous employment and because he professed a secondary interest in studying the methods of instruction at Harvard's law school. Nonetheless, Edwin H. Hall, who had already created a minor flurry with a letter to *The Nation* challenging the utility of a categorical ban on the receipt of money by amateurs for athletic performance, gave implicit support for Colson in the *Harvard Graduates' Magazine* of June, 1904. Hall insisted that the exchange of money was not really the problem. Instead, he returned to the conventional middle-class and genteel concerns over admitting "low morals, low intelligence, low aims, foul speech, bad manners, and trickiness" into collegiate sport by allowing persons other than regular candidates for a degree to play.[39] Seeking to have it both ways, the middle class and the gentility risked having neither.

Harvard was not alone in these problems, nor was the difficulty confined to the colleges. Fearing the evils of professionalism, Princeton and the University of Pennsylvania terminated the employment of their paid baseball coaches in 1906, with Harvard soon following their example. In *The Illustrated Outdoor News*, commentator Edward R. Bushnell showed more enthusiasm than insight in calling the move "a real innovation," since so-called graduates, or alumni, had often served as coaches during the late decades of the nineteenth century; yet his remark reflected the gnawing concern over the possible corruption of sport. Soon, however, this limited reform was imperiled when the three schools, along with Yale, Cornell, and Columbia, faltered in competition with Georgetown, Amherst, Dartmouth, and Brown — none of which had agreed to abide by the ruling against paid coaches. Georgetown's own record was spotty enough, particularly due to a scandal in 1904 over the school's decision to retain its star pitcher Crumley, who had earlier played four games for the Indianapolis team of the Western League. Officials at Georgetown had focused on intent, saying that Crumley had played merely "for the fun of it" and not for pay. Meanwhile, Harvard kept players out of games if they had competed in an "open" format that mixed amateurs and professionals. Columbia University was forced to dismiss its football coach R.P. Wilson, around the same time as the Crumley affair, for having included a "ringer" on the school's team. Seeking to clean up the athletic program, the University of Wisconsin experimented in 1904 with a special athletic society composed of varsity players who showed the pure amateur spirit. At Brown University, in the same year, a squabble took place between the Brown Corporation and the school's Athletic Board over the issue of including players who had been paid for summer games within the University Athletic Brotherhood.[40]

Among the urban clubs as well, there was confusion over the meaning of terms such as *amateur, commercial, professional* and *spectator;* and efforts to agree upon definitions usually failed miserably. As Samuel Crowther, Jr., observed retrospectively in 1905, the separation of the amateur from the "petty professional" was a tricky business; for, in fact, amateurism in the sense that Crowther meant it was largely a creation of the late nineteenth century. Without regulation of competitors in rowing, Crowther warned, the professionals would "drive every gentleman out of the sport"; and true amateur rowing would cease to exist. Yet the efforts of groups such as the National Association of Amateur Oarsmen, founded in 1872, normally met with limited success. Despite chiding of "masquerading amateurs," actual professionals continued to row; and the confusion of interests among oarsmen led many clubs into a long decline from 1885 into the twentieth century. Among the middle class and the gentility, where motivations were many and complex, the struggle to develop workable rules to govern and strengthen amateur competition was endless. Sportswriter J. Parmly Paret, commenting in 1906 on the Amateur Hockey League's ruling that five Canadian players were being paid by the Brooklyn Skating Club and hence must be barred from competition, summarized the sense of frustration and the suggestion of despair: "The greed of graft is a different kind in ice-hockey from that which has undermined the morals of most basketball players and many track athletes. The managers of the teams are much more at fault than the players themselves, and it is they who hold out the golden apple of temptation. . . ." It was not merely a problem of a few bad individuals; the system itself seemed at fault.[41]

The very clarity of the sporting system among the rich made it possible for them to avoid the ambivalence, ambiguity, and occasional sophistry that plagued the exponents of middle class and genteel virtues. Wealth—not virtue—was its own reward; and it was association with wealth that kept a sport worthy of further interest. At the same time, wealth served to guard and insulate a sport so that it remained not only limited in clientele but rarified in its social role. The rear-guard action of the rich in fending off the "sandbaggers" and preserving social distinction in yachting stands as an example of their successful defensive action. Whatever social benefit the very rich saw in sport was "social" only in the small sense, serving to sharpen lines of status.[42] But the effects of sport in individual gratification, in what Veblen called a renewed "clannishness," and in activity-oriented leisure were numerous and systemic. Untroubled by issues of moral purpose, the rich thus established the prototype of the sportsman as an unrestricted consumer.

What the defenders of the older tradition criticized as "monomania" in sport, whether among the rich or among the professionals, passed as a form of virtue among the ultra-rich. The wealthy Americans luxuriated in expensive yachts, "Sybaritic" clubs, and costly holidays. Yet the middle class and the gentility proved ineffective in stamping out their influence. In part, this may have been due to self-contradiction, as when Theodore Roosevelt expressed his belief that most men lived within forty-eight hours of a wilderness area and need only choose a companion to set out for a month in the wild. His glib prescription and its presupposition that the man could afford both the trip and any attendant loss of income suggest the limits of democratic thought and opportunity among the middle class and the gentility. At least the very rich made the best of it, turning a rather vulgar instinct for display into a form of candor. Thus impervious to the internally flawed arguments of their critics, the rich stood as a significant point of gravitation within the realm of sport and so also as a constituency lending sport an aura of legitimacy. It is an enduring irony that, given their privileged and powerful position, they had a largely radical effect, which finally touched the mass of Americans just as deeply as did the self-appointed protectors of American values.

CHAPTER **5**

From "Swooning Damsel" to Sportswoman — The Role of Women as a Constituency in Sport

WOMEN certainly became more active in sport by the end of the nineteenth century, and the idea that sport added to their well-being spread more widely in society than previously. Most study of this subject, however, has focused on presumed changes of character and behavior in women and on the role of sport in their quest for a measure of emancipation. In the process, the reciprocal impact that women had on sport has usually gone unappreciated. Although the place of women in American society was altering in the nineteenth century, so was the place of sport, as it gained importance among American institutions. Much of the literature analyzing women and sport at the turn of the century, then, has tended to treat women as the variable and sport as a constant, while both were actually altering simultaneously, though not identically. Thus, while sport was serving as an arena in which the social place of women could be newly delineated, it was also partly formed by those women who spurned the stereotype of the "swooning damsel," donned the habit of the sportswoman, and, gifted with a distinct consciousness, had impact as a separable constituency of sport.[1]

The impact of women on the emergence of sport to respectability and prominence depended on the intertwined factors of social power, role, and identity. Women who turned toward sport came from a functional minority in American society, experiencing constraints on the scope of their public lives and on the degree of activity even within their private lives. Further, the sportswomen formed only a minority among women in America, since some shied away from sport by preference and others

136

were effectively barred from it for lack of money and time. Even within a given economic group, women had differing sensibilities and attitudes toward sport. Cultural background created varying expectations among women as to the proper time and place for sport, as well as who should participate and at what ages. In short, the fragmentation among women generally carried over into their sport as well, and diversity reigned. In turn, the complexity of their origins and interests, which some have used as an indicator of political powerlessness, dovetailed with at least potentially discriminatory pronouncements about women's roles in society. Sport could aid women in "the reduction of their too corpulent curves," said fashion-conscious sportswriter Nixola Greeley-Smith. It might create a "revolution" in women's behavior, Anne O'Hagan claimed hyperbolically in 1901, reporting that games banished the often-cited female tendency to "nerves." Sportsman Edwyn Sandys claimed that sport would increase female fertility and strengthen the woman to serve as "the mother of a race of stalwarts of the future." In short, the purported functions and effects of sport were as varied as the kinds of people who made claims for it. As a result, the growing interest in sport among many women did not produce a unified and simple modification of their identity in American culture, except in one important regard.[2]

Relative to men, women remained disadvantaged and experienced discrimination. Relative to their own former state, however, many women enjoyed greater activity and a wider range in their means of self-expression and fulfillment. It was in this shift toward a comparatively broader scope of activities and toward the embrace of action itself that sport served a basic role in the emancipation of women. Even more, however, it was this same phenomenon which made women, whether emancipated or not, a significant constituency for sport. Diverse as they were, the sportswomen shared a sense of joyous renewal and regeneration and an underlying conviction of the worth of activity and the value of the material world. For these women, whether they aimed at social and economic emancipation or not, the "swooning damsel" yielded to the sportswoman. Although the persistence of discriminatory practices and attitudes remains an important factor in social history, the shift in the mode of discrimination, which more fully opened the realm of activity to women, was far more important to the history of sport. Like men, women shared in a practical, functional ideology of experience in which they were what they did. Irrespective of the degree of their emancipation, then, women expanded the range of activities through which they expressed their characters and formed their identities; and sport entered that range in important ways. While later critics have tended to question the extent of real economic and social gain among women in the late nineteenth century, it is clear that sportswomen of whatever background experienced a sense of freedom, change, and possibility which was little short of exhilarating. This enthusiasm and pleasure in action formed the common ground for the diverse expressions of women's sport, as well as the common base from which women of sometimes opposing views lent their endorsement to sport.

Corollary to the pleasure in action was the instinct of renewal, whether it was understood on a personal or a social scale. Here, too, the differences of opinion and emphasis were many. A champion of the Women's Metropolitan Golf Association in New York City, Caroline F. Manice emphasized the social and recreative role of sport rather than the value of competition. In an article published in 1904, she claimed that women found in golf, lawn tennis, and other suitable exercises a re-creation of the excitement and strength of their childhood days. Unlike men, who saw sport as "something to be enthralled in, to bet on and to fight over," women sought sport for diversion, and they remained good friends no matter who won or lost. Even in formal competitions, Manice insisted, perhaps the central aim was "to renew old and make new friendships." While Manice stressed a sense of community among women, others focused on physical regeneration. Edwyn Sandys, who saw sport as a means of strengthening women for childbirth, was only one among many who gave a literal meaning to regeneration as a goal of women's sport. The "natural sporting blood" should be sent rushing swiftly through their veins, and women would recapture the strength of their colonial foremothers.[3] With the rising sense that the human being was a developmental process more than a fixed entity, the whole notion of renewal for women as well as men became more pertinent; and sport promised to provide it. Like man, woman would achieve a kind of evolutionary development through carefully managed action. Convenient reductions from Darwin permitted men to assert women's inferiority, as G. Stanley Hall did in his studies on adolescence. Yet the overall thrust of developmental thinking greatly encouraged the movement of women outdoors and into the fields of sport. There they strengthened the very institution that supposedly strengthened them.

WOMEN'S SPORT AND SOCIAL RENEWAL

Although usually more restrained than men, women did pursue sport, liked it, and valued it highly. Some of them, ordinarily from the comfortable upper middle class, integrated it into their social patterns and sense of social renewal. In one definition of "social," this showed itself at lavish resorts such as Newport. But sport also seemed to turn the individual outward, restoring the sportswoman to a more general interchange with both men and women and renewing in her an amiable tone that flourished in the climate of permissible excitements. A frequent contributor to widely circulated magazines, Minna Gould Smith wrote in *Outing* in 1885 that sport served as a tonic to women's wilting spirits. The burdens of daily life seemed lighter, she insisted, after a "short, invigorating run on the tandem"; and the "fatigues and annoyances" of household duties vanished. The tandem bicycle itself suggested the woman's increased sociability, as she enjoyed comfortable exertion with her husband; and Smith affirmed that sport made the woman a more pleasurable companion for the man, as she shared his interest in the out-of-doors.[4]

The very emphasis on sport as a kind of fashion suggested its social quality. Cautioning women to guard against possibly harmful effects of a sudden turn toward sport, Minna Smith compared the enthusiasm for sport with a change of costume, calling it a "fashion of endurance" that could not be adopted as readily as the tweeds and flannels of the conditioned English sportswoman. Yet this was more than a playful remark; for it pointed toward a change in both behavior and tone. Taking the boom in women's sport as a given, Smith's remarks under-

The development of the "safety bicycle" encouraged greater use by women. In 1896, $60–75 represented as much as a third of a worker's annual income, marking "the wheel" as a plaything of the well-to-do — though some very wealthy women affected an indifference to the bicycle, except in a private setting. Color lithograph by the Strobridge Lithograph Co., 1896. By permission of the Library of Congress (LC-USZ62-28614).

score the fact that enthusiasm had reached a relatively high pitch. Taken in the context of middle-class culture, they hint at the sensibility that women's health lay in a social milieu and hence that women's place was not always within the home. Indeed, exercising with restraint, the woman bolstered both home and the larger society.[5]

Reporting on the growing devotion of women to cycling in the Chicago area, Smith indicated that the outdoor life was an effective curative for the "invalid woman"— one who suffered from sometimes imprecisely diagnosed ailments and had been kept within the confines of the home, often heavily dosed, and frequently on rest cures. A Chicago doctor, Alice B. Stockham, encouraged women to pursue exercise as a vigorous remedy for their complaints. As with the man, the woman now seemed a right candidate for a cure of action rather than rest; and Smith asserted that "exercise with the tricycle [was] better than medicines." Although such sportive behavior did not assure equality of condition for women, it encouraged a closer parallelism with the mode in which man experienced a sense of restoration and renewal. As men were supposedly vitalized by exchange of energy in the world of affairs and action, so did women's restoration increasingly seem linked to life in the larger world, even when it ended with service within the home.[6]

Customarily less concerned with the management of clubs, women who could afford it nonetheless began to exploit them as social centers away from the home. Elizabeth Barney reported in 1894 that women were commanding "their fair share of advantages," and they enjoyed a liveliness of personal exchange with their friends that gave them a greater sense of fulfillment and enhanced their equanimity. In the larger clubs, women used separate reading rooms, dining rooms, and sitting rooms; in the smaller ones, they shared more of the governance of the facilities with the men. In either case, however, the advent of the women imparted "a distinctly social tone, apart from sport, to all our sporting or country club life." Even if one took sport as no more than a pretext for social interaction, this alone virtually insured some tempering of woman's manner and style, some quickening of the activities that composed her personality.[7]

Women supposedly gained in quickness of thought, rapidity

of judgment, and accuracy of movement, thus making them more congenial toward men for whom these qualities were considered standard virtues. Even if the average woman's tennis game fell into an "easy game of 'lobs,'" as Elizabeth Barney judged, it lightened her spirits and enhanced her physical appearance. Such claims are significant not because, in any objective sense, the sportswoman was more fit and physically engaging, but rather because they suggest an altered notion of what one meant in using terms such as fitness and physical attractiveness. Just as clothing styles changed, so did body styles; and so, too, was there an altered sense of what was appealing in a personality. Sport became a part of this package of sensibilities; and a fit and attractive body was one that bore the physical signs of exuberant activity. Yet this concern over physical attractiveness was itself an indication of a basically social concern and of the enlistment of sport in its service.[8]

Although he thought that women needed to exercise more care to avoid overtaxing their bodies, sportswriter Ward Sanford also expressed satisfaction that women were engaging in sport with what he considered ever increasing frequency. In a sense, the very physiological weakness which Sanford and many others saw in women necessitated a greater effort in governing and guiding them to a modicum of health and strength through organized play and sport. Writing in *The Illustrated Sporting News* of June 13, 1904, Sanford insisted that girls "should no more be overtaxed physically than mentally, but the training of their bodies is no more to be neglected than the training of their minds." Similarly, those women physical educators who railed against sports such as basketball and discouraged other women from playing it did so out of their desire for the fuller and more pleasing physical development of their bodies. Lucille Eaton Hill, the director of physical training at Wellesley, dismissed it as a "rough-and-tumble game" unsuitable for girls and "likely to do more harm than good." Such experts further shared the views of other commentators who saw "masculine competition," such as the broad jump, the shot put, and hurdling as a distortion of the feminine qualities that united to form social grace. Restraint in the pursuit of their sport, then, was taken as a way of ensuring the social benefits of femininity.[9]

The ebullience of magazine writers and editors matched the enthusiasm of the sportswomen. Convinced that sport merited praise for bringing women out of their homes and into society, they cited approvingly the female contingent that was "following the hounds, on the golf links, at the tiller, in athletics [track and field], on the tennis court, on the turf, everywhere, in fact, except in the prize ring . . . ." Some claimed that women were, if anything, "more ardent devotees of the outdoor life than men." Yet the sportswomen proved specially victorious in turning sport into a social phenomenon or, perhaps more fairly, exploiting more persistently the potential of sport as a vehicle of social community.[10] Not obsessed with victory and inclined toward less abrasive competition than often appeared among men, women could pursue sport as an end in itself; and, in the process, they showed how sport could act within a group to strengthen a sense of cohesion by permitting individuals to share a common action.

To the extent that activities at country clubs segregated some women from men, to the extent that girls' sporting leagues occasioned a measure of rivalry with "a lot of top-lofty and unfeeling boys," and to the degree that college sport programs for women permitted a sense of isolation from the men's athletic craze, sport tended to encourage a feeling of commonality among women as against men, at least among those who shared social and economic backgrounds. This underlay claims, such as those of Christine Terhune Herrick, that women enjoyed a certain superiority in self-control, fairness, and the "sense of proportion," which she considered "that most admirable quality." Refinement in sport, Herrick thought, would aid in producing a "woman of the future" who would be "a much finer creature" than that of earlier times. Within this particular social sense, then, women could achieve a feeling of progress and evolutionary advancement. They might construe themselves to be morally better than men and different from them, as well as susceptible to different means by which these features might be realized.[11]

In the newer universities that pretended to fewer social distinctions than many of their Northeastern cousins, the correlation of women's athletic programs with social organizations further revealed the inseparability of some women's yearning for the experience of community activity and their sentiment toward sport. In Midwestern schools, for example, the traditional competition between different classes had emphasized their social identity; but, by 1904, there were experiments under way that enhanced it even more. At the University of Wisconsin, an intersociety basketball league emerged, permitting sorority members to play for the Greek-letter societies while retaining the prospect of playing on a conventional intramural team. Apart from its encouragement of sport — in this specific case, basketball — this measure tended to expand the circle of comradeship; and, even though the competitive drive thus gained some chance for expression, it still remained tied to a social purpose. At the University of Minnesota, strong interest in basketball showed itself among the young women, and enthusiastic teams played there, at the University of Nebraska, and elsewhere.[12]

In professional as well as collegiate sport, there were experts who sought ways of bringing women into the current of events. The ardent proponent of America's "national game" Albert G. Spalding, for example, believed that participation in golf, tennis, basketball, and cricket made women part of a broad national sporting community. Even more telling, however, was the rationale through which he gave women a role in baseball, a sport which he considered "too strenuous for womankind." He asserted that spectators actually participated in the game, while not sharing in the play on the field, by venting their enthusiasm in the grandstand. While the men played the game, women would use "smiles of derision for the Umpire" who gave an unfavorable call, or resort to "perfectly decorous demonstrations when it became necessary to rattle the opposing pitcher."[13] The feminine social mystique would bewitch umpire and opponent alike, and women would find their niche.

In making the psychological and social impact of rooting the key to women's participation in the national game, Spalding had also focused on what he believed to be their strong suit — the ability to explore the social dimension. The distinctions in role among men and women, which hardened into stereotypes, became evident for Spalding in a comparison of baseball with cricket. Although he wished to bar women from playing baseball, he considered cricket totally appropriate since it was, for them, an "Athletic Sociable" that did not "overtax their energy or their thought." Spalding suggested that the inferiority of cricket lay in its intrinsically slower pace, allowing men to adopt an improperly social emphasis in their approach toward sport. The man who played cricket, Spalding warned, thought his match was a chance to "drink afternoon tea, flirt, gossip, smoke [and] take a whiskey-and-soda at the customary hour."[14] Yet, while favoring discrimination between men and women, Spalding also identified in women a new and greater liveliness and a sharing in the social scene; and these were to a good degree the products of their sporting life.

RECREATION AND PROCREATION

Some middle- and upper-class Americans saw well-managed sport as a means to assure the biological future of the nation, which they thought was threatened by a decline in the birth rate among the traditional Anglo-American stock and the fertility of recent immigrants. Socially conservative members of the old gentility were among this cohort of fear, anxious for their values and social position. A drop in the birth rate among the white, Anglo-Saxon, Protestant stock, which became common knowledge late in the nineteenth century, brought them to conclude that "race decline" was under way and that extinction lay at the end of the road. Sport won attention from these people because physical activity and exercise seemed self-evidently pertinent to women's health and, specifically, to their capacity for childbirth. Logic alone could not say whether sport was beneficial or destructive to prospects for carrying a pregnancy to term; but it pointed to sport, as to other physical activity, as an area that required evaluation.

Those suffering such fears were not alone in their curiosity about the effect of sport on women's health. Physical culturists and educators, who hankered to clothe themselves in the mantle of science, provided an added impulse toward applying quasi-scientific disciplines to the study of female behavior and performance. Together with the strictures of socially traditional Americans who feared any disturbance of the relative status of men and women in society, this further encouraged the examina-

145

tion of sport in relation to differences, real or imagined, between men and women. In this way, distinct forces with varying objectives had a common effect in sorting and tempering women's sport in accordance with the goal of physical procreation.

Sportsman and writer Edwyn Sandys distinguished between activities that aided women and those that jeopardized their future health and ability to propagate. He approved of rowing, as long as it was in a moderate and noncompetitive format. He encouraged women to swim and to play golf, enthusiastically and happily but not to excess. These sports he recommended not because they offered self-fulfillment but because they would insure better childbearing. From his own vantage, Sandys saw no point in training women for public service — a role which people of his socioeconomic background considered most appropriate for men to anticipate in their sport; and he made no effort to guide women toward the professional careers. He even made no clear reference to the physical educators' belief in the intrinsic worth of the health of each man and woman in the land. Personal health assumed crucial importance for Sandys in the context of the national racial duty to conserve the old stock.[15]

A similar concern for breeding power guided B.F. Boller in the remarks he offered conservative German-American readers of *Mind and Body* in April 1900. Physical training for women seemed necessary to Boller, who apparently considered the argument from enhanced reproductive power to be the surest way of gaining support from readers for his proposals. He urged that girls be encouraged to play in organized games and to participate in the group exercises so dear to the turners. Recalling a concept whose origins receded into the classical age, Boller emphasized the importance of biological duty in encouraging the female toward sport: "If strong be the frames of the mothers, the sons shall make laws for the people." Much like Sandys, Boller believed that there was a sporting blood and a play instinct in women as much as in men; but he insisted that women's sport was even more important than men's because of the female function of childbearing.[16]

To be sure, Boller was patronizing toward the girls for whom he recommended sportive activities. In cloying voice, he spoke a plea on behalf of the imaginary girl-child in a tone that left the female at a certain social disadvantage:

> Do you blame us little animals, literally aching for the freedom of kittens, puppies, and lambs, if we demand of our teachers at least five minutes gymnastic or play-exercises at the end of every hour and a few full breaths of God's pure air? Especially when you remember that soon it will not be proper for little girls any longer to romp out of doors, with the boys; indeed it will be exceedingly unladylike; for then we must turn up our hair, lengthen our frocks, put on corsets, and "we can't be 'Tomboy' any longer."[17]

But such remarks were more than patronizing. They revealed Boller's fear that what German ethnics in America considered to be proper and decorous would militate against their further physical development and thus spoil the odds for the physical regeneration of the race. Although Boller's own conservatism on matters of convention and dress led him to doubt the appropriateness of sport for adult women, he became all the more concerned that the female be as fit as possible by the time that social convention should confine her. To Boller, as to Sandys, the duty of racial regeneration required appropriate play and games for females to condition them for motherhood, even though, in Boller's case, it was not clear that sportive behavior later in life would be encouraged.

Physical educator Dudley A. Sargent also identified female maturation with a kind of coquettish sexuality that had to be restrained in order to protect the development of males; and, in a way that echoed guidance writers such as the Reverend John Todd and Dr. Augustus Kinsley Gardner, Sargent implied that physical education and sport provided outlets that discouraged premature sexual curiosity and expression. In his autobiography, Sargent reminisced about the dancing classes and parties of the era before his own professional work began in earnest, much offended that "This hot-house physical education only wakens and stimulates a sex consciousness at a time when boys and girls should be unaffected and free." Even the gatherings sponsored by churches degenerated into "kissing games and so-called dancing" which "perniciously [weakened] the moral fiber of strong, healthy, clean boys and girls." By discouraging early sexual activity, using sport as a damper on enthusiasm for other forms of physical interest, Sargent thought that he was preserving the young for a healthier and more responsible life. Affected in part by his belief in rational physical education but also, apparently, by the notion of spermatic economy, Sargent added: "No one seemed to realize that there is a time in the life of a girl when it is better for her and for the community to be something of a boy rather than too much of a girl."[18] Athletics would sublimate sexual drives, the girls could be held in check while their physical development was outpacing that of the boys, and both male and female would be conserved through a critically dangerous period after which physical regeneration and renewal, through human procreation, could take place under rational circumstances.

Some advocates, admittedly touched by their own partiality to a sport in which they had invested much time and energy, argued that women could gain benefits from exercise for themselves and for their children. In *The Forum* of January 1896, cycling enthusiast Henry J. Garrigues promoted women's use of the bicycle for the benefits of good respiration, purification of the blood, and improved digestion, but even more for the curing of problems distinctive to them as a sex. Taking up the wheel would "overcome the impulsiveness and whimsicality which renders so many of them unhappy," Garrigues said, making them more orderly and rational. Most of all, bicycling would strengthen the muscle-bundles of the uterus so that childbirth would be undertaken under more favorable conditions. He embraced the doctrine of developing the whole body in a balanced way and considered the bicycle suitable to women except in periods of pelvic inflammation, "so common in their sex" (giving support to the barring of women from sport during menstrual periods), and while they were pregnant. Cycling especially surpassed horseback riding which, Garrigues warned, "if indulged in too much or at too early an age, is apt to produce a funnel-shaped pelvis, which abnormality may prove a serious obstacle to childbirth." Thus, fear for women's capacity for physical procreation loomed large in Garrigues's thinking, although he did not display a comparable zeal for preventing possible damage to the male reproductive system and to vulnerable male parts. He considered a fit and fertile body the summit of achievement for women, and so he valued the bicycle as the vehicle women could ride into efficient childbirth.[19]

Isaac B. Potter, the Chief Counsel of the New York Division of the League of American Wheelmen, added his support to the view that the bicycle offered women greater physical and mental health; and he considered it especially suited to them since exertion could be varied and flexible because of the very nature of the machine. Writing for *The Century* in 1896, Potter argued that cycling could be kept a "gentle exercise" for women — one that would cater to their purported craving for "change of scene" and the "delightful companionship of congenial friends," yet would not damage them physically or bring them to exhaustion. An instrument of at least partial liberation in that it brought women out into the open to recreate themselves, the bicycle had actually overcome traditional restraints on women's exercising in public by appealing to other traditional values that it supposedly could be used to save. If cycling made women more cheerful, it also supposedly prepared them to yield to male dominance in the world's activities and in the direction of the home. If cycling made them healthier, it was also to regenerate the race.[20]

Unlike cycling, sports such as football established an irreducible minimum of strenuous effort and violent contact for the participant that exceeded what most men and women considered the "weaker sex" capable of safely attempting. Moreover, the potential damage to the body seemed to them to be greater among women than men, either because of the body's supposed intrinsic weakness or because of what some termed its "greater complexity." Thus, the sorting of sports into those suitable to women and those dangerous to them often had overtones of the fear of "race decline" and of attitudes concerning female sexuality. In 1889, physical educator John S. White included tennis among sports that women might safely undertake, largely because "the strain is so short in the effort to reach and return the ball." White anticipated that continued severe exertion would wreak havoc on the inner organs of the girl or the young woman, and so he favored their participating in sport with less intensity than men, although with comparable frequency. The sports which White thought best suited women combined good manners and form with mild refreshment of the body, giving women a more active fashion for expressing themselves in society, while not encroaching on the bolder realm of male action. Thus, although one may fairly say that White, like many others of his time, typed the roles of men and women according to a deductive argument based on sex (the "man of action" needing "big lungs, brawny muscles and a constitution of iron"), it is crucial to the base of ideas behind the emergence of sport that he saw action and sportive experience as a proper means for the development of both men and women. Actions needed to be governed carefully, especially by sex, but they were key to robust and pleasing health.[21]

Women tended to be somewhat more oblique in describing the physical benefits of sport. Nonetheless, various women believed that exercise would have congenial medical effects. In language that compared closely to that of Edwyn Sandys, Mrs. Reginald de Koven wrote in the August 1895 issue of *The Cosmopolitan* that cycling would "bring delicate, fanciful women off their couches, and . . . rid them of vapors and nerves." These maladies were deemed to be caused by physical dysfunction, frequently of a sexual nature; and, while they had a social and psychological dimension, it was approached through the body as an organism rather than the mind as a separate entity. Bicycling would have effects on women that were analogous to those which sport had on men, strengthening their will and mental poise — again, terms which had a physiological rather than exclusively psychological connotation.

The effect which Mrs. de Koven expected cycling to have on women appears to have included the sublimation of sexual expression by concentrating on the sensual appeal of a fashionable exercise. She claimed, for example, that the bicycle was effective in "curing insanity" among women, citing "an authenticated case of an inmate of a retreat in Brooklyn who was restored to sanity by use of the machine." The meaning of this claim in the late nineteenth century was rich with sexual undercurrent, especially since the sexual organs were widely regarded as the causes of hysterical and insane derangement among women, often eliciting recommendations for radical gynecological surgery. When Mrs. de Koven claimed that the bicycle would help the woman forget "troubles and anxieties, real or imaginary," she is likely also to have meant that cycling would alleviate the physical problems that led to the anxiety in the first place. Thus, her proud boast that woman could go forth as a "rational, useful being" claimed more than her conditioning for entry into a world increasingly permeated by corporate values. It promised that she would not weaken the man's sexual potency by her own unregulated demands and "hysterical" presence; and, "no longer seeking for unhealthy excitement," she could focus on duty, rather than merely being driven toward gratification.[22]

Physical culturists sometimes picked up this theme, suggesting that proper physical development made women more attractive to men. Typical in its thrust and clear in argument was a compilation of the thoughts of the renowned strongman Eugene Sandow, prepared by Mercer Adam. Although Sandow and Adam thought the male body exceedingly beautiful, the American male perfected himself in the activities of a busy world. Women's beauty aimed at the instincts of men, according to Sandow. Their physical training was meant to acquire "grace of form and beauty of outline that attracts us in the sex," thus serving society by encouraging marriage and procreation. Meanwhile, sport was to give women other adornments to make them fit companions—"a lustrous eye, a clear skin, a bright intellect, a happy disposition, and a vivacious manner." They could enjoy rowing, swimming, skating, and many other sports—much the ones that John S. White also endorsed. Thus would they embrace the active, tactile, physically immediate world unfolding before them.[23] The woman was deemed beautiful not in a pose, but in patterns of action and movement. These added the crucial benefit of tempering her sexuality, enabling her to focus on childbirth rather than on "anxieties" and "unhealthy excitement," even as they strengthened her to undertake this racial duty.

THE IMPACT OF WOMEN PHYSICAL EDUCATORS

As experts in the new "sciences of the body," female physical educators offered additional arguments for women's use of sport, although these often paralleled those heard from other groups. Women physical educators held the human body and female anatomy in high regard and did not descend into ritualistic or stereotypical presumptions of female inferiority. Indeed, in a social sense, they considered women superior in the sensibilities which they carried into sport. Yet, because of the occasional similarity of their measures, the educators fell into a kind of "alliance of results" with groups that had other motivations and opinions. Some sport enthusiasts, for example, seem merely to have sought to preserve an etiquette in sport that was traditionally sexist. But women physical educators, like their male counterparts, were appalled at what they considered the unscientific and destructive emphasis on athletics for men; and they resolved to shield women from this evil force. Although there surely was an element of social control within their thinking, these were people who dearly loved the semblance of logic, who prized order and were comfortable with a structured and predictable life in which reason and expertise aimed at filling the gap for a waning tradition. Although these professionals can be seen as a source of some inequity when assessed according to the criterion of equal opportunity for men and women in sport, they nonetheless strengthened women's participation in an absolute sense and thus formed a part of sport's diverse constituency.

Unlike their male counterparts, the women educators were well placed to make good on their resolve to guard the students in their charge. Men's athletics had developed separately and independently from the sway of the men's physical educators, who thus had to fight for any influence over the forms of athletic competition. The women physical educators, however, enjoyed a wide-open field. They faced no entrenched women's coaching staffs, no retinue of paid trainers and handlers; and they profited from the stereotypical view that whatever competition women were allowed ought to be carefully restrained.

This affected the administrative structure of women's athletics, the choice of sports in which women would be permitted to compete, the level at which the competition would take place, and consequently the degree to which special training and coaching would be needed. As professionals, the physical educators, boosters of restraint, had a passion for dispassion and an emotional commitment to reasonable and sensible behavior. These attributes inclined them toward regulation of the realm of women's sport in a manner and to a degree literally impossible among men's sports, where male physical educators had entered the fray too late to be dominant. The educators' programs for women's athletics, then, assumed less dramatic proportions and flirted less with public display, dovetailing neatly with the preferences of the gentility. Nonetheless, within these limits, they reinforced the idea that women ought properly to engage in sport.

Women physical educators resolved to restrict competition to a more moderate or genteel level, always perceiving it as a component of physical education and not as an independent enterprise. Consequently, they were willing to sacrifice the commercial viability of sport as an entertainment for the sake of ensuring its efficacy as a means of physical education. For example, Senda Berenson adapted the rules of basketball to reduce its roughness and make it more suitable to the putative limits of women's strength; but this measure also reduced the excitement and dash of the game. Consistent with her professional commitment to the physical development of her charges, Berenson promoted adjustments in Naismith's game without concern over their damaging effect on women's basketball as a public spectacle. Indeed, the reduction of spectacle helped to confirm the support of many physical educators for this activity. Similarly, the women's version of the game remained decentralized and, for some time, unstandardized. With little impulse to intercollegiate competition, women's basketball became the subject of debate almost exclusively as a component of physical education, rather than as a part of a broad athletic and entertainment program. Questions centered on the game's compatibility with female physiology, on the degree and sources of roughness in play, and on the proper means to avoid developing star performers. In short, the key to the arguments was the personal health of the average player, not the public exhibition of inordinate competition.[24]

It is significant that the women educators chose this separate path consciously and in defiance of its possible "inequalities" with the course of men's athletics; and they pursued it because it seemed to be the course of superior reasonableness. In 1901, in *Basket Ball for Women*, Berenson affirmed that women should "profit by the experience of our brothers and therefore save ourselves from allowing . . . objectionable features to creep into our athletics." These injurious aspects revolved around the "win at all costs" attitude that prevailed in men's sport, including excessive training, commercialism, and the sacrifice of the team to the star. Lucille Eaton Hill, Director of Physical Training at Wellesley College, urged that women "avoid the evils which are so apparent to thoughtful people in the conduct of athletics for men." Significantly, the effort to keep athletics in appropriate balance often resulted in a total rejection of intercollegiate athletics for women. In this, the professional cadre was prone to concur.[25]

At socially respectable schools such as the "Seven Sisters," women physical educators were able to govern the participation of women in sport and in athletics according to their highest professional principles. In a sense, sport became a vehicle for the educators' sense of professional fulfillment, almost apart from their intent to impart reason and health to their charges. Balancing their objectives efficiently, they designed programs for the physical improvement of underdeveloped young women, maintained systems of graduated exercise and sports for all students, and allowed competition in sport to ascend only to those levels that they deemed conducive to good health and effective performance of social duties. Elizabeth Paine, who wrote a series of articles on women's athletics and physical training in colleges and universities for *The Illustrated Sporting News* during 1904, averred that both men and women needed "a well-ordered body and a goodly store of reserve power" to meet the demands of "these days of keen competition and exacting standards." In women's colleges, athletics served as a means for the attainment of health. The achievement of victory was secondary, and their separate path — leading toward health rather than to the extremes of competition — took them toward "independence of masculine tradition," as woman adapted "her sports and pastimes to her own needs along varied and original lines."[26]

At Smith College, Berenson demonstrated clearly that the physical educator could use sport as a means of improving the physical condition of students without succumbing to the seductions of unrestrained competition and the pursuit of victory as an intrinsically important goal. Sometimes called the "Mother of Basketball for Women," Berenson instituted a system of graduated participation in various sports, in which the severity of the sport and the intensity of play served as tools for the students' development, and in which the students' own limitations were permitted to govern the level of competition. Elizabeth Paine recorded the case of a student who entered college "unfit for hard work of any kind, weak and anaemic, and even the corrective gymnastic course was thought too severe for her fragile physique." Berenson's program provided for a steady increase in strength until, as a senior, the student had become one of the twenty strongest members of the class — "a vigorous, happy young woman, her health the most precious gain of her four years in college."[27]

As her series continued, Paine's reportage revealed a pattern among the upper-class schools. It included the emphasis upon personal development of all students that Smith so effectively advanced, the commitment to a view of the value of competition that smacked of Social Darwinism, and an insistence upon balance even within competition which harkened to the call of the genteel tradition. So determined were Bryn Mawr's educators that each woman be fit that they prescribed "individual corrective courses, no two precisely the same" for those who need special attention. Under close supervision from instructors, these "solitary toilers in the gymnasium" could be goaded and encouraged to achieve mediocrity. But even if they failed to experience so miraculous a metamorphosis as the case study from Smith College had presented, the women would in a sense become "competitive," against themselves and their dissolute habits, without ever having competed in an interschool competition. Those who were varsity athletes perhaps even better exemplified the spirit of Bryn Mawr, where, Paine said, "The Freshman soon awakens to the fact that she is permitted within the gates because she is one of the survivals of the fittest, past the first barrier of the entrance examinations, yet really only on the threshold of the striving for what is best in her four years of college life." "Life is one long competition," Dr. Louisa Smith, the director of physical culture, said, "so why not prepare for it in the gymnasium." But the Social Darwinist impulse itself was trapped in a maze of restraints. The college itself was "walled in for womankind," as Paine put it, nor did the Bryn Mawr staff hint much that women and men might rightly exercise any functional equality in sport. Nor did Dr. Smith approve of the "win-at-all-costs" competition that had become endemic among male athletes and their coaches. In the gymnasium as elsewhere, she judged, "Competition is wholesome only as it is carefully guarded and regulated."[28]

To visit Bryn Mawr in 1904 would have been, in part, to travel in time. For its sport programs retained objectives that had lost their persuasiveness in the men's schools, except among the physical educators. In another way, though, Bryn Mawr epitomized the aspirations of the professional physical educators — physical development for all, graduated participation in sport according to ability, competition subordinated to the purposes of cultivating the whole woman, and the glory of rational method itself. At Mount Holyoke, as elsewhere among the better women's colleges, the goal of the physical education and sport program was "to produce the fully trained womanhood so much needed in the world to-day."[29] The ambiguity within the women's schools centered in the essentially subordinate and occasionally patronized position that the physical educators accepted, one that harmonized with the goals of social traditionalists who resented change in the pattern of women's activities. The interplay of the specific professional concerns of the physical educators and the preferences of the social traditionalists worked to promote thoroughness in hygiene even as it prevented the building of an avenue toward excellence in performance and intensity in competition. Within this circumscribed area, however, the educators enjoyed considerable freedom to encourage young women to make use of sport and delineated a justification for it not unlike that offered for men's sport by the gentility.

Women took advantage of the milieu of sport to express themselves more viscerally than traditional taste had previously allowed, even if contemporary mores barred them from many playing fields. In basketball, the "fair devotees" of the game hissed every offensive play by the visiting team. At football matches, "delicate ladies who but a moment before shrunk from witnessing the 'brutal' game, with flushed cheeks and staring eyes wildly shriek their approval" of the violent downing of an enemy player. These, Dudley Sargent suggested ambiguously, exhibited some of the "recurring traits of our barbaric ancestry."[30] Well organized and managed, these demonstrations purportedly showed the surge of animal vitality that the preservation of the race required, albeit tempered by rational order and direction.

Advocates of a more deeply traditional society objected even to this display. For example, immoderate competition in women's basketball enraged and worried the editors of *Mind and Body*, whose views accorded well with traditionalist social sentiment in America. In May 1900, they commented on games between teams that had traveled "considerable distances" to compete with women from other schools. Such "viscious [*sic*] outgrowths" as the spirit of rivalry that almost blossomed into free-for-all fights on the court choked the seedling of "systematic physical training" in the higher schools. Although the American turners, whom *Mind and Body* represented, opposed athleticism and the obsession with victory wherever it appeared, the editors clearly achieved a new fervor because young women had behaved like bad boys. "Such public exhibitions of infuriation on the part of young ladies," they pronounced, "who thus vented their temper and obtuned their sense of propriety, even more than foot-ball-boys, should neither be encouraged nor tolerated by college authorities."[31]

The editors of *Mind and Body* shared the perspectives of the women physical educators, as well as of their male counterparts. Among those who communicated with the Milwaukee-based journal was Amy Morris Homans, the Director of the

Boston Normal School of Gymnastics and among the most influential physical educators at the turn of the century. Homans sought to promote "a more rational, self-controlled way of living" and to present "the ideals of 'the good life' as regards health and efficiency." Her students at the Boston Normal School, then, should learn how to use sport to develop in their charges the conventional traits of womanliness: "grace, poise, charm" and the like. As Helene S. McLaughlin indicated in an article for the *American Physical Education Review* in 1911, the athletic girl would not dress in loud masculine attire nor ape men's activities. Unlike her male counterpart, the woman athlete "plays for the joy of playing."

Although the path trod by women physical educators may have led toward a fuller life for their students and to a more rational one for themselves, it also veered sharply away from the road that the men had chosen. Male athletes thus had a free and open field in public sporting exhibition in which the belief in male dominance became a self-fulfilling proposition as women held themselves apart from the men's supposedly destructive and improper displays.[32] The other side of this coin, however, was that it enabled yet another group of women — and a visible and articulate one at that — to see merit in sport. Separation from men's sport meant avoiding contamination from excessive competition, from the hazards of professionalism, and from the subordination of the quest for health to the desire to win. From the vantage of the women physical educators, separation from the men went beyond equality — it meant superiority. While men squandered their opportunity to use sport for personal strengthening for competition in the world and yielded to the temptations of ego-gratifying and spectacular sporting display, women could reserve sport for the creation and regeneration of a rational way of life.

The multiplicity of viewpoints among the various advocates of women's participation in sport at the turn of the century paralleled the diversity among sport's constituencies more generally. Sport was a fashionable device through which to encourage the renewal of social ties and to strengthen one's identity by carving a niche in society. For others, some male and some female, sport was taken to serve regenerative functions of the most basic sort, enabling women to bear children more effectively and taming what some considered woman's tendency to sexual excess. Still others approached sport from the vantage of the rationalism and order that were much prized by the exponents of a managerial society based upon expertise. Coming from a welter of social and economic backgrounds, these proponents of sport had as many differences as commonalities of intent.

Yet the confusion of intent was less a problem to sport than it was to sport's exponents. As with the development of men's sporting programs and tastes, no one group or faction was able to envision quite what was to become of women's sport; and the comprehensive patterns which any one group harbored underwent a certain element of erosion and modification. Each group sought its special interests, and some achieved partial lists of successes and half-victories. But the overall picture was a patchwork in which the maker of one piece often worked in ignorance of others, or even in disagreement with them. Only retrospectively could one begin to identify within the whole a pattern in the results, while remaining skeptical that any one pattern of conscious intentions had achieved more than a restricted effect, however important it was.[33] The component parts of men's sport differed somewhat from those of women's sport; and the general pictures that emerged in each case proved sufficiently different so that later generations saw preliminary evidence of discriminatory causation. Yet the process at work in both men's and women's sport — the reliance on schematics to assemble the components into a working whole — was quite similar.

What lay beneath the audible debate over the purpose of sport for women was the commitment to the value of action as a means of regeneration and the assumption that women needed to have this experience of renewal and the active life as much as men did, even if they did so in a different way. The "swooning damsel" fell from fashion — or was pushed by the physical educators — and the sportswoman inherited much of her esteem. If one philosopher has said that the unexamined life is not worth living, the late-nineteenth-century sportswoman could have said that the unexperienced life cannot even be known.

In this context, the question of women's status relative to men, while important in itself, becomes something of an intrusion. What looms more critical in terms of the emergence of sport was the adjustment of women's sense of respectable means for exploring the world, of effective ways of conforming to the changing world view (of which they were themselves a part, in any event) that prized motion and a more exuberant style, and of available strategies for their own social and physical regeneration.

From Playing Fields to National Parks —
The Instinct toward an American Nationalism
in Sport and Recreation

THE instinct toward nationalism — which showed itself in America in such varied forms as the movement toward immigration restriction, overseas imperialism, and the standardization of a domestic culture — created a kind of constituency of sentiment favoring sports supposed to foster an identifiably American character. This group was not exactly identifiable by class or occupation, although many of the most ardent and vocal of its enthusiasts came from the comfortable middle and upper classes, but rather one which overlay groups definable in socioeconomic terms. To avoid a "chicken and egg" argument, one may suggest that the sense of the material world as truly real merged with the desire to determine that which was the distinctive character of each nation (seeing the nation as a concrete, physical entity rather than an accidental accumulation of whatever lay within arbitrary boundaries). A concept of "nationalism," then, came to be linked with the empiricist emphasis on the visible, tangible world. By a process of applying the general rule to the specific case, then, many Americans tested all actions, including a broad range of sports, for their suitability to an American character that was presumably in need of stabilization.

This deep-seated drive toward clarifying what it meant to be an American rode roughshod over the distinctive features of cultures which had given many of their members as immigrants. But the genius of the "melting pot," as then understood, lay in the fusion of diverse elements into a single and fundamentally stable whole. It was an effort to ensure stability in the midst of great change. The true American, according to Teddy

Roosevelt, was whoever acted like one. In *The Winning of the West*, whose first volume appeared in 1889, Roosevelt argued that the backwoods mixture of Germans, Huguenots, Irish, Dutch, and Swedes had become "one people" within a single generation lived out under the common conditions of the wilderness. The second generation, he asserted, "became indistinguishable from one another," "one in speech, thought, and character." The genius of American unity, then, lay in the willingness of people to adapt; and, since a race was defined largely by its experience and by the material conditions in which it was shaped, the preservation of European customs threatened the American identity.[2] So, too, in sporting behavior, difference presented more problem than promise. The decline of certain nineteenth-century sporting clubs suggested the extent to which cultural deviationism was becoming a liability. The Caledonian clubs and the *Turnvereins* provide cases in point.

The turners implicitly challenged the purity of an "American race," which was itself partly defined as an "English-speaking people," by cultivating the German language. They encouraged the study of German culture and political ideas; and they urged the maintenance of sport and exercise along lines that differed intellectually from the approach predominating in American culture. As Theodore Hough wrote of so-called Swedish gymnastics (another term for much of the turners' exercise program) in 1900, the turners began with an ideal image of the human body and a preconceived notion of what system of exercise would produce it. They were, in other words, both deductive and reductionist, while the stronger tendency in American culture lay in the direction of inductive experimentalism. The mass wand exercises, which so cheered the hearts of the turners, seemed tinged with passivity, monotony, and archaism. The precedence of formalism — in ideas as well as in actions — identified the turners with precisely that stream of thought in America that was pouring itself into a dry lake. Through the luckless coupling of foreign idiosyncracies (turner C.E. Ehinger once claimed as a great success of his group that it sharpened the "common [German] nationality of its members") and an obsolescent philosophical perspective (they opposed athleticism, record break-

Exuding energy, Theodore Roosevelt symbolized the supposed transformation of personality by transforming the body. In this 1885 studio portrait,
taken by George Grantham Bain, Roosevelt is dressed more appropriately
for a Wild West Show than for life in the Dakotas. By permission of the Library
of Congress (LC-USZ62-23232).

ing, and commercialism as well as experimentalism in the selection of sporting events), the American turners ran the risk of being—and of seeming to be—"un-American."[3]

The Caledonian Games in America provide a similar example. Scots immigrants recreated the Highland Games, including such events as the hammer throw and shot put, in order to preserve their native culture within the alien environment of the new world. Although the Caledonian Clubs that were founded to conduct the games and to host the accompanying social activities spread across the United States (as well as Canada), their membership remained overwhelmingly Scottish. By the 1870s, curiosity about the Caledonian Games had risen sharply among non-Scots who adapted certain of the events and various of the Scots' techniques in improving the quality of their own track and field programs. Yet the specifically Scottish character of the Caledonian Games, their "premodern" tolerance of social incursions and a tinge of professionalism, and the centripetal cultural implications of their programs doomed them in the world of late nineteenth-century sport.[4]

The association of special sports with particular races may have reached its apogee at the 1904 Olympic Games in St. Louis. On August 12 and 13, the organizing committee staged a series of special events called "Anthropology Days." They brought representatives from various peoples considered primitive and worthy of observation, putting them into competition with one another. Although these exotic guests did participate in some sports that regularly appeared on the Olympic schedule, they also displayed their skill at activities supposedly typical of their own cultures. The Pygmies, for example, took the laurels in the mud fight. An Igorot from the Philippines won the pole-climb. By contrast, a Patagonian was victorious in the high jump, and a Sioux Indian placed first in the 100-yard dash. Victory in each event presumably revealed ingrained skills gained through generations of practice, which had apparently become hereditary. Whether in traditional or special events, the competitors in "Anthropology Days" wore their native costumes rather than athletic garb—a visible sign of their racial differences. Ainus, Moros, and Kaffirs added to the diversity among the participants. Oddities though they were, the events may be taken as an authentic

CALEDONIANS.

COME a' THEGITHER.

AND GET THE NEXT

SCOTTISH-AMERICAN
JOURNAL

WHICH WILL CONTAIN A FULL REPORT OF THE

C.LEDONIAN GAMES

ORDER IT FROM NEWSDEALERS.

SCOTTISH-AMERICAN PRINT, No. 33 Rose Street, New York.

The emphasis on ethnic heritage served as a source of strength for some sporting clubs but set them at odds with Americans who believed that "alien" sports jeopardized national character. Lithograph, originally printed in color, by A.M. Stewart for Scottish-American Print, New York, 1885. By permission of the Library of Congress (LC-USZ6-515).

165

effort to assess the relative merits of different races; the nature of the game might reveal the character of the race.[5]

In short, ill-chosen sports might warp the American character, subverting whatever values a given group had decided exemplified the national tradition. The means and the settings for recreation and sport thus assumed importance far out of proportion to a common-sense assessment of the vagaries of child's play; for action was taken to be functionally equivalent to character. In the realm of organized play and sport, therefore, the sorting process was aimed at finding games that recalled the basic traditions that had formed "Anglo-Saxon" personality and character. In the realm of the open lands and great national parks, there was an effort to retain a material circumstance that had supposedly been instrumental in the shaping of that same character. From the playing fields through the great Western parks, American sport and recreation were thus formed and, in a sense, boosted by the instinct toward nationalism.

THE NATIONAL GAME AND "KING" FOOTBALL

It may be easy to see what was wrŏng about the sport of the turners and the Caledonians by seeing what was right about the major national sports, particularly baseball (the so-called national game) and football (which reigned as "King" on college campuses by the early twentieth century). Both sports appealed to the era's fascination with complexity, order, precision, and discipline; and the articulate sporting public embraced both sports — retaining the one and introducing the other to a wider audience, albeit a nonprofessional one. Each sport was linked to the land and the notion of regeneration through contact with natural forces as well as through subordination to established social demands. Moreover, each (not just baseball) enjoyed a myth of cultural and geographical uniqueness. Each was given a specific time and place of origin in the United States along with an individual creator in the case of baseball, and team-creators in football. If not unique, the myth of American particularism in these sports was conspicuous by its difference from the promotion of rowing, tennis, track and field, and the like, in which no such claim of America's special cultural and geographical identity was attempted.

Any "national" game could be so only if its geographic spread were complete. For this reason, baseball and football had the advantage of needing only small spaces with relatively limited support facilities. One could imagine a simple "pickup" game in either sport played on an open field, while, by contrast, a casual game of tennis still required precisely maintained minimum facilities. The comparative simplicity of the demands posed by certain kinds of ball games thus permitted their spread around the country without the preliminary requirement of spending time, effort, and money to create an environment in which to receive them. On the other hand, this does not answer the question of why these ball games, rather than others such as rugby or soccer, should have predominated. That depended less on absolute material conditions than on people's perceptions of sports and the ways in which they grafted onto some sports attributes which they considered specially American. If such an argument sounds circular, it should, since that was the structure of the thinking about sport at the turn of the century. Qualities that were supposedly American were imputed to football and baseball, which, in turn, were presumed to generate those values in the players.

Football had a special appeal because it combined the values of precision and order with a kind of gross physical force—a linkage that underscored the emphasis of the late nineteenth-century Americans on things and actions. Walter Camp, one of the most eminent of college coaches at the turn of the century, and Lorin F. Deland, who coached at Harvard, considered football outstanding especially because it had an "all-around *physical* effect on the player" (emphasis added). The sport required conditioning both of the trunk and of the extremities. It required agility—as tennis and baseball did—but it also demanded strength. In their book *Football*, published in 1896, Camp and Deland saw football as a composite of many sports, joining together the jumping, wrestling, running, throwing, and boxing of the old Greek pentathlon into a single sport. It was logical, comprehensive, physically demanding, reliant on ac-

167

tion. Disputes over the sport's value they dismissed as dispropor-
tionate nonsense, likening them to discussions of "certain rare
and exceptional diseases [such as hydrophobia]."[6] Football's emphasis on the physical, the material, the tactile — this was a key
underlying virtue which enabled it to make concrete any other
qualities it was believed to impart.

Just as the general theory of growth which turn-of-the-century
Americans harbored made them see all values as flowing from
various actions and habits, so within sport did moral qualities
develop in a naturalistic, organic way. Thus, games such as football and baseball were not merely *similar* to other actions in
their ability to create positive moral results. They were *equal*
to them. In a sense, one might even say that the process of experiencing the play of the sport was itself the actual process
of gaining and living the values that supposedly typified the
nation. Extreme pressure in a football game, for example, presumably taught "coolness" even as it taught toughness and the
"subordination of strength to will." Nor was the suppression of
temper a matter of courtesy. Walter Camp, for example, praised
it because it was likely to increase the chances of victory. As
a good pragmatist, Camp liked self-control because it was practical; it "worked." What seemed to be an improvement of morality was actually an improvement in efficiency, and vice versa;
and this symbiosis was achieved in an inseparable organic, physical growth and training of the individual. Moral attitude was
indistinguishable from its expression in action.[7]

At the apex of the system of functionalist morality suggested
by these remarks stood the person who coordinated the largest
number of specific tasks, combined the largest number of positive attributes within his own personality, and used the skills
requisite to convert resources and potential into action on the
field. This role could devolve from the coach to the captain
or to the quarterback on the field in football; and the sport's
promoters saw what they called "moral force" as a physically
practical force on the gridiron. "Moral" virtuosity, they believed,
enabled the cunning leader on the gridiron to realize Napoleon's maxim that in war the ratio between moral and physical
factors was three to one. For the American at the turn of the

168

century, however, it was superfluous to imagine a real distinction between the moral and the physical realms.

Suggesting much about their mentality, writers such as Camp extolled the particular and the concrete; and it was the concreteness of their favored sport — its defiance of what Homer Lea called "intangible complexity"— which served as an underlying theme of their remarks. When they compared football to war (something done in a far less detailed and serious fashion in later years), they did so with great particularity. For example, they distinguished between the study of military systems on the one hand and the study of battles on the other. Or, as yet another illustration, they discriminated between musing over grand strategy on the one hand and detailed examination of tactics and battle histories on the other. They noted that American students were especially interested in these latter battle histories — in other words, in the most detailed and most concrete form of study. In particular, the young Americans were presumably impressed by the way in which "a comparatively small body of soldiers has routed a force of twice its strength." Parenthetically, one may see in this a parallel to the American love of the underdog. But, for present purposes, it is even more significant to see the Americans' belief that moral power was directly transmutable into physical power — in other words, to see that physical conditions were component elements of the formula for national power and national identity. It was this formula that could create the appearance of snatching victory from the jaws of defeat.[8]

Their love of concreteness and physical detail made them emphasize that victory resulted from attention to detail rather than a good theory or a broad plan. In some circumstances, in fact, Walter Camp even suggested that the team should never be told the *theory* of the coach's defensive plan for fear that they would seek to substitute thought and finesse for hard, clean blocking. The learning of the plan could best be achieved in the process of carrying it out, Camp calculated; and in this perception we may see how totally defunct was the Germanic, idealist tradition of the turners and their ilk.

Even physical educator Dudley Sargent, who considered football too dangerous for the average student and considered injuries to be "its natural accompaniment," admitted that the game was perhaps the most accessible among college sports and had many advantages. He appreciated its ability to promote hardiness, fleetness of foot, quick perception, strong limbs, and presence of mind. It was less the nature of the game than the manner of its conduct that disturbed him.[9] But it is significant that even this rather sharp critic of football recognized in the sport those features which made it a sure bet as a national, and nationally accepted, sport.

Field sports (such as hunting and camping) had the advantage of bringing man into "closer relation to Nature than does football," Camp admitted. But he rejected this association of the contemporary American with the agrarian myth as being "out of the question with the young men in our colleges and schools, who have neither the time, the money, nor the location in which to indulge them." Despite much writing about the extension of greenery into the cities in various of the baseball or football fields, it is important to note that ardent promoters of the games, such as Camp, often saw it somewhat otherwise. For many of these people, at least on a conscious level, the national sport had little to do with vestiges of the older national myth. And a study of the actual policies of the national parks of the late nineteenth century and of the mentality that produced them would confirm this suppression of the old rural and agrarian myth. The parks resulted more than anything else from the surge of "monumentalism" within the American mind — the desire to search out monuments, created by Nature, which would serve as the American counterpoint to the man-built structures of Europe such as Chartres or the Parthenon. The recreation that Americans were to experience in the parks was far less the "wildness" of Thoreau than it was the road and highway program of Stephen Mather. The nonecological perception of the Americans running the parks showed itself in the penchant for giving natural formations names that implied construction, design, and engineering — for example, Zion's "Altar of Sacrifice" and "Great White Throne." So, then, it was a civilized and not a pure wilderness world that the promoters of the newly christened national sports had framed in their minds,

170

even those promoters who also backed the national parks as Roosevelt did. Not only were hunting and such sports no longer convenient for many Americans; they now seemed less desirable and less relevant, even as they had also been less susceptible of the myth of American exceptionalism.

On the other hand, football and baseball had the advantage of contact with the elements and, to a degree, defiance of them. Particularly in the case of football, the game proceeded even under adverse conditions—extremes of heat and cold, rain or snow. Thus, while the agrarian and rural myths may have been less prominent in the concerns of some of the sport's promoters than some commentators might suggest, the notion that American character was shaped in the chrysalis of the environment retained a certain ritualized presence on both the football field and the baseball diamond. Moreover, as Roderick Nash has pointed out, "wilderness" and openness are relative concepts whose personal meaning depends on the relationship of one's own pattern of expectations to the conditions one is encountering. From this vantage, on a personal level as well as a mythic one, the gridiron and the diamond could possess a certain tone of "wilderness" even in the midst of the city.[10]

Given the bias toward civilization and social organization in sport and recreation, which at least affected the middle class and upper class in America, it is no wonder that various other sports failed the criterion of sufficiency that baseball and football passed. For example, Camp and Deland asserted that tennis and track athletics were weakened by "the comparatively private character of the sport," which could never permit the development of esprit de corps as could football, baseball, or rowing in a crew. The emphasis that promoters of the national sports and pastimes gave to the "rugged individual" was restricted to his ability to act as a building block in organizations and in society.[11] This emphasis on the team and the group contradicted the individualistic character of many Western and mountain sporting activities. Even in those activities carried on in a public group, such as rodeo, the emphasis was on the individual performer rather than on a team; and, for that matter, the most significant team in rodeo may be construed as horse and rider. To people who imagined that sport was a form

171

of training for social leadership, that was hardly a sufficient model for running a country; and it may help us to see something more significant behind the off-the-cuff criticism that industrialist Marcus Hanna made of Roosevelt, when he objected to "that damn cowboy" in the White House.

Baseball's claim as a national sport, again, did not depend upon its rural associations, which in any case were much more myth than fact. Rather, baseball thrived because it had the same scientific complexity and social inclusiveness that promoters saw in football and thus matched as well as molded the purported American character. Compared to baseball, remarked the British writer Angus Evan Abbott in 1904, "there is no more exact and scientific game. The Americans have a genius for taking a thing, examining its every part, and developing each part to the utmost. This they have done with our game of rounders and, from a clumsy primitive pastime, have so tightened its joints, and put such a fine finish on its points that it stands forth a machine of infinite exactitude." Hardly the agrarian myth. So, too, American sportswriter Ralph D. Paine took issue only with Abbott's preference for cricket. "To compare baseball with crickett," Abbott opined, "is to compare the quick-swallowed cocktail with the quietly sipped bottle of port, the storming of Quebec with the slowly conducted, persistent Peninsular campaign. The one is an essence, the other a meal." Americans could satisfy their competitive appetites in less than an afternoon. But in that short space, as Paine noted, the national game could achieve a mechanistic precision.[12]

The nonrural, nonagrarian, nonregional character of baseball, as the Progressive-era American understood it, was all the more strengthened by the decision to attribute the game to a specific creator. Spalding and others thus not only gave it American roots, but roots that were nationalist, socially cohesive, and deferential. In one name, that of Abner Doubleday, were these characteristics united. Just as the American Civil War proved to be a crucial nationalizing experience, late-nineteenth-century Americans sought to lend this nationalizing and unifying quality to the sport of baseball by associating it with a Civil War general who had fought on the winning side. He was, moreover, a general in that Grand Old Army which had on its side the image of science, technology, and industry. In a sense, had baseball been rural, it ought to have been attributed to a Confederate such as Robert E. Lee. It was this metaphysical truth that overcame the practical hoax when Spalding praised what he termed the "righteousness of the verdict" of the Special Commission of 1907 in naming Doubleday as originator of the game.[13]

Despite his effort to create a viable myth of the American nativity of baseball, Spalding proved to be an extraordinarily innovative and often hard-nosed promoter of his favored sport. He carried the centralizing and monopolistic practices of business in the Progressive era over into the operations of his sporting goods empire, and he relied early on creative advertising and marketing techniques. Despite his insistence on the American distinctiveness of baseball, he also boosted it as a sport which would bring the benefits of reason, order, excitement, and discipline to other countries — all, of course, with the ancillary benefit of providing new business for his sporting goods firm. Significant as a demonstration of this missionary zeal was the world tour of a special all-star team which he assembled during 1888–1889. At the same time, he helped to mold the Progressive era's version of the hero — namely, the "star" performer whose efficiency and skill served as a ritualistic confirmation of the myth of the rugged individual. Full of paradox and complexity, his mind ranged from discipline as a baseball player and as a business executive to a jungle of accidents in the explanations and rationale he provided for his actions.[14]

In his book *America's National Game,* which certainly coincided with Doubleday's personal financial interests, Spalding obviously relished the pristinely American origin that he saw in the game. He said that it was appropriate that baseball was born in the preliminary stages of the Civil War (to use his phrase) and that it was the brainchild of a Union general. Baseball, he said, served to shape the peace through "a bloodless battle," as he called it. In a litany of alliteration, Spalding recited the sport's values: "American Courage, Confidence, Combativeness; American Dash, Discipline, Determination; American Energy, Eagerness, Enthusiasm; American Pluck, Persistence, Performance; American Spirit, Sagacity, Success; American Vim,

Vigor, Virility." Just as with football, so with baseball, Spalding claimed that the game had these qualities, in his words, "in quantity to spread over the entire continent." Baseball, quite simply, passed this geographic test for becoming a national sport; and it carried within it the long roster of components of the American spirit.[15]

Even sport analysts who dissented from the views of Spalding and the Special Commission as to the uniqueness of baseball's origins agreed that the game had *become* uniquely American in its effects. In the July 1901 issue of *Outing*, for example, Henry Chadwick, sometimes called the "father of American baseball," declared that this special transformation of the English game of rounders had created a manly field sport as distinctive to his people as cricket was to the English. Three years later, James L. Steele wrote that "young America looked askance at a game that required a day and sometimes two days to finish." Those Englishmen who had come to America failed to establish cricket as a national game because "the hustle and bustle temperament of Americans was not congenial to it."[16] Whatever the genesis of baseball, the game's suitability to the American character won widespread affirmation outside the United States as well as within it.

In an interview with Edward Marshall first published in the *New York Times* of November 13, 1910, Spalding described the psychological impact of baseball as corresponding precisely to the national character and, consequently, as a reciprocal creator of that character. Totally "undegenerate," the baseball player was "no thug trained to brutality like the prize-fighter," nor was he a gnomish "half-developed little creature like a jockey." Avoiding both physical oddity and moral perversity (which the residue of phrenology suggested were functionally the same, in any case), the baseball player exemplified the native American love of manly, skillful sport in the outdoors. Again, character could be formed in an interplay with environment that aped the logic of Frederick Jackson Turner. The beneficial effects of baseball would become permanent, as long as Americans devoted themselves to the game. As horse racing had resulted in better horse breeding, baseball, in Marshall's words, "resulted in improvement in man breeding."[17]

The actual practice of the game brought to fullness what already was innate in the native-born American; for it served to condition his physically, organically transmitted instinct. The naturalized citizen submitted himself to the discipline of baseball and, by acting as if he were an American, became one; and, apparently, he then passed the instinct toward this discipline on to his children through heredity. For all Americans, whatever their origin, the sport provided experience in a full range of actions and emotions in rapid combination and succession. "The game plays havoc with a boy's or a man's emotions," Spalding said. "In a day the player may well rise to the heights of victory and sink to the dark depths of black despair in a defeat." But the very exhaustion of the man's emotional capital liberated him and made him a more efficient player, and, by extension, a more effective citizen. The baseball player transcended the specific emotions of the moment even as he experienced them, setting them at a philosophical distance in perfect "self-poise." The end effect of a national sport was to create a committed yet efficient performer who "may well reach the super-point where he looks grave in victory and smiles with hope when he is vanquished."[18] Baseball, for one, transformed random instinct and zest into purposeful national character.

Football and baseball were thus taken to embody qualities that were quintessentially American, even if these qualities were readily discernible in other cultures or might even be regarded as defects by a twist of taste and judgment. From this vantage, it became possible to view these sports as shapers of American nationalism. But it remained necessary to show that football and baseball could be extended to all sections of the United States, transcending limits of culture, climate, and geography.

TENSION BETWEEN REGIONAL CHARACTER AND NATIONAL GAMES

As already implied, the development of a belief that there were certain identifiably national games took place during a time when Americans were becoming convinced that there were many perceptibly national institutions. This driving force, centrifugal in its workings, was nonetheless qualified by the centripetal impulses of regional distinctiveness within America — geographically as well as socially and ethnically. Moreover, claims

175

for national distinctiveness within American sport coincided with contemporary social scientists' assertion of the uniqueness of other national institutions; and all were attributed in part to the American land itself. As Albert Spalding promoted baseball as a natively American game, Edward Eggleston described Americans' long process of discovering the peculiarities of their physical environment and cultural patterns. As Walter Camp asserted football's power to shape the character of its players, Frederick Jackson Turner attributed American political and social values to a conditioning interaction between people and their geographical setting. The belief that institutions changed under the pressure of environment reflected the pervasive supposition that society and its components were organic, as has been suggested earlier; and character continually metamorphosed in response to the material details of living in a particular part of the world. Sharing the sense that life was process and inclined toward the bias that a physical environment created unique qualities in its residents, analysts of sport frequently ascribed the competitive achievements of athletes to the regions in which they lived. Unrestrained, such phenomena threatened national unity.[19]

If specific sports yielded particular results in shaping character and action, and if certain sports suited the geographical character of different parts of a country, it followed that populations in different regions were destined to differ from one another in bodily development and moral fiber. Mundane reportage of the regional patterns in sport at the turn of the century, then, actually outlined the differentiation and conflicts of physical type among various groups within the society. Environment and nurture became conditioning forces that could be conveniently and carelessly confused with race, partly on the ground that their power to affect an individual was comparable to that of heredity. Geography was a promiscuous influence for a mobile people. But when they chose to stay in one place, the promiscuity faded. Commonly grounded in their materialism and concreteness, environmental and racial determinants then emerged distinct but parallel.

This confusion of absolute and adaptable qualities perme-

176

ated the development of sport throughout the United States, and there occurred simultaneously an exploitation of regional styles and activities and a cultivation of sports that were national in scope. For people increasingly bent on experiencing life concretely, it would have been preposterous to ignore the distinctiveness of regional geography, even as it had conditioned sectional cultures. Yet their passion for rational order and effective management, coupled with their belief that a winning spirit needed to have the widest possible scope for its material expression, also impelled them to develop truly national patterns of participation and competition in sport. As a happy effect of this emphasis on a national athletics, those such as Theodore Roosevelt and Henry Cabot Lodge who opposed "hyphenated Americanism" might see in the major sports an ally in the effort to condition an American race and to counter the decentralizing effects of a diverse geography.

The decision of athletic boosters in the American West to imitate, as far as possible, the development of sport in the Northeast reflected their desire to be neither separate nor unequal. The New York Athletic Club served as the model for Pacific Coast Clubs such as the Olympic Club of San Francisco and the Multonomah of Portland, and the Western clubs aimed not at inventing novelties in sport but at performing better than the Easterners. Even the appearance of regional and Western journals devoted to sport expressed the quest for a truly national character and consciousness in athletics and recreation. *Chicago Field*, for example, provided rather broad coverage not only of sporting events that had a demonstrably national significance but from parts of the country that had previously been neglected by the major journals published in the northeast. Even more dramatically, *Western Field*, published in San Francisco from 1902 through 1914, sought to redress the imbalance that its editors had detected in American sport journalism by devoting their pages exclusively to activities in the Far West. Self-evidently useful in promoting subscriptions, this editorial decision also provided writers a chance to enumerate the athletic accomplishments of their local and regional teams. The "westward movement" of sport periodicals answered a need

177

Wealthy men with a spirit of technological innovation, seeking new forms of recreation, were swift to take advantage of the automobile. Shown here is the start of the New York to Seattle endurance crossing in 1909, the first attempt to take a motor car across the continent. By permission of the Library of Congress, George Grantham Bain Collection (LC-USZ62-33732).

178

that sportsmen of the region perceived; and even the journals devoted primarily or restrictively to Western sport formed, in that sense, a part of composite national sports coverage.

Yet the role of the regional journals proved inevitably ambivalent; and, if they functioned as components in a national system, they also drew unblinking attention to the real and material differences between sections of the country. *Western Field*, for example, extolled the unique beauty of Mount Rainier and hinted that all hiking, climbing, and fishing on its flanks acquired a distinctive character. A prominent geological fact, such as Rainier, created difference in the nature of specific sports; and these, by extension, could affect the character of the sporting public that practiced them. The Westerners attended to the special skills needed for successful fishing in the West, where different species offered new challenges to anglers. Even so, although the effects of environment were real, many Westerners consciously sought to transcend the peculiarities that depended on their geographical location and to become competitive within a national framework.[20] The price was to emphasize national over regional sports.

The medium through which sections of the United States could hope to converge in a national sporting consensus was athletic competition. The tour of the Cincinnati Red Stockings in 1869 exemplified a business venture that simultaneously fostered a national interest in and consciousness of baseball. Pacific Coast cities generated teams to meet the Red Stockings, sometimes by a virtual forced draft; and hopes brightened that the values associated with the sport would become general. At Seattle's Alaska-Yukon-Pacific Exposition of 1909, the promoters spent heavily to bring Eastern teams and crews to compete in the West. Although the fair's organizers used events with local color, such as war-canoe races, as near-theatrical entertainments, they took the athletic competition with the Easterners seriously and restricted themselves to traditional events such as rowing and track athletics.[21] The sports peculiar to a region could not be dismissed or wished away, but participation in a standard set of sports that had won national currency could bridge the differences among sections.

Among the sports that Seattle's boosters brought to the Alaska-

179

Yukon-Pacific Exposition was rowing—an activity that retained something of a Northeastern tinge and whose promotion in the Pacific Northwest represented something of a grasp at equality of status with the established clubs. Had it not been for the taint of professionalism that its ardent supporters never completely eliminated, rowing might have made a stronger bid as a national sport, although the full extent of its acceptance cannot be known; and, again, geography presented serious obstacles. Starting as a restrictively Northeastern avocation, rowing gradually spread across the country, with enthusiastic clubs even in rather unlikely spots. By the early 1870s, New Orleans and St. Louis had active clubs; the sport thrived in the Ohio Valley; and the Northwestern Association grew stronger. In 1878, clubs from Galveston to St. Paul formed the Mississippi Valley Association; and comparably enthusiastic oarsmen founded the Pacific Amateur Rowing Association, the Virginia Association of Amateur Oarsmen, and the Louisiana Association of Amateur Oarsmen. Regattas took place in Texas, and the holding of the National Regatta in Washington, D.C. in 1881 further encouraged the expansion of rowing into the American South. In the late 1880s, the Iowa Rowing Association was formed, while in Utah considerable rowing occurred on the Great Salt Lake.

Yet the sands shifted beneath the foundation of a national rowing system. Irregularities of geography ultimately forbade any absolutely national pattern from forming, and variations in climate sometimes added another burden to the load that the sport's promoters had to carry. Also, many clubs lacked adequate facilities and, according to Samuel Crowther, Jr., depended completely upon victory for continued support from members and associates. When some clubs retired from actual competition, they nonetheless retained membership in the National Association and propelled it into a quagmire of petty squabbles. Rowing in the Midwest dropped dramatically from the end of the 1880s on, with only the powerful Detroit Boat Club remaining important in the sport. Similarly, the National Regatta again took place, for the most part, in the Northeastern section of the country; and rowing's pretensions to prominence as a nationally inclusive amateur sport were confounded.[22]

Far more promising results came in the extension of football into all parts of the United States. By 1898, according to Walter Camp's retrospective All-American selections, quality of play in the game had attained sufficient distinction in the Midwest that the region produced its first national stars. The University of Chicago, Michigan, Nebraska, and Wisconsin for the first time broke the Northeastern monopoly in the selections. Minnesota joined this elite group in 1900, and Illinois in 1904. From sea to sea, football stars shone in 1910, as Oregon and Washington presented their first All-Americans.

The westward movement of football heartened its advocates, but the press of the game into the South occasioned elation. In 1906, Vanderbilt became the first Southern school to gain All-American distinction in the sport with their halfback Manier. Promoted in part by militant Americans such as Army General Leonard Wood, football in the Deep South distinguished itself at last with Alabama tackle Vanergraaf, a year after Texas gave the nation its guard Jordan.[23] Commentators had expected the hot and humid weather of the South to prevent the citizens in the old Confederacy from playing the game that had originated with the Northeastern elite. But this national, and nationalizing, game escaped this fate, as Southern gridders proved their stamina in the hot and often humid environment. The moral of this particular story was that football, once again, was reinforced as a game that was truly nationwide in its geographic scope; and its importance for the South lay in its service as a promoter of national values. As a corollary, however, the regional sports of other regions — rodeo for example — could no more serve this function in the South than coon-hunting could outside of it.

Speaking to a Harvard University audience as early as 1893, Francis A. Walker summarized the primacy of sports that were national in sweep. He gloried in the rapid spread of football into the Western and Southern states. It provided a sense of community and common interest, he observed; and its effects were enduring. Significantly, Walker praised the model that the athletic hero provided, believing that it led young men toward right standards and goals.[24] For, it must be noted, Walker held high office in the U.S. Immigration Service where he battled against slackened, diluted, or (as they put it) "hyphenated" Americanism. Football and any other national sport fought against this "hyphenation"; and they warred with equal spirit against sectionalism by putting regional games into a secondary and inferior status. Compared to a regional sense of sport, a nationally shared image would aid in the continuous renewal of shared values. Thus similar experiences of Americans in sport would endlessly nurture a national character.

LANDSCAPE AND ACTION

The notions of nationalism and identity expressed themselves with a distinctive force in American life in attitudes toward the land, the changing sense of landscape, and the transformations of the concepts of recreation which led toward a truly special invention of the time, the national parks. Their history offers a special test to control our understanding of all late nineteenth- and early twentieth-century sport and recreation; for it reveals the growing emphasis on activity over contemplative passivity, even while retaining the traditional emphasis on a nature which has been brought under human domination. Such concepts as landscape and recreation do not have absolute definitions but change in accordance with the conditioning of social and personal expectations. In the early nineteenth century, for example, the standard sense of what "recreation" meant could be described as "recovery through contemplation," at least when it referred to park areas. This showed itself in the horror which many Americans and even a greater proportion of foreign visitors felt over the rampant exploitation of Niagara Falls and also in the emphasis on the staid and contemplative city park, which eventually reached its apex in the work of Frederick Law Olmsted. This tradition, which had intellectual roots in the thinking of Emerson and especially of Henry David Thoreau, and which paralleled "luminism" in painting, gradually encountered grave competition from a more active sensibility that came to understand "recreation" as "refreshment through wholesome activity." This transformation in underlying attitude does much to suggest the basic changes in intellectual climate that were altering sport and recreation in general.[25]

One may argue with considerable accuracy that the land was always an important element in Americans' sense of their own identity; but it is also true that their sense of the land itself altered over time and, consequently, the identity they could invent for themselves did also. For present purposes, the growing emphasis on activity — on actions and events permitted or staged within the national parks, for example — is most compelling. Although there had been competing notions of "compatible use" within the national parks from their very inception, it is significant that the desirability of "improvements" which would encourage greater access and provide a greater diversity of activities for visitors within the parks increased during the late years of the nineteenth and into the early years of the twentieth century. Some park enthusiasts wished to transform Yellowstone into a spa in the European manner, complete with vast bathhouses served by the natural thermal springs, a small railroad, and a mechanical swing-bridge over the Grand Canyon of the Yellowstone River operated by a power plant at one of the falls. In the early twentieth century, the emphasis on road-building intensified; and parks such as Yosemite were provided with tiled swimming pools, ball courts, and other facilities that tended to diminish the natural experience of the parklands. Seen one way, these measures degraded an important American resource; seen otherwise, however, they suggest the deep commitment of Americans to the notion that recreation came through action and their tendency to confuse activity with leisure.[26]

The noted naturalist John Muir stood as a mediating and a transitional figure, clinging to Henry David Thoreau's conviction of the importance of quiet and contemplation yet also aware of the need to smash the careworn habits of the late nineteenth-century American by exposure to stunning natural marvels and scenery. Despite this latter penchant, however, even Muir aimed at bringing the citizen into close and working contact with nature in the particular and the concrete. The "scenery habit," which naturalists disdained, trivialized nature and its processes by turning it into a generality and, in a sense, into an abstraction. For Muir, then, scenery and stunning vistas were meant to liven the sensibilities of the visitor to the parks and enable him to undertake a thorough exploration of nature on its own terms. The geysers of Yellowstone, for example, would "charm and shake up the least sensitive out of apathy into new-

Naturalists John Muir, left, and John Burroughs believed that grand scenery could instill in businessmen an appreciation of deeper values. They are shown at the South Rim of the Grand Canyon in a photograph taken by hotelier Fred Harvey in 1909, three years after President Roosevelt used the Antiquities Act for the first time, to preserve the Colorado River's canyon system. By permission of the Library of Congress (LC-USZ62-13062).

ness of life"— or so Muir believed. Encouraging city-dwellers to journey to the Bitterroot wilderness, he promised the obligatory "lofty mountains steeped in lovely memophila-blue skies and clad with forests and glaciers, mossy, ferny waterfalls in their hollows . . ."; but he moved swiftly to assure the visitor: "When you are calm enough for discriminating observation, you will find the king of the larches." Thus, even as he extended the contemplative tradition, Muir revealed its potential for linkage with the cult of activity — namely, their common fondness for the concrete.[27]

Incapable of tolerating the notion that "conservation" should mean little more than the managed exploitation and use of the land, Muir failed to appreciate the degree to which the intrusions and "degradations" proposed for the parks represented the cutting edge of contemporary thought. The emplacement of an elevator to provide easy access to the Yellowstone River represented the technical and mechanical virtuosity of a people who loved machines and gadgets during an era when, as Siegfried Giedion has put it, mechanization was taking command. The concept of a stable ecology, which even Muir did not truly understand, seemed alien to the belief that progress inhered in change and that both were necessary to prevent decline and social ruin. The emphasis on monumental and spectacular display within man-made culture — in the transformation of the U.S. Capitol, the building of the Brooklyn Bridge, the development of the skyscraper (a kind of commercial adaptation of the Eiffel Tower), and the like — paralleled the fixation upon bizarre features within the parks. As Alfred Runte has pointed out, this tendency toward "monumentalism" (the perception of natural monuments as if they were the psychological and emotional equivalents in America for man-built structures in Europe such as the Parthenon or the cathedral at Chartres) was a prime motivation for the establishment of parks in the first place.[28]

One should add, however, that the Americans seemed to insist on having monuments that performed and did things. The very first of the natural splendors, whose wanton exploitation encouraged the effort to protect other areas from commercial depradations, was Niagara Falls — something that was an action as well as a sight (it was, after all, the Europeans who had to convince Americans that the management of the Falls was wrong). The magnificence of Yosemite inhered largely in its extraordinary waterfalls, pouring across ledges and breaking into veils along its great central valley. Indeed, so strong was the fascination for these literally moving scenes that firefalls were substituted when the waters were gone by late summer. So, too, in Yellowstone, action and performance were key. The thermal pools had to be alive, bubbling and venting steam. Sulphurous muds had to ripple and belch their fumes. Above all, the geysers must erupt. It strains the imagination very little to see the Progressive instinct toward rationality and predictability in the Americans' fastening upon "Old Faithful" as the central gem in Yellowstone — a geyser which combined the spectacular with a phenomenal regularity. This same instinct soon capitalized on the accidental discovery (by a soon terrified Chinese laundryman at the Yellowstone Lodge) that soap thrown into a geyser would cause it to erupt by altering the surface tension of the water. The park was not only a place in which Americans could recreate themselves by doing things — going on hikes, touring in automobiles, taking pack trips; it was a place where the park's own natural features did things. With the benefit of soap in thermal waters, there was no need to waste time waiting for nature to take its course; and the geyser would play a trick for the diversion of the visitors. This, of course, was the corruption of Muir's compromise; but it suggested, in a crude way, the continuing triumph of an unspoken ideology that extolled action and experience rather than contemplation and abstraction.[29]

The debate over the propriety of facilities, entertainments, and amusements within the American national parks largely paralleled the dispute between advocates of contemplative parks and play-parks in the American cities. Although Frederick Law Olmsted admitted of certain sportive amusements within Central Park, the main thrust of his genius lay in the creation of a pseudonatural environment — a tamed nature, which had itself been created by man, providing an illusion of natural harmony and order and an impression of human progress rising out of the natural order. Within specially protected lands, this instinct showed itself in special architectural forms, such as the naturalistic expressionism of the Great Camps of the Adirondacks in New York or, more formally, in the Ahwanee Hotel in Yosemite Valley. No such concealment was deemed necessary by the proponents of the play-park, who gave greatest importance to obviously man-made facilities for their recreation through games, play, and sport. Carried into the national parks from the city parks, this latter impulse justified the maximum possible facilities, which would thus provide the widest range of activities from which the visitor could choose. Again, activity and experience were set against contemplative passivity.

These perceptions of the national parks become particularly important to understanding the connection between notions about recreation and the sense of nationalism because parks were considered not only treasures to be saved but key devices through which the purported national values could be regenerated. From the more contemplative vantage, Muir certainly believed this; but Teddy Roosevelt also subscribed to this view, proving it in an ironic way when he incinerated an ancient tree near his campsite while on a hike with Muir. The exhilaration he felt seemed to him to be part of the sense of renewal and regeneration that he wanted for all Americans. The constant round of activities — hikes, drives, sails, and the like — that typified Roosevelt's outings represented something of a marriage between the landscape and human kinetics. Indeed, the emergence of kinesiology and variant studies of motion among humans seemed to be accompanied by the emergence of an energized, sometimes even animist, visual style in the paintings of Thomas Moran and especially Albert Bierstadt. As Scottish pathologist J. Bell Pettigrew, whose works were widely circulated in America, wrote in *Animal Locomotion* (1888), things must "move" to "have being"; and only when they were in motion were they "agreeable objects in the landscape." Life was equated with doing rather than with being; and the rising interest in sport was paralleled by the shifting interest in national parks as playgrounds rather than as sanctuaries.[30]

The instinct toward an American nationalism, then, affected the emergence of sport to prominence in a number of ways which dovetailed with the pressures generated by varying social and economic groups, as well as by still other intellectual and cultural forces. Two sports survived the tests of national distinctiveness, geographical extensiveness, physical address and immediacy, and the integration of personal excellence within the framework of the team. Other sports had their advocates, and they survived within a regional context even if they failed to achieve a universal acceptance. Even these, however, may eventually have capitalized on the image that football and baseball were able to attain, suggesting that sport in general was a reliable shaper of character.

In a broader context, the drive to shape character through action was replicated and elevated in the effort to regenerate American character through the recreation of an *ersatz* frontier. The national parks thus united some versions of the concept of wilderness with the Turnerian notion of the dependence of personal, social, and political values upon the material environment. In the great parks as on the city playground, the same experimentalist disposition made itself felt as Americans worked their way through an often hectic schedule of activities and sports. In search of recreation (whether the regeneration of the spirit or sheer fun), they showed their bias toward action in preference to contemplation, toward the concrete rather than the abstract, and ultimately toward sport rather than true leisure.

CHAPTER 7

Toward a New Image of the Body—
Champions of Movement and Action

IN his Phi Beta Kappa address at Harvard in 1893, Francis A. Walker claimed that a great change had occurred in attitudes toward the body during the century. He satirized the excessively intellectual student of the antebellum era as having a "towering forehead" and a "remarkable phrenological development," implying that his attempts to think had actually distorted his cranium. He accused early nineteenth-century moralists of equating physical strength with brutality and of considering exuberance the enemy of goodness. By contrast, Walker welcomed the rise of athletics in the colleges, favored the growth of sport among the students and in society as a whole, and suggested that intellectual and moral force were contingent on the health and strength of the body.[1]

Such views conformed to the opinions of his friends and fellow alumni Theodore Roosevelt and Henry Cabot Lodge; but they were rather overdrawn. Apart from the Muscular Christians, the antebellum years had seen ardent proponents of health reform and of new ideas about nutrition seek to gain a wide audience—with at least some success among the middle class. Moreover, phrenologists and physiologists pioneered in setting out theories that provided a physical basis for explaining moral behavior. Given these antecedents, Walker erred in presuming that a favorable sentiment toward the body was a novelty of the late nineteenth century. Despite them, however, he was right in believing that the magnitude and dispersal of that attitude had increased greatly; and the dispositions that had been largely the property of a coterie of precursors in the early nineteenth

189

century became the basis of much popular thinking in its later decades.

The greater novelty of the late nineteenth century—and the one more conducive to the rise of sport—lay in the reasons for the favorable view of the body and in the particular aspect that it assumed. In his vocabulary and choice of metaphor, Walker unwittingly revealed the emergence of a dynamic view of the body as an organism whose nature was known in its actions and movement. He ridiculed the antebellum Americans, accusing them of seeing the body as "a shell," "a prison in which the soul was confined," or "a wayside barn." Since the soul was separable from the body according to this view, the body had neither an integral relationship to the soul nor any vital force to ensure its own development. Like the wayside barn, the body was doomed to collapse. Like the prison, it was ultimately a burden and a disgrace. Like the shell, its worth came only from proximity to its contents. In place of this image of the body, which Walker drew to the point of caricature, there was now a more organic sense of the body that made matter and spirit inseparable. The organic vision emphasized movement and action as the signs of life and as its fundamental expression; and a static understanding of the body as a "shell" seemed, in the late nineteenth century, too close to the stillness of death. Unlike health, which might be understood as a fixed state without doing violence to logic, sport could not be seen except as a series of interlocked and overlapping movements. Sport was intrinsically action and process; and the advocacy of each created a sensibility that was more disposed toward the other. Thus, the growing belief that animal forms were most beautiful and most fulfilled when they were in motion supported a parallel belief that human health was at its greatest when the body expressed itself in action. Sport became a proof of health, as well as a source of it. Heroes came to be known for their actions more than their words, and whatever passed for values among them was inferred from their deeds.[2]

In a variety of fields ranging from religion through science to physical culture, many Americans turned toward an earthly model against which to judge their own bodily and spiritual development. They shared sensibilities and sentiment more than class or occupation; and they reconciled the tension between contemplation and action by obliterating the sharp metaphysical boundaries between spirit and matter or Heaven and Earth. Less than the image of God, these Americans sifted the history of man for the highest examples of coordinated physical, mental, and spiritual achievement, often ending with a celebration of Greek and Roman heroes. Yet they ultimately paid themselves their own greatest compliment by finding perfection in their own time. Having uttered a profound statement through Nature, God presumably endorsed the material world for what it already was, as well as for what it could become through evolution. Man thus became the most distinguished agent for continuous creation of a world that the Almighty had viewed with satisfaction and pronounced good. God thus receded from an active, preeminent, and limiting position in the world. Neither a Celestial Mechanic nor an Ideal, God stood as the first generator of species, races, and organisms that were obligated to tend to themselves. As the "crown of creation," man assumed lordship of its actions. It was a sensibility that enabled a human being to flirt with secularized divinity and to place his actions in an esteem beyond reason or proportion.

THE DESIGN OF MAN AND THE PLEASURES OF EXPERIENCE

The flowering of sport at the turn of the century expressed Americans' acceptance of life as an experience to be enjoyed rather than acquiesced in, even as it was also partly a result of this view. In seeking to relieve human suffering, reformers in effect posited happiness as normal. Scientists and physical culturists encouraged the view that human achievement could be raised, lending nearly mythic force to the well-developed body as a wonder of biomechanical design. The world afforded experiences in plenty, and the body was equipped to enjoy them. Praising the bicycle as an "engine of pleasure," the editors of *Scribner's Magazine* saw this tendency in Americans in June 1896: "When did any people before show so eager an appreciation of the enjoyment of life as the Americans are demonstrating by their enthusiasm?" Earth could be a range of joys, and the mundane bicycle propelled its rider toward the gratifications of physical experience. If sport trained Americans to pursue duty, it also permitted them to accept pleasure as a moral imperative. As Theodore Roosevelt asserted repeatedly, a life of obligation and duty brought joy and fulfillment to the individual, as well as purpose. Drawing from the same spring as Roosevelt, the editors of *Scribner's* emphasized Americans' growing disposition toward physical renewal, efficiently using discipline "so to regulate our journey through life as to improve the chances of living by the way."[3]

Although there had been a concern for the body among various figures in the early nineteenth century, it had not generally included an encouragement of sport as a means to achieve health or to express it; nor had it emphasized sportive activities as compared to calisthenics and systematic gymnastics. Health was not the same as sport, although many reformers much later in the century suggested that the latter could aid in achieving the former. Even prominent advocates of health such as Catharine Beecher and Thomas Wentworth Higginson conceived of it more as a stable condition than as a developmental process. Like grace, health was a state. Beecher also subscribed to the view that specific diseases and complaints resulted from the dysfunction of particular organs. This sense of the body more as an assemblage of component parts than as an integrated series of adaptive processes, which conformed substantially to the strong interest in heroic surgery, cauterization, heavy dosing, and similar extreme procedures, allowed a certain degree of optimism that diseases could be countered and ailments relieved. But the methods often tended toward the more dramatic and mechanistic solutions. Thus, although a pattern of secular acceptance of the body was beginning to take shape, the dominance of a vision of the body as a dynamic and developing organism did not follow automatically as one of its functions; and it was this latter view which, by emphasizing motion, proved more sympathetic to the rise of sport.[4]

Nonetheless, various developments in the first half of the century had contributed to the belief that health was a process and that the body was itself a pattern of movements and systems which linked physical and moral behavior. Although Muscular Christianity gave explicit support to such a doctrine of linkage, phrenology offered implicit encouragement in a comparable direction. The effort to detect a specific organ or physical zone of the body that corresponded to a particular part of the brain suggested that the body was a pieced-together mechanism whose rules could be learned, although its behavioral inclinations could best be altered by radical excision such as lobotomy. So, too, the phrenologists' conviction that the elements of character conformed to thirty-seven separate "organs of the brain" conflicted with a unitary model of the mind and undercut the notion of a disembodied soul governing the actions of man's body. Significantly, the phrenologists — who were often deists — usually equated physical ailments with moral failings. An author of works on anatomy and digestion, Dr. Andrew Combe declared that he had "sinned" when he was troubled by a toothache; and Horace Mann once declared a dyspeptic stomach to be "an abomination in the sight of God." The phrenologists' view of character as the relative balance of various organs in the context of external forces savaged the concept of free will and undermined the concept of personal sin in its traditional religious sense. Moreover, the notion that moral and social evil was contingent upon a physical organ that might be adjusted tended to impeach the doctrine of original sin and the assertion of the fundamental evil of mankind. In fact, Nathaniel W. Taylor, Professor of Theology at Yale in the 1840s, specifically rejected the doctrine of the fundamental corruption of man; and phrenologist George Combe declared that the advocates of religion had better put their readings of the Bible "into harmony with natural truth." Thus, in proposing to explain human behavior, the phrenologists exiled metaphysical forces to little other than a decorative role; and they edged toward the belief that, if human temperaments manifested the condition of specific organs, then changes in behavioral pattern could alter the temperaments.[5] The importance of action was thus personalized, while the source of individual will was largely externalized.

Changes in medicine further encouraged the perception of the body as a process, even as the advancements themselves often followed from that view. Radical or "heroic" treatments, which involved a major change of bodily state, were gradually discredited during the nineteenth century; and there was a decline in the enthusiasm for bleeding, heavy dosing, and radical surgery, even as medical discoveries made such heroic attempts seem increasingly outdated and ineffective. Meanwhile, proponents of nutritional reform, such as Sylvester Graham, who lectured on behalf of phrenologists Lorenzo and Orson Fowler, emphasized the importance of rational living as the basis for health. In short, it was a lifetime commitment and a lifelong duty. In this respect, they paralleled the phrenologists' assertion that the only way in which to strengthen moral faculties was to exercise them. Thus, gradually, medical reformers, nutritionists, and phrenologists all anticipated the need for a theory that explained individual change within the limits of the human species as a type — a theory of bodily development and personal behavior that merged nature and nurture.[6]

Thus, although they lacked the explicit emphasis on movement and action which became relatively common toward the end of the century, these forerunners had no doubts about the contingency of the body's health on the individual's behavior, nor about the reciprocal effect of one's bodily condition upon one's moral vigor. Such views were becoming commonplaces at the turn of the century. In 1906, Dudley Sargent, who shared the view that physical activity was inseparable from moral practice, wrote that specific exercises developed "different traits, qualities, and characteristics through their effect upon the muscles, lungs, heart, brain, and general nervous system." Sargent's claim that particular sports produced distinct attributes elevated material action to an uncommon eminence over any separate mental or spiritual realm. In their keen concern for nutrition, training, and weight-control, those Americans who promoted physical culture also showed their belief that the human body was more a process than an entity. It could be shaped and reshaped, altered to different purposes and tasks, changed with time and taste.[7]

The practical and scientific study of the body encouraged its acceptance. Man's physical form did not bar him from God, nor did it prevent his spirit from soaring. The upward lifting of the soul occurred only in the physical achievements of the body, and God's quiet endorsement of the process came in the fact of evolution itself. There was no disparagement, then, in the dispassionate study of the body. Seeing man as an animal did not debase him, because the final comparisons with other creatures revealed the special gifts of the human. Even more, assessing the human being with something akin to objectivity empowered man to make the most of himself. Understanding the body gave the expert power to develop it.

The shaping of a whole personality, then, depended in great part on a proper conditioning of the body. A word that would become commonplace in the training of athletes and in experimental psychology, *conditioning* assumed the sense of "bringing into a good condition or state" by about 1890 in the United States. Although *condition* occasionally referred to personal health and fitness as early as 1860 in England, its common usage then pertained to horses and commodities. The application of variant forms of the word *condition* to human subjects, then, did not occur until about the time that the human being was accepted and analyzed as a developing animal, rather than as a fixed and largely unchanging creation of God. Turning to a study of the body that they considered morally and philosophically neutral, Americans proved receptive to new studies of "animal mechanism," whether undertaken in the United States or in Europe. E.J. Marey's *Animal Mechanism: A Treatise on Terrestrial and Aerial Locomotion* was included within D. Appleton and Company's International Scientific Series in 1879. Not only did Marey seek to subject the human animal to scientific and dispassionate analysis, but he also introduced his study of man under "Terrestrial Motion (Bipeds)," pairing it with the quadrupedal locomotion of the horse. Marey's man could hardly be confused with a static object, molded by God from mud and slime. He displayed what he was through what he did, and his identity as an organism could be known fully only through studying how he moved.[8]

In America, the researches of Eadweard Muybridge and Thomas Eakins into the exact structure and dynamics of the motion of various animals reflected a similar bias. In his studies of human movement conducted at the University of Pennsylvania in 1884–1885, Muybridge accumulated 100,000 negatives that held images of a wide range of sporting activities and an assortment of other forms of work. Included were running, the broad jump, the high jump, lifting dumbbells, throwing and catching a baseball, throwing the javelin, catching and throwing a football, swinging a bat, rowing, wrestling, boxing, and various acrobatic feats. Both men and women performed for the photographer, the latter, for the most part, professional artists' models and the former mostly personnel at the University of Pennsylvania — the professor of physical culture, fencing and boxing instructors, and a well-known pugilist. The disciplined use of nudity, without which the studies would have been absurd, showed a frank acceptance of the propriety of the naked body, at least within the framework of scientific inquiry. As a side-benefit, the analysis of human motion in sport and other work aided the redefinition of modesty in one's own person. Scientists making preliminary use of Muybridge's photographic data adopted a rigorously empiricist and unsensational tone that made consideration of the human body in action no different from the study of a horse in its paces or a dog on the loose. All were equal in scientific validity and in ethical neutrality.[9]

Appleton's International Scientific Series also featured the thoughts of Alexander Bain, emeritus professor of logic at the University of Aberdeen, who devoted his attention to *Mind and Body* and to the physical basis of perception and noesis. In 1894, Bain provided a revised version of his views, updated to reflect the most recent findings in physiology. In *The Senses and the Intellect*, he outlined a theory of volition that identified the willpower not as a fixed characteristic and assuredly not as a "gift" but as a physically conditioned transformation of instinct through experience. "Physical learning" could create new and intense levels of volition; and the spirit of victory, of which Henry Cabot Lodge spoke, became more precisely and quite literally a habit and a product of action. The cultivation of the physical — emphasized by the physiologists' and Bain's equation of the pleasure-pain principle with the basis of instinct — correspondingly meant that popularizers of this theory could identify athletic conditioning with the preparation of socially efficient world conquerors whose deeds fueled their own will to power.[10]

American experts in physiology, psychology, nutrition, and other fields pertinent to sport also knew of the experiments of Ivan Petrovich Pavlov, even though some embraced some of his specific results without attending to their broader implications. The nutritionist Horace Fletcher, for example, delighted in the inducement of salivation by conditioned reflex because he believed it proved that "earned appetite and thorough mouth-treatment of food are preliminary necessities of easy digestion, and that disturbance or shock of any sort during the process [may] stop digestive proceedings and endanger health." But there was an underlying agreement between Pavlov and his American admirer. In a 1906 lecture at the Charing Cross Medical School in London, Pavlov devoted scientific study to "the so-called psychical processes in the higher animals." To presume that such psychical processes were real, Pavlov said, "would be transferring ideas from [the investigator's] own inner world to nature. . . . The naturalist must consider only one thing: what is the relation of this or that external reaction of the animal to the phenomena of the external world?" As William James did, Pavlov doubted the universal validity of subjective observation and concluded with a study that aimed only at experience and conditioning and sought the day "when the human mind will contemplate itself not from within but from without." Pavlov's explicit goal was to exert extreme control over human behavior. For his part, Horace Fletcher shared the enthusiasm for objective, scientific, and external study of the human animal; and he praised especially the researches of Russell H. Chittenden, the director of the Sheffield Scientific School at Yale. Chittenden sought to discover the exact quantities of food, water, and nitrogen needed for the "smooth running of the [human] machinery"; and he argued that moral and ethical decisions depended basically on the physiological condition of the body. He specifically attributed poverty and vice to improper nutrition, adding a peroration that "Poverty, crime, physical ills, and a blunted or perverted moral sense are the penalties we may be called upon to pay for the disobedience to Nature's laws." Chittenden had reduced morality to a well-balanced and economical diet. In Pavlov's terms, an external reaction of "vice" followed from scientifically inaccurate use of the dietary "phenomena" of the external world.[11]

Fletcher further viewed sport as an auxiliary to the efficient study of the body, and he believed that the Sheffield Scientific

197

Shown here in a photograph of 1920 when he was leaving Yale's Sheffield Scientific Laboratory, Professor Russell H. Chittenden pioneered in the development of a calorimeter — a device for measuring heat produced by the human body under stress, instrumental in providing a scientific basis for the study of sport as a variant of work. Photo by Bain News Service. By permission of the Library of Congress, Biographical Files.

School's proximity to the Yale gymnasium and its well trained personnel gave it a special edge in conducting profitable research. Nearby, in Middletown, Connecticut, was a new calorimeter by which to cross-check measurements of metabolism completed at Yale. In describing the results of his own test under the calorimeter, Fletcher used the language of machines and industry to a degree that makes unmistakable the metamorphosis of person into an adjustable object:

> The author had just demonstrated the possibility of running the human machine on half the heat, on one-third of the fuel, and with only one-tenth of the waste, as represented by the waste, or ashes of digestion. Not only was this done while in pursuit of the ordinary activity of present-day life, but under stress of 'Varsity-Crew exercise, as reported by Professor Chittenden and Dr. Anderson. Had this demonstration been made relative to steam engines or electrical motors, the information would have been revolutionary in establishing new values for things industrial and commercial.

By a simultaneously scientific and imaginative act, Fletcher placed control of his body outside of himself. He stripped from the intake of chemicals into his body such words as "food" or "dining" or even "eating" as altogether too metaphorical and, as Chittenden put it, altogether too flattering of "our personal pride to have a well-supplied table, and to eat largely and freely of the good things provided." Food was "fuel," the body a "machine," excrement "waste," and the goal of the candid researcher ought correctly to be not the elevation of man's morals but the achievement of "immunity from the common diseases which now afflict mankind." Physical research and physical activity had as a first and functionally primary aim not spiritual but corporeal health.[12]

Yet the distinction between physical and spiritual well-being did not have any true metaphysical merit. To speak of mind and body as separate clouded what Alexander Bain called "The only tenable supposition . . . ; [namely, that] mental and physical proceed together, as undivided twins." Bain rejected a gross materialism that subordinated the mind to bodily processes and external stimuli, but he also believed that modern physiology

199

demonstrated the falseness of immaterial principles. Even Thomistic advocates of an isolated intellect had to admit that "purely intellectual operations such as memory depended upon material processes. He explicitly denied that "the mind used the body as an *instrument*" because saying so would give a prior and separate existence to the mind and reduce the body to a mere tool through which the mind wrote out its thoughts.[13]

Physical educators shared the belief in the coordinate importance of mind and body and applied it to actual training practices. They opposed an artificial split in the methods of educating the young, which segregated mental development from physical training both spatially and temporally. Theodore Hough, whose "Review of Swedish Gymnastics" appeared in *Mind and Body* in May 1900, called the schoolroom a "direct hindrance to normal physical development" of a child. Forcing children to sit still in desks usually designed without reference to human anatomy and depriving them of play discouraged physical development, and the consequent deficiencies in bodily health would in their turn yield moral and mental illnesses. Nature, Hough insisted, "does not make the adult man as a machinist does a piece of mechanism, by completing one thing before beginning another." The human being was not only complete as an organism but indivisible into component parts without killing it. So, too, they agreed that the human organism was not a fixed fact but a process. As Hough said in 1900, "In actual life, Athene does not spring full-fledged from the brow of Jove, nor Venus from the foam of the sea." In most unromantic detail, he added: "For one hundred and seventy-five thousand two hundred hours the most varied physiological activities have been at work to the man or woman of twenty years."[14]

An uninterruptible and perfect mutuality existed in mind and body; and the body produced effects on mind and thought as certainly as the articulated thoughts generated in the mind governed specific acts in the material world. In his book *Mind and Body*, published in 1879 and intended for a popular literate market, Bain offered a detailed example:

When physical nourishment, or a physical stimulant, acting through the blood, quiets [a] mental irritation, and restores a

200

cheerful tone, it is not a bodily fact causing a mental fact by a direct line of causation: the nourishment and the stimulus determine the circulation of blood to the brain, give a new direction to the nerve currents; and the mental condition corresponding to this particular mode of cerebral action henceforth manifests itself. The line of mental sequence is thus, not mind causing body, and body causing mind, but mind-body giving birth to mind-body.[15]

Bain concluded that physiological findings proved the validity of "conjoint causation," thus giving a suitably empirical imprimatur to his thesis.

The universe itself proved his point, he believed; for the invisible forces moving the planets inhered in matter, expressed by terms such as "inertia" and "gravity." Concluding with a remark of Priestley and Ferrier, Bain suggested the impertinence of asking questions that exceeded the bounds of what one pragmatically needed to know: "'Why introduce a new entity, or rather a nonentity, until we see what these multifarious activities of matter are able to accomplish?" For Bain and his intellectual allies, life was but one substance with two properties that existed as a "double-faced unity." Using the language of the Athanasian Creed, he resisted "confounding the persons [or] dividing the substance." In the metaphors of the logician and in the physical experiences he considered, the destiny of perfectible man became apotheosis on earth.[16]

The application of scientific method to sport endowed athletics with physiological economy, and it made possible the transfiguration of the individual athlete. The sportsman would play until he actually incorporated the jointly physical and moral virtues. "It is possible to 'practise' Healthy conditions until they become a very part of oneself," wrote tennis champion Eustace H. Miles in 1901. The well-trained sportsman would be physically, intellectually, and morally complete; and his physical exertions were indispensable to this accomplishment. By devoting public attention to "some of the most important things in life," among which Miles included constipation, the new physical culturist freed man from the chains of "terrible depression," and from "unhappiness, restlessness, and inability to work."[17] Nor did happiness refer only to an attitude of the individual imagination. It improved health by changing the red corpuscles of the blood in a manner that Miles neglected to specify. The imprecision did not deter him from seeing a reinforcing interplay between aesthetic and physical contentments, and he accepted the "pursuit of happiness" as worth almost endless sacrifice. The very choice of words—happiness, contentment, as well as "aesthetic," "graceful," and "physical"—gave verbal imprimatur to the human body and the material universe. The quest to improve the individual human form escaped the bounds of utilitarianism and veered toward narcissism. "Exercises and Games . . . ," Miles wrote, "should lead us to consider our members and faculties, and to compare them with those of the brute creation, and they should make us not only thankful that our bodies are so wonderfully made, but also determined to use and develop these bodies by the best possible means. . . ."[18] The design of man and his capacity for physical expression evidently demonstrated divine approval of the physical culturist and sportsman.

CHRISTIAN MINISTRY AND THE ADVOCACY OF SPORT

Ministers and religiously enthusiastic laymen showed increasing concern over the behavior of young people at the turn of the century, much as secular reformers did; and they often turned to sport and other activities presumably appealing to the young in order to guide them toward right living in this world and salvation in the next. At the same time, however, they emphasized the earthly presence of Christ and described the Lord as an affable, bold, and strong man whose life proved his enthusiasm for the joys of this world. In a broad range of denominations from Baptists to Congregationalists, there arose spokesmen who depicted Christ as primarily a man of action, thus seeking to appeal to the inclinations of the young by drawing out qualities which they believed most closely resembled those valued in their society. At the same time, they thus turned Christ into a hero and Christians into his fans.

Moralists advanced "the life of Jesus Christ," even more than his words, as the most eloquent expression of theological and social perfection. In increasing numbers, they shared the favorable opinion of the human body and of the material world that physical educators held, propelled by their belief that God spoke through evolution and hence that the created world enjoyed his blessing. Moralists and theologians enlisted Christ to support their programs for moral and social reform, claiming that the New Testament gave evidence of his approval of worldly experience. In 1906, Cornell University professor Jeremiah W. Jenks asserted that Christ showed "no trace of asceticism" and that he did not "object to the social customs of his times in themselves." The criteria of his approval were the social utility of the customs and the degree to which they served the Father.[19] In *Life Questions of High School Boys,* published in 1908, Jenks affirmed that "Our enjoyment of life comes largely from the gratification of our tastes." He used ball games as examples of the way in which young men should be conditioned into right conduct, and he approved of play when boys entered it with concentration and commitment. Jenks strongly suggested that honest, amateur sport deserved praise, and the "clean" athlete's courage was no less praiseworthy than that shown on the battlefield. Promoting a coherent view of religion as suffusing all activities in daily life, Jenks included playing ball among the pursuits likely to develop a religious character as much as giving to the poor and helping one's parents. Although the chapter and verse verifying Christ's prowess as a ballplayer remain obscure, "his acts and character" embodied the core of ideals to which Americans must aspire.[20]

The Young Men's Christian Association (Y.M.C.A.) encouraged the new and positive appreciation of the body. As early as the 1850s, exponents of Christian reform such as Henry Ward Beecher urged that adults provide orderly and wholesome exercise for boys so that they would gain in physical vigor while staying "separate from temptations to vice." Gradually, associations in the major cities devoted themselves to building gymnasia and establishing physical training programs, all of which presumed the basic dignity of the body. Although the Christian leaders often had to hire retired circus performers or prize fighters who lacked their religious fervor, they remained committed to physical activity because, as a New York writer put it in 1889, "the body is a temple of the Holy Ghost." At length, the minister supported a moderate pursuit of sport as a part of the complete development of human capacity and personality, and he considered it a fit ally to practical theology. Enthusiastically, he noted:

> . . . the Devil has no patent right on these athletic recreations, and it is only pusillanimous in us to yield to him an exclusive privilege, when he has no claim that can stand. I do not mean that every one should make it a point to get the muscle of a stroke oarsman, or the agility of an acrobat in a circus; but I do mean that every one should remember that it is as much a duty to cultivate the body as to cultivate the soul, and without this twofold and harmonious training, religion would become irksome, and study a weariness to the flesh.

Another preacher observed in *The Watchman* in 1885 that the gymnasium, which had once been considered "a wicked place, a place for pugilists to get a muscle, a training school for manufacturing Heenans," now provided greater curative power than anything else on earth.[21]

The emphatic preference of the Y.M.C.A.'s organizers for a full and rounded development of the individual accorded perfectly with the professional instincts of the physical educators, and this commonality of viewpoints hastened the establishment of ties between the two groups. Within the Y.M.C.A., the distinguished head of the Springfield Training School Luther H. Gulick encouraged the use of sports for the physical development of young men. Gulick shared the positive opinion that Y.M.C.A. promoters had of the human body, declaring it a "wonderful combination of the dust of the earth, and the breath of God." He claimed Christ as the model of human perfection and described him as the savior of "the whole man, body, mind and spirit."[22] With no sense of blasphemy, Gulick thus spoke of Christ's concern for mankind much as he did of his own work as a physical educator. Sharing the commitment of contemporary psychology to the coordinate importance of mind and body, Gulick sought to save souls in bodies. Unlike his more hidebound predecessors in the Y.M.C.A.'s gymnasiums, he celebrated sport as a magnificent and effective means of training mind and spirit as well as body. From the organization's convention of 1889 on, Gulick set himself to designing and implementing training programs that would supply directors of physical education to numerous sites around the country. Amos Alonzo Stagg joined Gulick at Springfield in the early 1890s to coach a football team of "Stubby Christians," and Gulick promoted basketball indefatigably. The Y.M.C.A. movement became the home and sponsor of basketball, much as the colleges were to football. To suit the needs of urban businessmen, for whom he considered Naismith's game too strenuous, W.G. Morgan invented volleyball. To coordinate and regulate participation in these "gymnastic games," as he called them, Gulick sparked the establishment of a Y.M.C.A. Athletic League. Sports had taken their place as vehicles of spiritual and corporeal reform. To the 1901 convention of the Y.M.C.A., President G. Stanley Hall of Clark University spoke with magisterial approval: ". . . the future historian of the church of Christ will place this movement for carrying the gospel of the body as one of the most epoch-making."[23] If the body enjoyed a gospel, Gulick and the advocates of sport became its prophets.

The editorial board of the Young Men's Christian Association contented itself with mortal models as well as divine. To shape the thoughts of young men, they promoted the ideas of Henry Ward Beecher, who identified the body as "the most precious gift that God has given us, aside from the soul." Man had an obligation to respect his body and to preserve it. Beecher likened the "squandering" of physical strength to the wanton destruction of "beautiful pictures on the wall and magnificent statues" in the niches of a great estate. Association Press encouraged the belief that physical activity and sport insured a clearer functioning of the mind and a firmer development of the will. In 1920, for example, F.H. Cheley collated *Stories for Talks to Boys* and reprinted testimonies from the lives of great men to prove the moral merit of exercise. He quoted the *Boston Herald*'s story of William Cullen Bryant swinging a chair in place of Indian clubs, historian George Bancroft indulging in daily horse-riding, and Gladstone gaining mental strength through physical labor in cutting trees. Cheley also cited physical educator H.H. Moore, who praised Lincoln for prowess as a wrestler. Moore also applauded Gladstone for his commitment to cricket, football, walking, and boating. Cheley himself reminded readers that Harvard's President Eliot had gained his capacity for work through rowing, fishing, riding, and hiking. A boxer and oarsman while in college, Eliot had been able to make a great contribution to the nation's affairs "because of his splendid body."[24] So far from being a "vessel of sin," the human body deserved attention for its enrichment of moral life and as an embodiment of it.

Proponents of a "social gospel" argued that spiritual regeneration was facilitated by improving the material environment, implicitly accepting the power of the physical world in spiritual practice and belief. Thus, they pointed not only to an empirical approach to religious service and doctrine, but also toward an altered view of the material world and of the human body. Many prominent authorities nodded their approval of well-regulated games and sports. Phillips Brooks, Episcopal Bishop of Massachusetts from 1891 to 1893, accepted any activity that made a boy become "a strong and good man," while Josiah Strong called play not only "natural and normal" but even "a divinely ordered thing." John L. Alexander, the first executive secretary of the Boy Scout Movement and an enthusiastic collaborator in the work of the Y.M.C.A., promoted games and sports as part of the solution to the "boy problem" in an edition of essays released in 1912, *Boy Training*. Lee F. Hanmer contributed the thought that the child who played fair at tennis would not cheat in business and that obedience to the rules of basketball encouraged loyalty to the laws of the state. Alexander himself observed that adolescence "marks the beginning of team work and team work is only an expression of social cooperation." He added his approval of the Public School Athletic League in New York and of the Sunday School Athletic League, which aided "the Sunday-school in dealing with the adolescent by recognizing his physical needs."[25]

More broadly, Professor Simon Patten of the University of Pennsylvania proclaimed that "Enthusiasm and the missionary spirit come with the growth of physical vigor." Washington Gladden, in *Applied Christianity*, justified amusements as "a means of refreshing the mind and replenishing the strength of the body" and recognized that recreation could shape character. In 1902, the Congregationalist minister Gladden endorsed the teachings of Theodore Roosevelt about the "strenuous life" before a Yale

University audience and for readers of *Social Salvation*. The prominent Professor of Church History at the Rochester Theological Seminary, Walter Rauschenbusch, recognized the common person's need for leisure and recreation in *Christianizing the Social Order*. The Y.M.C.A's Social Service Commission, which included the Reverend Henry Sloane Coffin among its members, as well as Gladden and Rauschenbusch, lauded play as the means of stifling "the lust of [vice]." Not only did the Commission tolerate sport; in their 1912 report, they urged the churches to provide "the moral leadership in athletics in America." Members further endorsed Simon Patten's argument that amusements served as attractive media for moral and religious lessons.[26]

A considerable literature appeared that was devoted to the sports and pastimes of young men, providing them guidance in their leisure activities and a sense of purpose in their pastimes. The Y.M.C.A.'s Association Press published books to promote "Symmetrical Boy-development," such as *Boy Training*, edited by John L. Alexander. G. Walter Fiske of the Oberlin Theological Seminary contributed a volume on *Boy Life and Self-Government* that promoted play, games, and sport as means to aid youth in the "struggle for manliness" and identified "boy life" as the "epitome of race life." The play instincts would serve to promote socially responsible action in the "gymnasium for citizenship," even as they would make the boy a committed and activist Christian. Authors such as H. W. Gibson contributed information on *Camping for Boys*, and George H. Corsan promoted swimming, diving, water sports, and lifesaving in *At Home in the Water*.[27]

Clarence C. Robinson, the Secretary of the Boy's Department of the International Committee of the Y.M.C.A., enthusiastically supported the participation of working boys in sports such as baseball, football, gymnastics, swimming, and track athletics. Properly supervised, the boys would avoid gambling halls and pool rooms, and they would be less inclined toward profanity and drinking alcohol. Correct use of sport would make it a "large factor in his character development," according to Robinson, who clearly believed that the environment in which the boy spent his leisure hours conditioned the habits he would acquire.

The Secretary sensed a similarity between physical recreation and moral regeneration, both of which were evolving and developmental experiences. Comfortable in an allusion to the theology of conversion, Robinson urged adults to guide boys through sport and other "re-creations" so that they would come to know "what it means to be 'born again' for one's work." By attending to the boys' leisure-time activities, the adult Christian would gradually condition them to become responsible members of the community. Robinson even claimed that the religious reformers had virtually monopolized the movement to bring physical rehabilitation and amusement to the public, as, for example, in the playground movement. In this Robinson suggested the extent to which the Y.M.C.A. had come to accept the material world as a worthy vehicle through which to approach salvation.[28]

Those promoters of religion who advocated social reform aimed to use sport as a method for ingraining Christian virtues, and they believed that the athletic contest captured the spirit of a boy and elevated it through emulation of Christ. George Walter Fiske, Professor of Practical Theology at Oberlin College, extolled sport for requiring team-play, healthy competition, "alertness of mind and muscle," cool temper, and quick judgment. Sharing the Y.M.C.A.'s belief that the minister must start with youth where they were, Fiske reported Henry Sheldon's findings that 61 percent of all boys' spontaneous clubs boosted athletics. These might help the adolescent gain the habits of cooperation and subordination that would only attain fulfillment when "he finds a personal Master again in Jesus Christ." At the very least, sport in a Christian environment replaced frivolous activity in an atmosphere heavy with sin. The "sissy boy" who failed to recapitulate the history of the race "probably needs a good stiff dose of out-of-doors games," Fiske said. As proper development of the body conditioned the individual toward the salvation of the soul, he aspired toward radiant companionship with God. The adolescent must "be on friendly terms with Jesus Christ," Fiske stated, and enjoy the Master's protection, ideals, love, and comradeship. Give the boy the heroic model of an activist but disciplined Christ, they concluded, and "you have armed him with all the panoply of God."[29]

THE BODY AS A REALIZED IDEAL

For Christian ministers of the Social Gospel, the human body became a form of holy writ and revelation. For them, individual human beings gave specific existential meaning to a general divine plan. In turn, man assumed personal obligations to complete God's natural design — to recapitulate in each person the history of the race, in a sanctified version of G. Stanley Hall's theories, and to uplift the race by slow stages of evolutionary progress. So lofty a goal required not only a general sense of destiny but specific models against which the American could test his actions and according to which he could assess his growth. Secular exponents of sport and physical recreation willingly accepted the endorsement of clerics; and many, such as Luther Gulick, who made crucial contributions to the work of the Y.M.C.A., sincerely advanced Christ as the realized ideal for man to imitate. The literal body of Christ, taken as the vehicle and motor of his actions, became a symbol of the unity of goodness and action that Theodore Roosevelt had claimed to be the high duty of all Americans to achieve. Yet the physical indistinctness of Christ might have obstructed or at least confused the campaign for physical regeneration. Secular models substituted for Christ in increasing numbers; and the hero, who was defined by action and whose actions were equated with character, merged to a renewed importance in secular life and to a novel significance in sport. As movement and action took hold of Americans' mentality, sport became a means for the pursuit of earthly perfection. Given its association with sport, classical culture became a new source of models for the American.[30] As the adaptation of Christianity to evolutionary thought had encouraged a more positive appraisal of the body, the classical age's emphasis on the coordinate importance of mind and body contributed to the eminence of recreation and sport as agents of personal and racial fulfillment.

Thus, elements allied with both the sacred and the profane fastened upon concrete symbols and representations of the values they favored. For those who remained deeply influenced by Christianity, the transformation of even the physical depictions of Christ suggested the importance of care for the body and a vigorous, active life. In a sense, Christ became a hero, a spiritual athlete dying young for the sake of the transcendent victory; and the gradual appropriation by athletes of the status of demigods reciprocated for the emphasis on the humanity of Christ, without which his heroism could not have existed. At the same time, however, the enhancement of the image of the human body occurred in the secular environment with the assumption of the basically pagan imagery of classical Greece and Rome. Simultaneously, the high esteem of the classics fell upon the body and the sporting activities to which it was put, but the association with paganism excepted the body and sport from some of the more demanding moral strictures of conventional Christianity. Christ was becoming an earthly version of a transcendent model of body and soul; but man was reciprocally grasping toward his own perfectibility. Physical culturists, physiologists, and others came to see their own intervention as central to a nationwide attainment of this high physical estate.

The differing assessments of the body and its proper activities reflected differing senses of modesty and an altered sensibility. As late as 1875, President Buckham of the University of Vermont had objected to public athletic display as a pagan spectacle. He declared it "beneath the dignity of a free-born Vermonter to expose their muscle in public, like gladiators in the amphitheater." Yet by the turn of the century, sportswriter Arthur Ruhl included Buckham among the men of "good old New England stock" who had guided the small colleges which "were coeducational or strongly sectarian, or both. In the first there was likely to be a feeling that there was something incompatible between athletics and a decorous gentlemanliness, and in the latter sport was looked at askance as flippant and of the flesh fleshy."[31] For Ruhl and his contemporaries, sport could be both gentlemanly and ladylike. Far from being frivolous, the association of a pagan past with the Christian present gave evidence of human progress.

Some athletic performers employed classical imagery self-consciously, sometimes because of the high esteem in which they held their own competitive efforts. William Muldoon of New

Posing as "The Fighting Gaul," William Muldoon illustrates the element of spectacle in gladiatorial sports. Theatrical poses and pagan imagery probably contributed to the broader acceptance of bare skin in public. Photo by Falk of New York, taken in 1888, toward the end of Muldoon's championship years in Greco-Roman wrestling competition. By permission of the Library of Congress, Biographical Files.

York, for example, began his career as a wrestler in 1876 at the age of thirty-one, competing as a heavyweight in the Police Championships in his home town. Five years later, after winning the American Greco-Roman wrestling title from Thiebaud Bauer, Muldoon devoted himself to the sport fulltime. For his costume, Muldoon adopted the motif of a Roman gladiator, with studded breechcloth and thonged sandals. In promotional photographs as well as his matches, Muldoon was otherwise naked, revealing a fit and imposing body of which some considered him inordinately proud.

Another specific example of the classical pagan image came in the somewhat hulking form of a woman wrestler with the ring-name of Minerva. Wearing rugged boots, close-fitting tights, a tunic-style short dress, and ankle bands, Minerva was often seen in the midst of a veritable garden of barbells and dumbbells. Her image (and perhaps her "persona") freed her from the mundane reality of Hoboken, New Jersey, her home town; and the posturing that characterizes her photographs involves the acceptance of different standards of conduct from those generally accepted in her day and place. In her costume, she transcended wickedness by undermining the standards for judging it. She also attained a kind of cultural freedom comparable to that which Isadora Duncan, Ruth St. Denis, and others touched through their use of loose clothing evocative of the classical and pagan age.

To be sure, the images of paganism were in part an attempt to generate public interest in commercial properties. Yet the specific nature of the promotional campaigns and the specific identities established for the athletes encouraged the acceptance of previously suspect sports ventures and new manners in the presentation of the body. The primary vehicle for the establishment of the pagan image — the outlandish costumes that provided such basis for contemporary fascination — deviated from the disciplinary, regulatory, and standardizing institution of "team uniforms." From the first known use of team uniforms by Harvard crews through their commonplace employment by the end of the nineteenth century, these had sanctioned activities that otherwise might have been dismissed as frivolously individualistic. The use of such team uniforms, moreover, itself underscored the prominence accorded to group activities; and the sports that enjoyed extensive press coverage, alumni interest in the case of colleges, and recognition from intellectuals and social commentators often promoted the team.

Yet, on its own terms, classical costume constituted a special kind of "team" uniform, worn by somewhat self-indulgent but deeply disciplined proponents of the worth of the body. It appealed to spectators — as many as 3,000 when Muldoon wrestled Edwin Bibby in San Francisco in 1883. As his police and military uniforms had represented a preexisting identity that he could adopt through enlistment and use as a shell for a mundane existence, his cultivation of the new Roman costume grasped at an almost transcendent status. Moreover, to the extent that it assumed value as a model in itself, Muldoon's body was superior to the particular methods that shaped it and even to the purposes to which it was put. A Theodore Roosevelt might have considered that self-indulgent; but there were respectable Americans who no longer presumed that self-indulgence was always a vice.

Intrinsic in Muldoon's transformation was the revelation of his body, or most of it; and it is important that the manner in which he made this exposition was as significant as the fact that he did so at all. Closely tailored and spare, Muldoon's costume emphasized his good proportions and well-developed physique. It not only had the practical advantage of freeing him of encumbrances for wrestling; it was a way of calling great attention to the attributes of his body even apart from his physical performance. As much as it constituted an aid to Muldoon's performance in the ring by its sparsity and an assist to his image by flattering his impressive physique, Muldoon's costume was the feathering of the peacock, the uninhibited flaunting of the body in general and male beauty in particular in a society that still questioned the propriety of the exposed female ankle. This celebration of the well-developed body as the result of intensive training and dedication implicitly certified the value of body-building and physical culture as the means of achieving it.

The celebrated wrestler Georges Hackenschmidt took the final step by discarding pseudo-Roman costume and posing in the nude in imitations of classical statues. Hackenschmidt thus embodied the aesthetics of harmonious development. Certain other athletes and strongmen — such as Eugene Sandow — followed the same course. Not only in the fullness of their nudity, but in the use of the body as a vehicle of expression, these personalities hinted that mere flesh might achieve a limited transformation when it was suffused with a balanced and well-developed human spirit.

The promotion of a classical image of human perfection was far more than a sensationalist eccentricity. Many women concerned with the advancement of their sex in American intellectual, industrial, and social life promoted Greek, Roman, and neoclassical models as the concrete manifestations of their proper destiny. In *The Women's Athenaeum,* published in 1912 and concerned in large part with the physical appearance and condition of the American female, Emily Grant Hutchings of St. Louis stated bluntly that art in the Greek classic period reached its "highest perfection." Hutchings emphasized the artists' creation of a system of measurements and proportions for the human body, observing that they aimed at "a summing-up of the most beautiful proportions in many beautiful bodies." Although all parts of the body corresponded to one another in magnificent balance, the Greek artist started with "an ideal of perfection" that Hutchings believed must lead to aesthetic slavery. By contrast, the Dutch and Italian painters produced ugly paintings when using living models, because they had to rely on "peasant women whose bodies were far from beautiful" and because their limited knowledge of anatomy did not arm them to compensate imaginatively for the physical defects of their subjects. Although Michelangelo merited some recognition for imitating Greek sculpture in the *Pietà,* Hutchings thought him a thrall to images of gross force. His women, she noted disapprovingly, "look as if they could not only follow the plow but take an active hand in the destruction of the universe." At some length, Hutchings celebrated a combination of "classic ideas" and "realism" as the contemporary ideal, and she breathed dynamic change into the fixed shell of the Greeks' perfect form. For the catalogue of specific proportions that she provided to guide women in their personal development did not stand as an end in itself. The human form gained value as the "physical expression of the ideal human being"; and Hutchings hastened to warn her readers that both civilization and right living — heredity and conditioning — controlled their appearance. The proportionate body expressed "the well balanced mind and the perfectly rounded character." Moral development and cosmetic attention generated bodies evocative of classical art, yet superior to it because they shared the reality of life and change.[32]

The physical culturist Minna Gordon Gould shared Hutchings's belief that physical action generated beauty, and she made even more explicit Hutchings's bias in favor of movement and change. Gould reminded readers of *The Women's Athenaeum* that "all organic bodies require motion as a means of life, and she recommended exercise not for any straining of the muscles but to keep the human being and its human body moving together in concert. Attending to exercise and games, the enlightened person would see the body not as "bestial" but as "the temple of the immortal part of us," which would be "sculptured into Divine beauty by the divinity within." The inner, dynamic force in the human being shaped a body that ever more closely approximated perfection.[33]

Trained physical educators shared the desire for harmonious development of the body. Mary Coolidge Fish called health, grace, and strength "Woman's Birthright" and encouraged their attainment through physical education and sport. A graduate of the Sargent Normal School of Physical Training and, in 1912, a professor of physical education at the University of Kansas, Fish cautioned against excessive ambition in sport, arguing that "prolonged nervous strain" in matches could be destructive. True to her mentors' philosophy, she encouraged activities that pleased the participants and counteracted their tendency to exercise only spasmodically. Fish strongly endorsed "fancy" dancing, in which students expressed themselves in organic, fluid movement while costumed in the neoclassical style. But she also encouraged the use of sports and games, since the ready enthusiasm of the players played directly into the hands of the physical educators. Among the activities that deserved praise were tennis, rowing, skating, volleyball, handball, field hockey, basketball, and golf. Whatever program the women entered upon, however, her goal remained a "happy medium" that accorded with the classical vision of the "golden mean."[34]

The painting and sculpture of the "high culture" of turn-of-the-century America reflected the pervasiveness of the classical ideal as it was animated by a strong dose of naturalism. The great American museums built collections of classical art and, in some cases, acquired copies of outstanding Greek and Roman statuary in the galleries of Europe. Leading this campaign, Louis Palma di Cesnola, director of New York's Metropolitan Museum from 1879 to 1904, conducted excavations while American consul at Cyprus and retained a passion for classical culture throughout his tenure. Widespread enthusiasm for archaeology itself reflected the penchant for the ancient world that set amateurs to digging and made their finds fashionable. In their companion taste for Renaissance art, turn-of-the-century upper-class Americans discovered an earlier effort to recapture the classical spirit; and late Victorian art drew upon both traditions in a "search for idealism" that was alive with action.[35]

The difference of opinion among art experts as to the perfect classical form frustrated the more practically oriented educators, yet there remained a strong sense that "the best types of ancient statues" made possible a standard vision of perfection in the human body. To this end, physical educators who specialized in anthropometry were expected to provide great service. Measurements of statues could be compared to those of living persons, and those humans who captured the essential spirit of the classical aesthetic could become models for the mass of people. This mixture of classicism and what Emily Hutchings called "realism" could be marketed commercially. According to the editors of *The Women's Athenaeum*, American state universities relied on the "ideal of classical art" in cutting dress patterns, thereby establishing it as a norm of the correct American body. In addition, the living persons singled out by anthropometrists could give information about exercise, diet, and the multitude of habits that manifested themselves in the body. The editors of *The Women's Athenaeum* compared the Venus de Medici and the Venus de Milo with Lily Langtry. The "Jersey Lily" enjoyed an ambiguous resemblance to the Medici statue, which had an attractiveness of "physique" but the "suggestion of mental power reduced to the lowest." The writers may be accused, perhaps, of a touch of snobbery in their judgment of Miss Lily; and they may have read from her career to her form, rather than from her body-type to her mentality. "Beauty," the editors noted in the end, inevitably expressed "character which can be judged from results recorded in life." Actual experience attested to beauty; arbitrary conceptions of an ideal that had no correspondent in the actual world were unauthentic.[36]

Scaled down to actual evolutionary experience, perfection for man came to be defined in human terms and, at the risk of paradox, within the limits of human genetics. The standards by which humans could judge their development lay within the history of the race. Thus Dr. G.W. Fitz told readers of the *Harvard Graduates' Magazine* of September 1893 that there was an "ideal condition" of the human body but that it did not express itself through an act of Platonic imagination. In an argument suggestive of Hall's recapitulation theory, he argued that savage nations and Greek sculpture provided evidence that the "potential savage perfection" existed in all times and that each member of every generation had the opportunity to reproduce it. The infant needed only the right kinds of activity, both mental and physical. Fitz attributed a decline in the physical caliber of Americans to "our highly differentiated, conventional life with its pure mental ideal." Distorted emphasis on the mind invited deterioration in the body, which, not immediately but eventually, would become genetically fixed. The savage showed symmetry, as did the Greek heroic ideal; and the American should pursue it as well. Active, practical, and balanced, each young American would experience forces and stresses comparable to those that had formed the "ideal structure" of man in remote times.[37]

Commenting in 1904 on "College Boating in the Sixties," Clarence Deming showed that humans could consciously mold their bodies to achieve distinction in performance, and he also revealed the extent to which the image of the perfect man had changed from the era of the Civil War to the turn of the century. Admiring the victorious Yale crew of Wilbur Bacon in the 1860s, he reported on their "theory of reducing flesh" according to which the ideal oarsman was wiry, thin, and light.

217

The Yale crew of 1865, coached by disciplinarian Wilbur Bacon, shows what a later writer called "the greyhound look." By the end of the century a different approach, emphasizing muscle-mass, had become dominant. Both views assumed that coaches and other experts could tailor malleable bodies to the needs of specific athletic tasks. *Outing*, July 1904, 414.

Through austere and somewhat bizarre dietary control, the typical Baconian rower became especially adapted to his duties: "his fleshy outline is of the greyhound type; his muscles are knotted, not rounded; the ribs are barred clearly below the dark skin." Deming rejected the specific idiosyncracies of Bacon's prescription for success, but he embraced its purpose. A new image of the rowing athlete prevailed at the turn of the century, governed by the exponents of "the 'beef' theory of large muscle fashioned by training into the highest economies of unity and skill." Bacon and Deming both believed that a conscientious coach could sculpt a crew and also that changing their physical form and condition would improve performance. There they parted company. To remain consistent in seeing specific athletic success as the result of an exact match between the corporeal instrument and the sporting chore, Deming needed to accept a discoverable hierarchy in the design of human machines. Successful though they were, then, Bacon's crew had to be judged empirically invalid in a comparison with the "large muscle" crews of the turn of the century. Indeed, part of the Yale crew's success in the 1860s stemmed not from the superiority of their method but from their having a method to which they adhered religiously. With the all but universal acceptance of one training system or another, an orthodoxy would, and did, emerge. So unusual had the almost emaciated look of Bacon's oarsmen become by the 1900s that Deming included a photograph of them, naked to the waist, to underscore the greatness of the transformation.[38]

Physical educators sought to complete each human body by using particular sports and distinct patterns of muscular development as they suited specific cases. They insisted upon order and balance in place of riot and excess. As Lucifer sinned through inordinate ambition, colleges corrupted themselves and their students by overzealous athleticism. Physical educators rejected exclusive reliance on any one sport because it created a moral distortion that showed itself in bodily eccentricity. Dudley Sargent claimed that he could recognize oarsmen, ballplayers, and gymnasts "from their peculiar muscular development." He even alleged that he could distinguish between a starboard and a port oar, the pitcher, catcher, and shortstop from the rest of

219

the nine, and the special event of the gymnast. Developed in mind and in body with muscles and powers balanced, the whole man embodied the principle of harmony; and, precisely because professionals such as Sargent believed that there was a "limit to human capability," they could also hold that physical perfectibility was not only conceivable but practically attainable. Performing to the fullness of one's powers gave existential consummation to the individual. As American pragmatism banished idealistic presuppositions about philosophical categories, principles, and essences, the physical educators adopted a corporeal and empiricist version of perfection in which symmetry of the parts made the human organism transcendent as a whole.[39]

J. Bell Pettigrew suggested how man could achieve greatness in movement and action. A distinguished pathologist from Edinburgh, he explained to American readers in 1888 that the discovery of natural laws of motion endowed man with power to harness it, enabling him to act as the synthesis of animal capacities. Every mode of animal locomotion assumed exceptional importance by exemplifying the "beneficence and design" of God. In his book *Animal Locomotion,* published in D. Appleton and Company's International Scientific Series, Pettigrew postulated that the love of motion was universal, and that all animals had missions to perform. The execution of naturally dictated motions brought God's plan of flux and organic growth to fulfillment in experience. This process brought all living beings who followed its demands to a kind of perfection; for "Even the most exquisite form loses much of its grace if bereft of motion." Symmetry best showed itself in motion and action, further proving that the aspects of animal perfection grounded themselves physically and showed themselves empirically. "The rigidity and stillness of death alone are unnatural," Pettigrew said. "So long as things 'live, move, and have being,'" which was a coexisting and interdependent phenomenon, "they are agreeable objects in the landscape." Change thus became the "present solace and future hope" for man, a promise that the world actually incorporated the seeds of progress and that he could, through scientific imitation of God, make them flower.[40]

G. Mercer Adam, who compiled the statements of physical culturist Eugene Sandow, believed that modern scientific study,

Plate 59 of *Animal Locomotion*, published in 1887 by the University of Pennsylvania, illustrates Eadweard Muybridge's technique of setting up cameras at regular intervals on a numbered grid and shows one of the earliest starting positions designed by professional coaches. The runner's position, resembling a frozen instant in a run, enables him to "fall into" the race at the sound of the gun. By permission of the Library of Congress (Lot 3309, Cage A).

221

particularly in exercise physiology, enabled man to approach "the consummate beauty of physical form" with an efficiency and a prospect of success far exceeding even the ancient Athenians. Microscopic study of cells, Adam said, "revealed almost the secret of life itself, with its ever-recurrent motions of waste and renewal." Exercise increased the motion of the cells markedly. Quoting the English authority on physical education Archibald Maclaren, Adam reported the discovery that hastening the rate of the regenerative cycle of human cells brought such an "advance in size and power" that "the ultimate attainable point of development is reached."[41] Human perfectibility became possible in the new age of scientific study of the body, which itself could achieve completeness and fulfillment within the range dictated by the state of genetic development of the race.

Sandow himself typified this perfected human form. Simultaneously, the young Prussian achieved "the classical ideal of physical beauty" and, on arrival in America, made it seem "that the advance-guard of a new order of physical beings had descended on our planet." Publicist Adam backed his hyperbole with scientific testimony recording the opinions of professors Virchow, Rosenheim, and Vanetti that Sandow was "one of the most perfectly-built men in existence." Dudley Sargent called him "the most wonderful specimen of man I have ever seen" and compared him to Apollo and Hercules. An anonymous member of the New York Athletic Club identified the key to Sandow's perfection when he said: "I have seen athletes with almost as big muscles, but never one with the all-round development Sandow possesses." Nothing in excess, all muscles of his body had been brought to fullness and balance. It was a miracle of physical balance, order, discipline, and organization.[42]

The presentation of Sandow's achievement in vocabulary rich with classical reference and allusions raised him to special distinction. The poses in which he was photographed captured the spirit of classical sculpture, enhancing his identity as a living masterpiece. As with marble so with flesh, man could sculpt and finish a form that actually perfected the physical characteristics that were potential genetically. The similarity between Sandow's physique and Greco-Roman sculptural tradition did wonders for the strong man's public image. Even more, how-

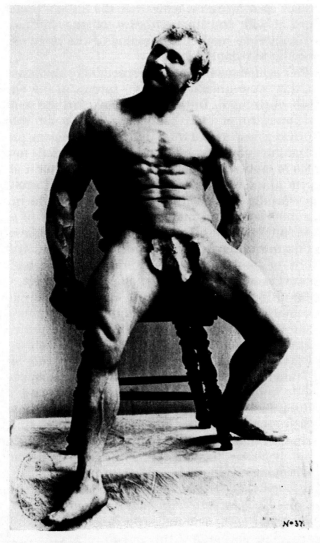

Eugene Sandow, wrestler and strongman, was heralded as the most perfectly developed man in the world. He published guides on bodily development and circulated nearly nude photographs of himself, becoming perhaps the most successful male pinup of his time. Many of his poses imitated classical statues. Photo by Napoleon Sarong of New York. By permission of the Library of Congress (LC-USZ62-2793).

ever, it lent convincing evidence that the human body could be shaped at will; and the persuasive balance and beauty of Sandow's physique made this molding of the body seem not only possible but laudable.

Sandow's achievements enjoyed respectability and favor partly because they were linked to action—success in the wrestling ring, feats of strength. In this way, he avoided the semblance of mere narcissism and self-indulgence; but he also thus positively turned a neoclassical form into a living, moving presence. To say that the body was at its most beautiful and its most perfect when in motion, moreover, was also to say that it attained fulfillment in the very process of experience that formed it, as it was performing the specific actions that set out the practical limits of one's being and character. It was a theory of aesthetics, then; but it was also a manifestation of the philosophical disposition toward experimentalism that undergirded the acceptability of sport and the public display of the body.

Disparate as were their motives and special interests, various advocates of sport, physical culture, and bodily development had a common effect in placing emphasis on motion and in seeing movement and action as the normal and proper state of the human person. In motion, as Francis Walker suggested in his 1893 Phi Beta Kappa address at Harvard, modern man might attain a practical version of perfection. He spoke poetically of the "sublime passion" for the human body and the care for its form that was taking hold of the nation, finding in the body "their greatest delight." Observing the popularity of classical sculpture in his own day and favorably noting the high esteem of life classes in contemporary art schools, he pined for the conditioning of a human paragon through the labors of the physical educator. The ideal man would communicate through actions and deeds, a hero without words—or else one whose otherwise trivial words acquired value from his deeds. Although more articulate and more effusive than some other observers, Walker captured the essence of an informal constituency of Americans who were swept up in the enthusiasm for the body, in the ability to shape it, in the pleasure of using it, and in the satisfaction of valuing it. "The Vision of the Apollo may yet rise," he said, "to the view of thousands, out and up from the arena at Springfield, as erst it rose before the thronging multitudes of Olympia."[43] Even if the process proved to be endless and if further uplifting refinement always seemed possible, the goal of physical wholeness and fulfillment in the material world had become current. Sport had united the pursuit of godliness and the pursuit of happiness.

CHAPTER 8

Sport and Mentality

THE context in which sport assumed importance within American culture was that which led William Dean Howells to say, in 1895, "It seems to me that we are always mistaking our conditions for our natures."[1] Change was possible; and what appeared to be character hinged upon mutable circumstances, practices, and customs. Against such assumptions, sport could readily be seen to shape character. After all, what did not?

Americans came to believe that actions formed character, rather than simply reflecting one that had already been determined. The process was reciprocal, and it was also ambivalent. In the older categorical thinking of the physiocrats and the early phrenologists, behavior conveniently corroborated preexisting character. But for those who aimed to reform society, behavior could be governed by will. One was not predestined to a life of evil or ruin, although one might seal that fate by indulging in actions that led to it. Much of the latter—the newly dominant strain—can be seen in the perspective of William James. His philosophy was, in a sense, equivalent to a psychology, while both his philosophy and his psychology depended upon a profound belief in the authenticity of the material world —that it existed, that it was truly real, and that nothing which could not be tested experimentally could usefully be discussed as if it were real. For James as for others, action and movement became the vocabulary of the soul.

The rise and eminence of the athletic star exemplified the growing fixation on action and experience. As David Voigt has suggested, the promotion of the star performer was largely a marketing strategy adopted by owners of sports franchises. Yet, as Neil Isaacs has noted, the sports star embodied a new understanding of the meaning of the word *hero* in American culture — one identified not by his character but by his deeds. The moral range among stars underscores this shift — a Christy Mathewson revered for his upstanding personal life, and a Ty Cobb admired despite his seeming indifference to humane concerns. Their common ground was a scientific attitude toward baseball, along with their success in translating knowledge into victory on the playing field. Mathewson himself obliquely supported this view when, questioning the adulation accorded Babe Ruth, he rated the scientific complexity of baseball above its brute strength. By extension, Mathewson valued continuing, regular excellence over the fluke; and thus the hero was the repeated victor in a whole course of contests rather than in a daring "one-shot" performance.[2]

The vision of the body as a dynamic process, rather than a fixed entity, made it and its actions the living and continuous expression of whatever might be called "spirit." Crucial to this sense of the body as the culmination of its own activities was the general thrust of evolutionary science more than its specific observations. Evolution meant that man was in motion, that all things were in motion. If one accepted a doctrine of creation, it became continuous; and an altered God became somehow closer to man while man became necessarily closer to the rest of creation. This sense of the world as a nexus of relationships allowed the rise of analogies rooted in energy and dynamism. The proliferation of sports training machines that used electricity, for example — however bizarre and ineffectual — reminds one of the widespread understanding that life itself was "electrical." In discussing the proper conditions for sexual copulation, Dr. Augustus Gardner urged that man and woman "have this function when the sun is up in the heaven, so as to furnish electric states of the body." On a more metaphorical level, Theodore Roosevelt served as the embodiment of national energy and vigor. Energy was deemed instinctual, even if its forms seemed scientific; and exerting rational control was the one safeguard against letting energy deteriorate in contingency and chaos.[3]

In one sense, turn-of-the-century Americans betrayed the primacy of the material world in their own minds. Yet, at the same time, they reached toward a reintegration of mind with body and of spirit with matter. The sense of unity that had been part of the Puritan gift had been jeopardized by Newtonian physics and by the Enlightenment. Thus, scientific discoveries in the nineteenth century only added to the psychological strains imposed upon a culture founded in the dream of coherence and community. Though often cited as an age of rampant materialism, the late nineteenth century was actually another moment in a continuum of materialism sanctioned in science at least since the seventeenth century. What the late nineteenth century offered that was special was, ironically, a hope of seeing spiritual meaning within material circumstances and of restoring a sense of purpose to what otherwise must be random and pointless existence. The "search for order" in the management of life signified this to the extent that it restored a sense of goals toward which life could be managed. The development of psychology and, later, of psychoanalysis argued strongly toward a unity of spiritual and physical phenomena, even if they often dissented from the notion of an immortal soul.

Despite the high ethical tone which many advocates of sport and the "strenuous life" adopted and urged on prospective followers, their position nonetheless contained a moral threat of the most fundamental sort. Yet it was in this very danger that much of sport's appeal lay. The acceptance of the material world (exemplified by Margaret Fuller's statement "I accept the universe" and Thomas Carlyle's "Gad! She'd better") and the reciprocal doubt about the dimensions of a spiritual universe led to what David W. Noble has called "the sacrilegious quest for an earthly paradise." For all the talk about moral goals for physical exercise, there was an intrinsic danger that means would lose their ends; and action, as a substitute for virtue, would become its own reward. This risked severing sport from the moral and intellectual realm where some of sport's advocates had first drawn strength — cutting the tree from its roots. It also threatened to deprive sport of social interconnection and responsibility. If sport became an end in itself, it could easily escape all control except that generated from within. Such limits — largely technical — would make sport, in a settled and civilized era, a parody of untamed nature; and the playing fields and the arena would ape the mythic American Eden.[4]

Indeed, the emergence of sport as part of mass culture in America hastened precisely such a redefinition of how one played the game and, even more, of why. Rationales that had been worked out painstakingly by middle-class and upper-class Americans to reconcile new behavior with old values became mere slogans in the mouths of those catering to the masses. As for the working class and the broad middle class of the twentieth century, the elaborate theorizing of an earlier time had little pertinence. Sport, amusements, fun and games — all were seen as a given, requiring no explanation or justification. Against this turn, the older and more traditional mentality had no adequate defenses, except perhaps a retreat into a few sports either too expensive or too arcane to attract the masses. Yet, by their own earlier accommodation to sport as they themselves understood it, the middle- and upper-class advocates of sport had hastened its integration into the broader scene of American life by removing themselves from potential opposition. Although the rise of sport as a key element in American mass culture is surely among the key consequences of the actions taken by the middle and upper classes, it certainly was not what they had in mind. Nor were they directly responsible for all specific actions that led in this direction. That is a story of its own.

Although later sports enthusiasts tended to fasten on the explosive action of organized sport, the turn-of-the-century advocates were equally attentive to its intricate restraint. Few institutions so persuasively promised to "tame the beast" within man without losing the benefits of the beast's great energy. Whether conceived as a kind of repressed sexuality or used as a curative for both lassitude and overindulgence, sport addressed Americans' concern over sex during the Victorian age and grasped at a naturalistic solution that retained the primitive while aspiring toward social progress. The comparisons between sport and war depended on the similarity with which they linked primal force to sophisticated management — in other words, on the tailoring of nature to the precepts of the new managerial society. It was this meld of natural, primal power with organization and rationality that William James identified as crucial to American culture in approving sport as a "moral equivalent of war." In a society impatient with metaphysics, rationality and social control were the substitute for contemplation; and, for James as for others, sport assumed a role in linking contemplation and action.

In this age of appreciable change, Americans engaged in a quest for meaning — the moral side of a "search for order"— in which the fusion of contemplation and action loomed as an aching need. On the American scene, it was long customary to confuse thought with purpose or destiny; and the activities of Americans as a whole were thus transformed into a doctrine of missionary zeal and manifest destiny which in turn strengthened the dubious dogma of American exceptionalism. In a small way, the obsession with certifying some sports as distinctively American reflected this thirst for a sense of special purpose and meaning, which, as Edith Wharton suggested, was nearly synonymous with American "innocence." This innocence, this exceptionalism, this sense of America's distinctive purpose, even though largely built on myth, assumed the functional goodness of man if he were in an environment uncorrupted by artificial social institutions. The emergence of sport, corresponding temporally with the resurgence of religious perfectionism, renewed the American tendency to assume the perfectibility of man and society. It was a legacy of the Enlightenment. It was an inheritance from Puritanism. It was the myth of Jacksonian democracy. It was the cultic belief of the scientific experts. In all, it was a firmly lodged component in the American system for dealing with life and its complexities. The sometimes narcissistic pursuit of the perfect body as the badge of the perfect personality and soul was, ironically, a reconciliation of materialism with moral perfectionism. The ultimately enthusiastic reception of sport in America would not have been so easy without these preconditions.

Americans did not need to undertake such intricate considerations of psychology and personal dynamics to be affected by them, nor did they need to reconcile them consciously and coherently with sport. As Carl Jung has pointed out, realities of the *psyche* may exist independent of the realities of the *physis*.

The fact that something may be physically impossible, or at least improbable, does not impeach its psychical truth or psychological impact. But the assumption of underlying order despite material differences added to the effectiveness of the constituent groups making sport a common institution. Each group could deceive itself, when necessary, and expect its special vision of sport to become reality. The odds against them, posed by their differences with other constituent groups, did not automatically break their faith in sport's future as each narrowly defined it. Moreover, as they experienced sport in ways that they had not anticipated, each group could adjust its own mythic sense of sport until some common vision began to take hold.[5]

Sport's respectability — that is, its rise to approved institutional status — came through a social parallel to atomic "critical mass," hinging on the variousness of views about sport's proper form and function. Once sport achieved a certain frequency and distribution, it tended to generate new conditions and advance its own acceptance. It thus became part of the background presence of the culture, a piece in the whole of community life, and one whose very strength inhered in its complexity and seeming self-contradictions. Neil Isaacs has referred to sport as an edifice, suggesting that it needs building codes and maintenance to keep it from collapsing. Yet a more apt model may be a town instead of a megastructure — some complex of related, interacting, but separable elements. They vary in importance over time; and the deterioration or collapse of one structure in the "town-system" does not doom all others, even if it makes moving through the rubble uncomfortable. On the other hand, a certain magnitude (or "critical mass") and diversity (or difference in role) determine its survival as a separate institution. This complexity largely accounts for sport's strength in resisting and repelling serious challenge. Any truly effective attack on sport would need to be conducted on the whole gamut of fronts from which it had originated.[6]

There should be little cause to wonder, then, that change has often come slowly in sport as part of the social system, given the complexity that contributes to its institutional strength. Sport was a series of facts transformed into a myth, and a myth perceived as if it were a fact. Debates over its merits could constantly be shifted from one set of terms to another, from the practical to the ideal, from the actual to the theoretical, from the factual to the mythic. This very form of "double-think," which paralleled seeing spirit and matter as a "double-faced entity," made rigid insistence on the purely factual realm seem unconventional and perhaps even perverse.

A few examples of this psychological and functional complexity make it more clear. Later barriers to ending discrimination toward women in sport seem to stem largely from the fear of women that helped to shape it as an institution. Suggestively, men advocating doctrines of female inferiority also used sporting activities — such as the periodic hunting trips of the Reverend John Todd — to escape fuller familial relationships. Similarly, genteel traditionalists feared women's entry into sport as a potential encroachment on a male domain. Men may have perceived sport more as an intimate and personal sphere than as a social and public one, at least in some circles; and this would help to explain their resistance to women's full participation in sport. The sexual isolation of the male in most sport made it an institution into which men might flee, spend their time, use their energies — avoiding confrontation with women and defining personal values in a largely homosocial environment. Taken as a means of avoiding social contact and fuller heterosexual relationships, sport recalled Tocqueville's observation that males centered on money-getting, a worldly activity that was at once consuming and individualistic. It separated one from women (given the conventions of society), put one in the association of men, sanctified narcissistic self-aggrandizement, and had limitless potential to absorb one's attention. In a later age, when the practical power of the American dream faltered, its mythic properties remained vital in the physical realm of sport. But the male-centeredness of the American economic dream invested itself in sport as well — replete with its ambivalent attitude toward women, its egoism, its male-bonding, and its provision of structured activities that saved men from developing their own patterns of relationship toward women. The intertwining of such psychological and material factors so enmeshed men and women that gender-determined behavior became difficult to alter.[7]

As religion had earlier undergone a "feminization," sport now was largely masculinized; and the two different institutions were not antithetical in role. In its pretense toward regenerative functions, it approximated a religious sensibility for men, albeit material and secular. As Frederic Paxson perceived, sport could be viewed as a "safety valve" in a society where opportunities for free expression and change were diminishing. Even more, it was Paxson's genius to integrate sport into the American ideology of regeneration and to see in sport a behavioral pattern aimed at renewal, simply by linking it to a mythic sense of the land and nature. Sport proclaimed excellence as normal. It smacked of perfectionism, defied age, and scorned death. As hero, the sportsman became the symbol of masculine sacrifice, an Arminian champion whose largely self-generating character assured his successes. Sport was, to a considerable degree, the masculinization of the regenerative myth, even while sparing the more static myth of the "leatherstocking."[8]

Such underlying shifts in the emotional and social basis of sport made it far more agreeable to the devout Christian and far more respectable to the indifferent one. The advocates of sport, whatever their background or goals, universally called attention to its presumed ability to govern the players' will. Success in sport depended on the subordination of the individual to the group in the case of team sport, or on the submission of the individual to an externally established discipline, whether in a team sport or not. This appealed to the long-standing desire of religious leaders, especially those of a conservative or evangelical stripe, to break the "willfulness" of children. Yet it did so in a way which avoided the complications of relationships between male and female, an especially nice advantage in an age when sexuality seemed unusually troublesome. The advocates' emphasis on discipline, order, and hierarchy portrayed sport as a professionally managed supplement — perhaps even an alternative — to traditional agents of discipline such as family and church. Sport involved extreme, even excessive, commitment; but it did so in the name of discipline and order. So sport became a ritual of risk in a society which, although built on venture, increasingly aimed at predictability and insurance.[9]

Sport personalized, concretized, and institutionalized American man's mythic interplay with nature and the continental environment. As Elting Morison has suggested, Frederick Jackson Turner saw the American frontier as a kind of technical system in which Americans established a foothold in an abiding nature. But its merit depended upon the survival of the great bulk of nature as an unconverted and unharnessed force. Neither pure civilization nor absolute nature, American culture occupied the middle ground where the linkages between the two occurred. Even so did sport shun the extremes and serve as a mediator between them.[10]

The imagery of sport provided ties of its own between nature and civilization. For example, sport linked man and machine by suggesting parallels in the workings of both. At a time when man's "feel" of his own society and his relationship to nature on the grand scale had altered, the emergence of sport suggested a reconciliation of man and nature—of man's quality as an animal and his placement in a large natural context, even though it had been modified by the machine. In this respect, the complexity and fluidity of sport resembled the complexity of American attitudes toward nature and represented turn-of-the-century man's hope to have the best of all worlds simultaneously. The study of the human body, which accompanied the growing interest in sport, treated the body as if the "crown of creation" had been mass-produced to specifications in a sacred factory, even as it was finished to perfection in a profane gymnasium. The machine model provided a certain image of the body—efficient, balanced, powerful, but without nonfunctional excess parts—that encouraged the concept of a balanced muscular development advanced by the physical educators and began to set a standard that would last at least a century. Animal vitality took partnership with rational education, man with mechanism, and civilization with nature. The sharp antinomy was blunted.[11]

Neat assertions of a discrete cause for a simple effect fail to account for the rising respectability of sport. The complex and sometimes countervailing forces within sport militate against simple explanation. Yet, at the same time, they suggest the importance of sport as a part of the ongoing cultural development of America. Key areas of historical change in the late nineteenth

234

and early twentieth centuries — with respect to the family, sexuality, social organization, business patterns, attitudes toward modernization and the notion of progress, and many other areas — not only developed contemporaneously with sport but interacted with it in myriad ways. Somewhat like binary stars, they merged into phenomena with identifiably discrete elements which, while autonomous, could not exist without each other. Sport was not a mirror of society but a part of it. More than a microcosm of other elements, sport was a new pattern in the social fabric, novel as an institution, with so many open ends and so many raw edges that it could grasp hold of the double-faced entity that was the American experience and the American mentality.

Notes

PREFACE

1. Surveys of American sport include Betts, *America's Sporting Heritage, 1850–1950* and Lucas and Smith, *Saga of American Sport.* An adaptation of the Turner thesis to the topic is Paxson, "The Rise of Sport." A survey of writings in sport history is Edelman, "Academicians and Athletics," although much has been published since its appearance. For an attempt to set out a typology of what is modern about sport, see Guttmann, *From Ritual to Record.* But also note Caillois, *Les jeux et les hommes;* Loy, "The Nature of Modern Sport"; and Dunning, "The Structural-Functional Properties of Folk-Games and Modern Sports."

2. A survey of early American sport is Holliman, *American Sports, 1785–1835.* On spectacle in a related culture, see Wiles, "Crowd Pleasing Spectacles"; also see Woods, "James J. Corbett: Theatrical Star," for a different slant. On pedestrianism, see Moss, "The Long Distance Runners of Ante-Bellum America." One study of horse racing is Chance, "Fast Horses and Sporting Blood." Concerning early rowing, see Crowther and Ruhl, *Rowing and Track Athletics;* and on the first intercollegiate organization, see Lewis, "The Beginning of Organized Collegiate Sport." On the suppression of sport, see Jable, "Pennsylvania's Early Blue Laws"; and for information on opposition to bloodsports see Jack W. Berryman, "The Ending of American Blood Sports," paper presented at the American Historical Association's 86th meeting, Dec. 1971, New York.

3. The omission of a definition of sport here is deliberate. However, on the spirit of play and its contrast with what he calls "serious activity," see Huizinga, *Homo Ludens: A Study of the Play Element in Culture.*

4. See Higginson, "Saints, and Their Bodies" and, concerning the advice to Dickinson, Edelstein, *Strange Enthusiasm.* Also note Lewis, "The Muscular Christianity Movement."

5. See Persons, *The Decline of American Gentility.*

6. See Kohn, *American Nationalism;* Ryan, *Womanhood in America;* Jones, *The Age of Energy;* Chafe, *The American Woman;* Lasch, *Haven in a Heartless World.*

7. On various responses to evolutionary theory, see Persons, ed, *Evolutionary Thought in America*. On "anti-modernism," see Lears, *No Place of Grace*. Also see Wiebe, *The Search for Order*.

8. Morison, *From Know-How to Nowhere*, 104; Jones, *The Age of Energy*, 17; Lasch, *Haven in a Heartless World*, 23.

9. See Jones, *The Age of Energy*, 14, 343–45.

CHAPTER ONE

1. See, e.g., Lévi-Strauss, *The Savage Mind*.

2. A classic study of religion and the concept of renewal is Frazer, *The Golden Bough*, particularly with respect to the sacrificial instinct.

3. On Puritanism in New England, see Miller, *The New England Mind*. Not all religions equivocated on the questions mentioned; but those long in America were hard pressed to reconcile traditional beliefs with changing conditions in the world.

4. Concerning the Puritans' attitudes toward temporal ritual, see Thomas, *Religion and the Decline of Magic*, especially 51–77 on the intertwining of belief, mentality, and perception of the visible world. On the rising sympathy for the Arminian position in early Protestant culture, see Greven, *The Protestant Temperament*.

5. See Mary Ann Meyers, "Gates Ajar," in *Death in America*, ed. Stannard, referring extensively to nineteenth-century Mormons such as John A. Widtsoe, James E. Talmage, and George A. Smith. On the Mormon experiment, see Arrington and Bitton, *The Mormon Experience* and Arrington, *Great Basin Kingdom*.

6. On transcendentalism and religion, see Hutchinson, *The Transcendentalist Ministers*. Concerning transcendentalists' views on the body, see Park, "The Attitudes of Leading New England Transcendentalists toward Healthful Exercise."

7. For a consideration of Phelps's book in the context of changing attitudes toward death, see Ann Douglas, "Heaven Our Home," in *Death in America*, ed. Stannard. For studies that seek to build a framework on attitudes toward death, see Stannard, *The Puritan Way of Death* and Ariès, *Western Attitudes toward Death*.

8. This does not require subscription to a formal religion or advocacy of a specific creed. Indeed, the exact opposite is true — the impulse toward belief quite outside conventional religion. See, for example, Jung, *The Archetypes and the Collective Unconscious* and *Answer to Job*.

9. See Adorno, "Veblen's Attack on Culture," in Adorno, *Prisms*, especially 81. Concerning the application of an almost religious sensibility toward the machine, see Henry Adams, "The Dynamo and the Virgin."

10. See Giedion, *Mechanization Takes Command*, a remarkable work that anticipated the interest in "mentality" rather than the documentary history of elite groups.

11. The information presented here concerning the history of the bath

comes largely from Giedion, *Mechanization Takes Command*. Also see Troyat, *Daily Life in Russia.*

12. The quotation appears in Giedion, *Mechanization Takes Command,* 634.

13. Contrast entropy with the emphasis on motion and activity in the work of Eadweard Muybridge, Thomas Eakins, and E.J. Marey.

14. See Giedion, *Mechanization Takes Command,* 659.

15. Concerning the body and its relationship to changes in culture, see Kern, *Anatomy and Destiny,* especially "The Body Electric," which describes the Victorian attempt to understand the dynamics of human behavior in terms of nervous system, electrical energy, the transmutation of asceticism into control and power, and the need for joys in the present life.

16. See Brohm, "Twenty Theses on Sport," in Brohm, *Sport — A Prison of Measured Time,* 174. Brohm comments on the matter of sublimation at some length in "The Myth of Educative Sport" in the same book. He specifically calls sport a "libidinal substitute," a means of exploring the body — limb by limb, organ by organ — through controlled and self-inflicted punishment. Hence sport becomes a mortified form of the pleasures of sex and a specific sublimation of death. It becomes a rather perverse way of handling uncontrollable desires, intense anxiety over erotic pleasure, and a compulsive thrust for control. On the tension between pleasure and pain, see Brown, *Life Against Death.*

17. See especially Brohm, "The Significance of Physical Leisure in the 'Leisure Civilization,'" in Brohm, *Sport — A Prison of Measured Time,* 88–101. For Marx, "leisure" meant simply free time.

18. See Brohm, *Sport — A Prison of Measured Time,* esecially 23. Brohm's observation that pain is a deep attraction in sport somewhat parallels late nineteenth century claims for the importance of pain to creativity, as, for example, in the works of Nietzsche. See Kern, *Anatomy and Destiny,* particularly "The Body Electric." All of this is complicated by the fact that there is no clear scientific definition of pain. See, however, Zborowski, *People in Pain,* as well as the work of Matisyohu Weisenberg. Also, for Brohm, problems related to oedipal identification, fantasy, and the like resolve themselves perversely in the narcissism of sports teachers and coaches, in father-figure syndromes (as with coaches and their teams), and in the homosexual quality of friendships in sports.

19. A useful study suggesting Americans' tendency to endow the machine with almost animate qualities is Marx, *The Machine in the Garden.*

20. An interesting study of the efforts of the working class to set their own patterns of play and sporting activity in one northeastern city is Roy Rosenzweig, "Reforming Working-Class Play: The Development of Parks and Playgrounds in Worcester, Massachusetts, 1870–1920," a paper presented at the Conference on Political/Social History, SUNY College at Brockport, Oct. 1978. As an example of industrial paternalism, Henry Ford at one time paid his workers not only according to his evaluation of their productivity but also to his assessment of their morals. See Flink, *The Car Culture.* For a case

study of a company that found sport useful in improving productivity, see Schleppi, "'It Pays.'" On paternalism and recreation in the H.J. Heinz Company, see Alberts, *The Good Provider.*

21. The rise of therapeutic intervention is explored in Lasch, *Haven in a Heartless World.* For a short consideration of Priessnitz, see Giedion, *Mechanization Takes Command,* 662ff.

Although electrophysiology was evidently studied relatively little in America as compared to Europe, there was much interest in the neurosciences from the 1870s onward. The psychologist G. Stanley Hall, for example, had worked at the physiological laboratory established by Henry Pickering Bowditch at Harvard. H. Newell Martin, an outstanding biologist who was deeply interested in the nervous system, was appointed to the Johns Hopkins University; and one of his brightest students, Henry Herbert Donaldson, worked as an instructor in psychology with Hall. See Robert G. Frank *et al.,* "The Neurosciences," in *Advances in American Medicine,* ed. Bowers and Purcell, II, 552–613, which also has an extensive bibliography. Concerning the impact of anesthesia, see Francis D. Moore, "Surgery," in the same volume, 619ff. For information on Lister, see Wangensteen and Wangensteen, "Lister."

22. Tyler, *Freedom's Ferment* places Grahamism in the context of the emerging quest for women's rights. See also Fletcher, *The A.B.–Z. of Our Own Nutrition;* Atwater, *Methods and Results of Investigations of the Chemistry and Economy of Food;* Atwater, "The Chemistry of Foods and Nutrition"; Atkinson, "The Food Question in America and Europe"; and Levenstein, "The New England Kitchen and the Origins of Modern American Eating Habits." Dudley A. Sargent comments on Chittenden's experiments at Yale in his *Physical Education.*

23. On the concept of spermatic economy, see Barker-Benfield, *The Horrors of the Half-Known Life.* Indeed, the fear of exhaustion of human resources paralleled worry over running out of natural resources. On the latter, see Hays, *Conservation and the Gospel of Efficiency.*

24. Concerning the development of institutionalized research and parallels in other areas of American life, see Morison, *From Know-How to Nowhere.*

25. The quotations from Brooks Adams come from his *The Theory of Social Revolutions* and his essay, "The Heritage of Henry Adams," introducing Henry Adams, *The Degradation of the Democratic Dogma.*

26. See Spalding, *America's National Game.*

27. See Roosevelt, "Degeneration and Evolution" and Collier, *England and the English from an American Point of View.*

28. The information concerning Todd is based on Barker-Banfield, *The Horrors of the Half-Known Life.* Todd also contributed to *The Herald of Health and Journal of Physical Culture — Advocates a Higher Type of Manhood — Physical, Intellectual, and Moral.*

29. The quotations appear in Barker-Benfield, *The Horrors of the Half-Known Life,* 156–57.

30. It would appear that avoidance of sexual "vice" and desirable moral character were nearly synonymous for Gardner. The specific refer-

ences are from Barker-Benfield, *The Horrors of the Half-Known Life*, 21 and 231.

31. The concern over stimulation of the senses was widespread. Levenstein points out that the failure of the "New England Kitchen" occurred partly because of the blandness of its food — deemed virtuous by the old New England stock, but merely boring to the southern and eastern European immigrants. See Levenstein, "The New England Kitchen and the Origins of Modern American Eating Habits."

32. See Beard, *Sexual Neurasthenia*, 102–3.

33. See ibid., 103. Engelmann's researches are reported in Meyland, "Harvard University Oarsmen," 372–73. Earlier studies of the physiological effects of sport include Darling, "The Effects of Training" and Finlay, "The Abuses of Training."

CHAPTER TWO

1. Lodge, "Speech at the Alumni Dinner, Harvard Commencement, June 1896," in *Speeches and Addresses*, 293. According to John A. Garraty, Lodge shied away from organized and team sports in his youth, preferring solitary rowing and occasional sparring. But even if Lodge's interest in sport was largely retrospective, it was significant; and his later emphasis on the worth of team sports reflected his mature opinion.See Garraty, *Henry Cabot Lodge*, 24. However, also note Lodge, *Early Memories*, 69 and passim.

2. Hughes toured America (and New England schools especially) during the years when Henry Cabot Lodge was an undergraduate at Harvard. According to Crowther and Ruhl, *Rowing and Track Athletics*, 39, the crew at Cornell was formed specifically in response to urging from Hughes when he was in Ithaca. On the more flexible and adaptive tone of the genteel tradition, see Greven, *The Protestant Temperament*, which is suggestive despite dealing with an earlier period. This argument also conforms to Persons, *The Decline of American Gentility*.

3. On the American "gentry," see Persons, *The Decline of American Gentility*.

4. Lodge, "Speech at the Alumni Dinner, Harvard Commencement, June 1896," 293.

5. Ibid., 293. Lodge cited the American Civil War for its beneficial effect on national character and will, as did his friends Theodore Roosevelt and Francis A. Walker (who guarded the interests of the old blood lines while serving with the U.S. Immigration Service). For an argument correlating reflections on the Civil War with the quest for a moral equivalent to war in the form of sport, see Frederickson, *The Inner Civil War*.

6. Roosevelt, "Morality and Efficiency," in Roosevelt, *American Ideals*, 35. For Roosevelt's youthful athletic interests, see Putnam, *Theodore Roosevelt, The Formative Years*, 142ff; also see Pringle, *Theodore Roosevelt*, 34ff; and Hagedorn, *The Boys' Life of Theodore Roosevelt*, which saw 35 printings by 1940. In addition, see Klein, *In the Land of the Strenuous Life*, 245 and

NOTES TO PAGES 34-44

249, and Roosevelt, *American Ideals*, xvii–xviii. Richard Hofstadter detects anti-intellectualism in Roosevelt's assertion of "character" over intellect. But Hofstadter equates "character" with "morals," missing Roosevelt's sense of it as a single word for the "realizing of ideals." Thus Roosevelt admired historian James Ford Rhodes and Arctic explorer Peary as much as a Carnegie or a Morgan (indeed, more so) since they embodied the mind-in-action which was true character. See Hofstadter, *Anti-intellectualism in American Life*, 207–8.

7. Roosevelt, "The American Boy," in *The Works of Theodore Roosevelt, XII*, 130–31. Failing to distinguish between war and sport falsely equated two autonomous variables. Others did use a language of equivalence, claiming that "Baseball is War!" (to cite Albert Spalding), but not Roosevelt or Lodge.

8. Efforts of Harvard alumni to regulate and manage sport and athletics include Hemenway et al., "Important Suggestions on Athletics"; White, "The Constitution, Authority, and Policy of the Committee on the Regulation of Athletic Sports"; and Gardiner, "The Graduate Athletic Association." Alumni also sought to reform specific sports, often influenced by physical educators. See Emmons, "Needed Football Reforms." For opinions from several college presidents, see Butler, "Shall Football Be Ended or Mended?"

9. See Sargent, *Physical Education*, 53–55. Sargent began as a gymnast and performed in a traveling circus. Born in Belfast, Me. in 1849, he became physical director at Bowdoin College at the age of twenty. He spent the late decades of the century overseeing the program at Harvard.

10. Sargent, *Physical Education*, 57, 69; Roosevelt, "The American Boy," 128–29, 132, and "Manhood and Statehood," in *The Works of Theodore Roosevelt, XII*, 212.

11. Hall, "Some Relations Between Physical and Mental Training." For an analysis of Hall's significance in education, see Cremin, *The Transformation of the School*. On Hall's influence in psychology, especially with respect to adolescence, see Kett, *Rites of Passage*.

12. Boller, "Physical Training," 26.

13. Hough, "A Review of Swedish Gymnastics," 50–51.

14. Although their family origins and economic backgrounds would not always have suggested their inclusion in an American gentry, many Army and Navy officers came from established and distinguished families. More important, the emphasis on tradition and on a moral tone of sacrifice, service, and discipline united the military to the gentry. Although a common economic and social background was at best incomplete, the sharing of values was general. Significantly, an officer was considered a gentleman in an age that did not use the term loosely; and officers were welcome as members and guests of exclusive clubs.

15. Story, introduction to Lea, *The Valor of Ignorance*, xix–xx; Lea, *The Valor of Ignorance*, 27.

16. Ibid., 40–42.

17. For Brooks Adams's specific remarks, see *The Law of Civilization and Decay*, vii–xi.

18. Adams, *The Degradation of the Democratic Dogma*, 142. This work and its companion letter to teachers of history were drafted in 1910.

19. Roosevelt's review of *The Law of Civilization and Decay* is reprinted in *The Works of Theodore Roosevelt*, VIII, 259–60. Brooks Adams's remarks concerning "energetic material" recall and resemble the language of the "spermatic economy" and the fear of exhaustion.

20. Roosevelt, review, in *The Works of Theodore Roosevelt*, VIII, 259–60.

21. Roosevelt, "Degeneration and Evolution," 96–97, 101, 108.

22. Hough, "A Review of Swedish Gymnastics," 49–50. For a balanced view of Shafter, see Cosmas, *An Army for Empire*. Apart from his obesity, Shafter had a reputation as a bully, a failing that Roosevelt specifically disparaged in "The American Boy."

23. Specific references to the Tennis Cabinet and to Roosevelt's other activities are in Gardner, *Departing Glory*, passim. Other tennis partners included Henry L. Stimson and James Garfield.

24. "National Rifle Tournament" [a photographic essay], 6–7, 10–11; "President Roosevelt in Yellowstone Park," 8–13, 22.

25. "D-e-e-lighted to Hear It," 2.

26. "The Strenuous Relatives of President Roosevelt," 7, 17.

27. The athletic events associated with the Paris World's Fair of 1900 were actually the games of the Second Olympiad, held contemporaneously and listed in the Fair's program simply as "International Games" (much to the chagrin of the Baron Pierre de Coubertin).

28. On Wood's activities in sport, see Lane, *Armed Progressive*, 20–21; also, Clifford, *The Citizen Soldiers*, 38–39. For the Army, an extended march in training was usually called a hike. Further, while at the Presidio of San Francisco, Wood took troops to Sequoia National Park for field exercises, further confusing civilian and military hiking.

29. Wood to Hamilton Holt, 26 September 1914, quoted in Hagedorn, *Leonard Wood*, II, 149.

30. Clifford, *The Citizen Soldiers*, 6.

31. Parkhurst, "The Practical Education of the Soldier," 946–50. I am indebted to John Langellier for calling much of this material to my attention.

32. Foote, "Military Gymnastics," 243–45.

33. "Comment and Criticism" (May 1891), 662–70.

34. "Comment and Criticism" (Nov. 1892), 1182–86.

35. Donworth, "Gymnasium Training in the Army," 508–15. For a popular survey of sport at Fort Riley, Kansas, see Cantwell, "They Led the Life of Riley," 106–28.

36. Evans, "Why Athletics Should Be Fostered in the Navy," 5. Evans had commanded the U.S.S. *Iowa* under Rear Admiral Sampson in the defeat of the Spanish Admiral Cervera off Santiago.

37. "A Great Athletic Body," 2. College catalogues included military drill in the physical training program. See, for example, the *Harvard University Catalogue* for 1895–96, 521ff.

38. Godkin, "Athletics and Health," 457; Roosevelt, "Manhood and Statehood," 212.

39. James, "The Moral Equivalent of War," in James, *The Writings of William James*, ed. McDermott, 668.

40. Ibid.; James, "The Moral Philosopher and Moral Life" (1891), reprinted in James, *The Will to Believe*, 213. For a nearly sarcastic "immoral equivalent" of war in "periodic saturnalia" so that their horror would act as "vaccination against the sure pestilence of war," see Bourne, "Twilight of Idols" (1917) in Bourne, *The World of Randolph Bourne*, 193–94. Also note Bourne, "The Undergraduate," 197–98.

41. Roosevelt, "The Manly Virtues and Practical Politics" (1894), in Roosevelt, *American Ideals*, 40–41; Roosevelt, "The American Boy," 130–31. On Roosevelt's desire for moderation in sport, see Lewis, "Theodore Roosevelt's Rule in the 1905 Football Controversy," 717–24, and Moore, "Football's Ugly Decades," 49–68, which overstates Roosevelt's influence. In the 1904 season, 21 players died, and another 200 were injured. Some 30 players died in the 1909 season.

42. See Clifford, *The Citizen Soldiers*, 58, 94.

43. Adams, *The Law of Civilization and Decay*, 164ff.

44. Gettell, "The Value of Football," 139–42. On the impact of wartime athletics upon subsequent civilian sport, see Lewis, "World War I and the Emergence of Sport for the Masses." Also note Camp, "Industrial Athletics"; Foster, "Why Our Soldiers Learn to Box"; "How Uncle Sam Has Created an Army of Athletes"; and Lewis, "The Military Olympics at Paris, France, 1919."

CHAPTER THREE

1. Fletcher, *The A.B.-Z. of Our Own Nutrition*; Taylor, *Scientific Management*.

2. Sargent, *Physical Education*, 82, 84. Only half in jest, Edward R. Bushnell wrote: "Athletically speaking, what is a minor college, any way, but one that can furnish good practise for the large universities, always taking care not to subject them to defeat?" Bushnell, "The Minor Colleges' Gridiron Outlook," 2.

3. Sargent, "Strength Tests and the Strong Men of Harvard," 513–25.

4. Sargent, "The Hemenway Gymnasium," 169–80; Putnam, "Required Gymnastics at Harvard," 30–36; Greenleaf, "Student Diet at Harvard," 171–83; and Sargent, *Physical Education*, 82.

5. Sargent, *Physical Education*, 52, 55, 58. On the need to limit exercise properly, see Hutchinson, "Exercise and its dangers," 601–7, and "Real Danger of Athletics," 168–73. Also see Darling, "Medical Supervision of Athletes," 190–96.

6. McKenzie, "Building the Physical Side of College Men," 4.

7. Hall, *A Collection of College Words and Customs*.

8. Metzger, "Who Will Win the Intercollegiate Regatta of 1906?" 9.

9. Quoted in Camp, "Harvard's Rowing Invasion of England," 8; Metzger, "Who Will Win the Intercollegiate Regatta of 1906?" 9. Although Metzger thought it foolish to oppose daily workouts, other writers recommended recuperation and rest to ward off "staleness." See Darling, "The Effects of Training."

10. Bushnell, "Colleges and Schools," 146.
11. Stauffer, "Why George Woodruff Went to Coach Carlisle," 4–5; Bushnell, "Football Prospects of the East's 'Big Six,'" 4.
12. Downey, "The Middle West's College Baseball Champions," 6.
13. Paine, "Harvard's Athletes for 1904," 22. The precise explanation for the gradual increase in the emphasis on winning among students and alumni at Ivy League schools remains unclear. However, those calling for improvements in the athletic program at Harvard, for example, sought success against members of their own kind at other Ivy League schools, hinting at some accommodation of gentility with competition and also at the maintenance of class distinctions. Thayer, "Harvard's Loss of Athletic Prestige," 31–37.
14. Lang, "The Problem of Professional Rowing Coaches," 2. Also, on amateurism in rowing, see Crowther and Ruhl, *Rowing and Track Athletics*.
15. Bushnell, "With the College Athletes" (27 Jan. 1906), 17. The phrase is from Roy A. Thomas, who had coached at the University of Pennsylvania and was irritated by their lack of commitment to his sport. Thomas, "Teaching Baseball—Major League Comment," 6.
16. Ibid., 7. The coaches were Thomas McCarthy, John J. O'Brien, Frank Rudderham, and John Irwin respectively.
17. Bushnell, "With the Colleges Athletes" (20 Jan. 1906), 17. By context, the term *trainer* here means *coach*.
18. Crowther and Ruhl, *Rowing and Track Athletics*, 110–11; Ten Eyck, "Relative to Crew Rowing—Sculls versus Sweeps," 2.
19. Sheldon, *Student Life and Customs*, 239. The term *trainer* can refer to a person with a principal role in a sporting endeavor, as in boxing or horse racing. Even there, however, the emphasis on expertise is clear, despite differences in terminology from football or baseball. In the latter case, usage distinguishes between *coach* and *manager*. To make matters more complex, *trainer* was sometimes used to mean the coach of a team. Here, however, *trainer* will be used to refer to a person working primarily as an aid to a coach and his team.
20. *Oxford English Dictionary*, s.v. "Training."
21. See Willoughby, "When Sandow Visited California," 72–77.
22. The *Post* article is featured in Brousseau, *Looking Forward*, 291.
23. Ibid., 292.
24. Ibid.
25. Ibid., 290.
26. Ibid., 294. Recall that various scientists speculated on the importance of electricity in the body, as in the nervous system. Thus, it is no surprise that popularizers sought to market products by pretending to be on the cutting edge of science.
27. Ibid., 292.
28. Edwards, "What the Year Has Brought Forth at Princeton," 11; Kaempffert, *The Book of Modern Marvels*, 229, 230; Camp, "General Prospects of Yale's Football Champions," 11, which shows a primitive tackling dummy evi-

dently regarded as something of a novelty and a proof of the forward-looking attitude of the teams.

29. Kaempffert, *The Book of Modern Marvels*, 231–34, has examples of machines used in training for baseball. Illustrations of rowing machines accompany Paine, "Columbia's Athletic Prospects," 4–5.

30. "Penn. State—Athletic Stars of Pennsylvania—Mercersburg," 12.

31. Courtney, "Teaching College Men the Art of Rowing," 2; Hutchins, "Reconstructing the Game of Football," 2; "Mishaps of the Football Campaign," 2. A strong attack on football is Clurman, "Is It Not Time for Parents to Act?" 5. Also see Thwing, "Football: Is the Game Worth Saving?" with opinions from various college presidents.

32. Handley, "The Outdoor Swimming Season of 1906," 132–33.

33. Daniels, "How American Swimming Was Revolutionized," 2. In addition to his work in journalism, Handley was a successful swimmer and captain of the team at the New York Athletic Club.

34. Green, "Looking After Baseball Players' Physical Side," 2; Orth, "The Pitcher's Viewpoint of the Game of Baseball," 2; "The Younger Experts' Newport Tennis Duel," 13.

35. Fletcher, *The A.B.–Z. of Our Own Nutrition*, xii, 22; Williams, "The Chemistry of Cookery," 773–80.

36. MacFadden, *Physical Culture Cook Book*, iv.

37. Mathews, ed., *A Dictionary of Americanism*, II.

38. Sangree, "How a Big League Baseball Team is Prepared," 6.

39. "A Mutiny with a Moral," 2.

40. "Is Athletic Training Overdone?" 2.

41. Crowther and Ruhl, *Rowing and Track Athletics*, 227–28.

42. Godkin, "The Athletic Craze," 422.

43. Allen and Olmsted, "Schoolboy Athletics in American Schools," 2; Stearns and Browne, "Schoolboy Athletics from the Master's Viewpoint," 2.

44. Huntington, *Home and College*, 14, 30–36, 41–50. Note that Higginson was not primarily an advocate of sport, let alone athletics, but rather of fitness and health, even though he later supervised studies of the relationship between athletics and health. See van Allen, "Vital Statistics of College-Bred Men."

45. Godkin, "Athletics and Health," 458.

46. Sheldon, *Student Life and Customs*, 245–47. Also see Richards, "Intercollegiate Athletics and Faculty Control," as well as White, "The Constitution, Authority, and Policy of the Committee on the Regulation of Athletic Sports." President Eliot is quoted in Sheldon, *Student Life and Customs*, 242.

47. Hartwell is quoted in *Report of the United States Commissioner of Education*, 558–59.

48. Wiebe, *The Search for Order*, 112–13.

CHAPTER FOUR

1. Hofstadter, *Social Darwinism in American Thought* states the concept of status anxiety. Bannister, *Social Darwinism* is its sharpest and best cri-

tique. Persons, *The Decline of American Gentility* remains useful. The pertinent point here is not how much socioeconomic difference there was among groups nor how uniformly they divided along class lines or family background, but rather that there were differences in sensibility — obvious in behavior and the literature about it — which appeared inside class lines and across them. In short, the structure of society is less the issue here than the patterns of mentality; and, although often related, they are not always so. Nor are they identical.

2. Boyle, *Sport — Mirror of American Life* recognizes the role of the very rich in advancing certain sports. Significantly, he doubts that his readers will believe him.

3. Veblen, *The Theory of the Leisure Class*, especially 255–72. Also see Collier, *England and the English from an American Point of View*, 228; Martin, *The Passing of the Idle Rich*, 6.

4. "Fox Hunting in an Automobile," 10.

5. *Illustrated Outdoor News* 1 (Dec. 1906).

6. Thomas, "Teaching Baseball," 7.

7. Spalding, *America's National Game*, 6.

8. Barney, "The American Sportswoman," 276.

9. Macdonald, *Scotland's Gift*.

10. Curry, "Yachting as a Sport for the People," 10–11. Also see Spahr, *An Essay on the Present Distribution of Wealth;* King et al., *The Wealth and Income of the People of the United States*. In 1904, when Curry called yachting universal, bacon cost 18¢ per pound, butter 28¢, sugar 30¢, and a five-pound sack of flour sold for 16¢. In short, the industrial worker of 1904 could buy and use a small power launch if he ceased eating, spent nothing on shelter, had no medical expenses, and used the boat rarely enough to keep his fuel bill low.

11. Curry, "Yachting as a Sport for the People," 10–11.

12. O'Hagan, "The Athletic Girl," 734–35.

13. Barney, "The American Sportswoman," 268, 269–73, passim.

14. Ibid., 265–66.

15. Burton, "Hats and Boots for the Sportswoman," 18–19; "Modish Raiment for the Sportswoman," 16.

16. Barney, "The American Sportswoman," 266.

17. "The Sportswoman," 16.

18. Strong, "Great Britain's Famous Women of the Hunt," 8–9.

19. "Dogs of High Degree and Their Titled Mistresses," 8–9.

20. Sargent, "Ideals in Physical Education," 223.

21. See Chandler, *Strategy and Structure* for a consideration of vertical and horizontal integration in the context of American business.

22. I am indebted to David K. Wiggins for references to the accounts of nineteenth-century travelers in America.

23. See Bradley, *Such Was Saratoga* for its role as a resort.

24. Bledstein, *The Culture of Professionalism* discusses the concept of enclosure in "Space and Words," 46–79. Bledstein specifically refers to sporting spaces, such as stadiums and country clubs, 6off.

25. Van Rensselaer, *Newport,* provides much information on life during the fashionable summer seasons.

26. Ibid., passim.

27. Even the Prince of Wales was unable to arrange for Sir Thomas's admission into the Royal Yacht Squadron.

28. "Scenes from Sporting Life," in O'Connor, *The Golden Summers* is valuable.

29. Morgan is quoted in O'Connor, *The Golden Summers,* 131.

30. Elliott is quoted in ibid., 135.

31. The phrase comes from an obituary of tennis champion "Dicky" Sears, quoted in ibid., 146.

32. See Persons, *The Decline of American Gentility,* 43, 50, 65.

33. Allen, *The Great Pierpont Morgan,* 188–94; Satterlee, *J. Pierpont Morgan.* A useful and engaging study suggesting the social role of leisure and sport is Hoyt, *The Vanderbilts and Their Fortunes.*

34. Potter, *People of Plenty* deserves attention as a way of modifying Frederic Paxson's application of the concept of the "safety valve" to sport. Much as Potter suggests that the contours of American character were formed with respect to abundance, one may profitably assess how abundance has shaped American sport.

35. Sheldon, *Student Life and Customs,* 232–35, 237–38. Also see Roosevelt, "'Professionalism' in Sports," 187, 190–91.

36. Hemenway et al., "Important Suggestions in Athletics," 191–96.

37. Gardiner, "The Graduate Athletic Association," 344–51. Also see Sargent, "Ideals in Physical Education," 221–26.

38. Godkin, "The Athletic Craze," 422–23.

39. See "Rowing," a subsection in the "Athletics" column, *Harvard Graduates' Magazine* 12 (March 1904) 449; Hall, "The Money Rule in Athletics"; Hall, "The Pitfall of Athletics."

40. Bushnell, "With the College Athletes," 14.

41. Crowther and Ruhl, *Rowing and Track Athletics,* 161–62, 164, 169ff, 178ff. The extended quotation is from Paret, "Importing Canadian Professionals for Ice Hockey," 8.

42. Roosevelt, "'Professionalism' in Sports," 188–89.

CHAPTER FIVE

1. Although some of sport's advocates may be grouped by social and economic interests, the identification of women as a separate constituency is somewhat more subtle. Ranging from the working class through the heights of industrial and financial wealth, women lacked socioeconomic coherence. Yet, to the extent that women were legally and socially disadvantaged with respect to men, they may be said to form a "class" of sorts. More critically, to the extent that they had consciousness and sensibility different from men (whether they confirmed or challenged inequality), women assumed a separable identity.

2. The quotations are from Greeley-Smith, "New York Women and the Art of Fencing," 4–5; O'Hagan, "The Athletic Girl," 733; Sandys, "The Place That Woman Occupies in Sport," 11. Sandys blamed men for woman's removal from sport—men who "bowed about the limpid figure, who penned sonnets to its eyebrows, hung on its whispered words, swore it was the perfection of feminine grace and beauty." Ryan, *Womanhood in America* is a good study of women in the nineteenth century. Also see Chafe, *The American Woman*. The idea that economic factors affected women's perception of their roles appears in Gilman, *Women and Economics* and in the work of Thorstein Veblen. A similar view is expressed in Nearing and Nearing, *Woman and Social Progress*, in which they also rely on Dudley Sargent's studies to call for dress reform. On that issue, also see Bloomer, *Life and Writings of Amelia Bloomer*.

3. Manice, "Women and Their Relation to Outdoor Recreation," 6; Sandys, "The Place That Woman Occupies in Sport."

4. Smith, "Women as Cyclers," 318.

5. Ibid.

6. Ibid.

7. Barney, "The American Sportswoman," 263–64.

8. Ibid.

9. Sanford, "Girls in Athletics," 2; "Two Views of Athletics for Women," 5.

10. Editorial, *Illustrated Sporting News* 2 (2 April 1904), 2.

11. Ibid.; Herrick, "Schoolgirl Athletes on the Track and Field," 14–15.

12. "Wisconsin's Athletic Girls," 6.

13. Spalding, *America's National Game*, 11–13.

14. Ibid., 7.

15. Sandys, "The Place That Woman Occupies in Sport," 11.

16. Boller, "Physical Training," 25–26.

17. Ibid.

18. Sargent, *An Autobiography*, 36. Also see Barker-Benfield, *The Horrors of the Half-Known Life*, particularly concerning notions about male sexuality and the danger of proximity to women.

19. Garrigues, "Woman and the Bicycle," 582–87.

20. Potter, "The Bicycle Outlook," 786.

21. White, "The New Athletics," 46–52.

22. See de Koven, "Bicycling for Women," 392–94. Although Barker-Benfield, *The Horrors of the Half-Known Life* has been criticized over the question of actual frequency of hysterectomies and ovariotomies, what is crucial here is the association of sexual organs with hysteria and insanity.

23. Adam, *Sandow on Physical Training*, 156–57.

24. See Smith, "The Rise of Basketball for Women in Colleges," 18–36.

25. Ibid., for quotations from Berenson and Hill. Also see Berenson, *Basket Ball for Women* and Hill, *Athletic and Out-Door Sports for Women*.

26. Paine, "Physical Training in Women's Colleges—Smith," 3.

27. Ibid., 4.

28. Paine, "Athletics at Women's Colleges—Bryn Mawr," 6.

29. Paine, "Athletics in Women's Colleges — Mount Holyoke,"4.
30. Sargent, "Ideals in Physical Education," 225.
31. "Women and Basketball," 60.
32. For material quoted in this paragraph, I am indebted to Judith A. Davidson, "The Homosocial World of Intercollegiate Athletics," unpublished paper, presented at the 1978 meeting of the North American Society for Sport History, Windsor, Ontario.
33. For a significant preliminary description of diversity of interests and purposes among women in the late nineteenth century, see "The Paradox of 'Woman's' Sphere," in Berkin and Norton, *Women of America*, 139–49.

CHAPTER SIX

1. The literature on nationalism is large. For an overview, see Kohn, *The Idea of Nationalism* and also *American Nationalism*. In the American case, however, more useful specific studies are Marx, *The Machine in the Garden;* Potter, *People of Plenty;* and Boorstin, *The Americans*. Significantly, all of these authors emphasize the importance of things over consciously formulated ideas in American culture.
2. Roosevelt, *The Winning of the West*, I, 1–27, 92, 108. The belief that conditioning and environment shaped one's racial inheritance helps to account for widespread fear among whites over participating in sporting events with blacks — not to say this was an exclusive cause.
3. Hough, "A Review of Swedish Gymnastics," 52–53. The term *Swedish gymnastics* was also applied in America to the physical training taught by the German turners. A valuable analysis of the decline of formalism is White, *Social Thought in America*. Also see the example of Ehinger, "Report to the Executive Committee of the North American Gymnastic Union," 195–98.
4. This paragraph relies on Redmond, *The Caledonian Games in Nineteenth-Century America*, an informative study.
5. References to "Anthropology Days" appear in Schaap, *An Illustrated History of the Olympics*, 76. On Carlisle, see Stauffer, "Why George Woodruff Went to Coach Carlisle," 5.
6. Camp and Deland, *Football*, 47–52.
7. Ibid., 48–49. Thorstein Veblen pointed out, with barbed wit, that the so-called manly virtues might not be quite what they were cracked up to be. For example, self-reliance and team-spirit could as readily be described as truculence and clannishness. Veblen, *The Theory of the Leisure Class*, 268–69.
8. Ibid., 48, iv.
9. Sargent, *Physical Education*, 102–3.
10. On changes in the meaning of "wilderness," see Nash, *Wilderness and the American Mind*.
11. Camp and Deland, *Football*, iii, 53, note D. It is appropriate that all of the sports cited for praise were team sports, including "boating," which

referred to competitive sailing with organized crews in some usages and to rowing in a crew in others.

12. Paine, "Why Baseball is the Greatest American Pastime," 5–6, 17.

13. Spalding, *America's National Game,* 19.

14. I am indebted to Peter Levine of Michigan State University for sharing preliminary findings from his study of Spalding.

15. Spalding, *America's National Game,* 4–9.

16. Chadwick "Old Time Baseball," 420–22; Steele, "How the National Game Developed," 333–36.

17. Interview with Spalding by Edward Marshall, first published in *New York Times,* 13 Nov. 1910, in Spalding, *America's National Game,* 534.

18. Ibid., 538.

19. See, e.g., Eggleston, *The Transit of Civilization.*

20. See Mrozek, "The Image of the West in American Sport," 3–14. For convenient access to microfilm versions of *Western Field* and *Chicago Field,* see Mrozek and Richards, eds., *Sports Periodicals.*

21. See Northam and Berryman, "Sport and Urban Boosterism in the Pacific Northwest."

22. Crowther and Ruhl, *Rowing and Track Athletics,* 168–87.

23. For data on early football, see Weyand, *American Football,* passim, 467–74. Weyand captained Army's football team in 1915.

24. Walker, "College Athletics," 13.

25. An interesting assessment of ideas behind the national parks is Runte, *National Parks.* Also see Ekirch, *Man and Nature in America.* Luminism and transcendentalism are linked in Conron, "'Bright American Rivers'"; also see Miller, "Kindred Spirits."

26. On proposals to modify the parks, see selected passages in Sutton and Sutton, *Yellowstone.* On access and roadways, see Buchholtz, "No Trail Too Steep," 96ff.

27. Muir, *Our National Parks,* 2–3, 17–18. Also note Bradshaw, "Trying Out the Future," which observes that more places have been named in honor of Muir in California than for any one else.

28. Giedion, *Mechanization Takes Command* reveals the deep impulse toward machine-solutions. On monumentalism, see Runte, *National Parks.*

29. On the forced eruption of geysers, see Sutton and Sutton, *Yellowstone.*

30. The tree-firing appears in Buchholtz, "No Trail Too Steep." On movement, see Pettigrew, *Animal Locomotion.*

CHAPTER SEVEN

1. Walker, "College Athletics," 2–4.

2. Ibid.

3. "The Point of View," paragraphs on the subject of "The Rule of the Bicycle," 783–84. In *The Social Basis of Religion,* Simon Patten, professor of political economy at the University of Pennsylvania, observed that in the

20th century "a pleasure economy has displaced the pain economy" of earlier years.

4. For Beecher's views on the origins of diseases, see Ann Douglas Wood, "'The Fashionable Diseases': Women's Complaints and Their Treatment in Nineteenth-Century America," in Hartman and Banner, eds., *Clio's Consciousness Raised*, 1–22. Also see Betts, "Mind and Body in Early American Thought" and Park, "'Embodied Selves.'"

5. Davies, *Phrenology, Fad and Science;* George Combe, *Notes on the United States,* particularly I, 206ff., and II, 44ff., 148ff.; Andrew Combe, *Observations on Mental Derangement;* and Sizer, *Forty Years in Phrenology.*

6. See Regina Morantz, "The Lady and Her Physician," in Hartman and Banner, *Clio's Consciousness Raised,* 38–53, but especially 45. Also see Davies, *Phrenology, Fad and Science,* 109.

7. Sargent, *Physical Education,* 76. Also Camp and Deland, Football provides an excellent example of the intensive study of training and shaping the body, especially 296–315.

8. See *OED,* II, 786–88. The use of the word *conditioner* first assumes meaning as an agent to improve physical condition in the Dec. 1888 issue of the *American Farmer* (Chicago). *Conditioning* assumes a comparable meaning in *Land and Water* in 1889 in connection with dog biscuits. Also see Marey, *Animal Mechanism.*

9. See Muybridge, *The Human Figure in Motion. Animals in Motion,* an abridgment, copyrighted in 1899, included some human figures along with a majority of nonhuman subjects, suggesting the indiscrimination between the human being and traditionally "lower" forms of life. Also see Dercum, "A Study of Some Normal and Abnormal Movements Photographed by Muybridge," in Muybridge, *Animal Locomotion,* 108–33.

10. Bain, *The Senses and the Intellect,* especially 265ff.

11. Fletcher, *The A.B.-Z. of Our Own Nutrition,* 180. Pavlov's early lectures had already been circulated in the U.S. by the publisher, Lippincott; also, Pavlov, "Scientific Study of the So-Called Psychical Processes in the Higher Animals" (1906) in Pavlov, *Lectures on Conditioned Reflexes,* 82, 95; Chittenden, "Physiological Economy in Nutrition," quoted in Fletcher, *The A.B.-Z of Our Own Nutrition,* 73–74.

12. Fletcher, *The A.B.-Z of Our Own Nutrition,* 53–54; Chittenden is quoted in Fletcher, 77. Chittenden makes clear that consumption of rich foods and excessive quantities constituted conspicuous consumption, a mere display to signify status but one that damaged health. The circumstances of the test procedures appear on 60–71.

13. Bain, *Mind and Body,* 131. In his essay on "Human Immortality," James still asserted that the "special stream of consciousness" formed in the unity of the mind and body would pass away as if it had been a veil. In the same essay, he dismissed fears that individual immortality is impossible because there would be insufficient space for the souls throughout eternity. Sir Arthur Conan Doyle also tied material events to spiritual forces, although he saw the physical world depending on the spiritual realm rather than equal to it.

World War I, for example, became a gigantic clash between spirits in which nation-states on the physical earth were mere pawns. See, Meikle, "'Over There,'" 23–37.

14. Hough, "A Review of Swedish Gymnastics," 51–52.

15. Bain, *Mind and Body*, 132.

16. Ibid., 195–96. Also see Bain, *The Senses and the Intellect*.

17. Schmidt and Miles, *The Training of the Body*, 45–46, 49.

18. Ibid., 52–54.

19. Jenks, *The Political and Social Significance of the Life and Teachings of Jesus*, 73–83. Jenks was Professor of Political Economy and Politics. Also see "An Old Boy," *Notes for Boys (and Their Fathers)*, 115–23. The author sees all wholesome acts as forms of religious devotion and rates various sports and games according to their personal and social worth. Also see the lucid essay "Evolution and Theology in America" by Stow Persons, in Persons, ed., *Evolutionary Thought in America*. But note the skeptical Gill, *The Evolution of Christianity*, which sees modern ideas about God as independent of the supernatural. Despite theological differences, all agreed on the worth of the body.

20. Jenks, *Life Questions of High School Boys*, 16, 27–28, 62, 70, 138–39. Also see Stevens, *The Teaching of Jesus*, by a Yale theologian who argued that Christ considered man worthy but demanded constructive action from him. In *Jesus' Principles of Living*, 76, Jenks claimed divine approval of games and sports by inferences drawn from the New Testament. Kent and Jenks wrote: "[Christ's] reference to the game played by the children on the streets indicates that he was familiar with it and suggests as a boy he was fond of sports with which to relieve the tedium of the monotonous life at Nazareth." The little children whom Christ ordered his disciples to allow near him "recognized that he sympathized with them in their love of play."

21. Beecher is quoted in Hopkins, *History of the Y.M.C.A. in North America*, 32. But a critical view of the Y.M.C.A. is McBride, *Culture Clash — Immigrants and Reformers*, 62–83. The minister from Troy, New York wrote in Boston's *Young Men's Magazine* 2 (April 1889), 7, quoted in Hopkins, *History of the Y.M.C.A. in North America*, where *The Watchman* is also quoted, 248.

22. Hopkins, *History of the Y.M.C.A. in North America*, 255.

23. Ibid., 251–70, provides an account of Gulick's work introducing sport into the Y.M.C.A.'s programs.

24. Cheley, *Stories for Talks to Boys*, 108–10.

25. Alexander, *Boy Training*. Brooks and Strong are quoted on 80–81. The direct quotation from Alexander is on 161. In his introduction to Alexander's book, Chief Scout Ernest Thompson Seton speaks of a boy passing through the "well-known stages of race development," in which he recapitulates the racial history. "Babies are little helpless animals, Small boys are monkeys, Boys are selfish brutes, Lads savages with no real religion . . . ," and so on through life. Dr. William Burdick, in his essay on "Adolescence," recommended that first attention be given to the trunk muscles and to developing arms and thighs which "came to our use in the fish age."

253

26. See Patten, *The Social Basis of Religion*, 209; Gladden, *Social Salvation*, 148–49; Rauschenbusch, *Christianizing the Social Order*, 417, and Rauschenbusch, *The Social Principles of Jesus*, written as a voluntary study course for the Y.M.C.A.; Social Service Commission, Y.M.C.A., *Social Service Message*, 57–59; Peabody, *Jesus Christ and the Social Question;* Mathews, *The Social Teaching of Jesus.*

27. Association Press advertisements ran in their own publications, such as Robinson, *The Wage-Earning Boy*, 109–11.

28. Ibid., 32–33, 38–40. Assessing sports for their moral value is Edwards, *Popular Amusements*, 104.

29. Fiske, *Boy Life and Self-Government*, 116, 189, 105–6.

30. There was considerable interest in neoclassical style in art and architecture during the antebellum years, shown in various public buildings and notoriously in Horatio Greenough's statue of George Washington, draped with a toga and naked to the waist. In the late part of the century, however, classical forms were offered as guides for individuals to follow in developing their own bodies.

31. Crowther and Ruhl, *Rowing and Track Athletics*, 282–83. However, S.F. Taylor, President of Missouri's Stephens College said, in 1904, that a man who played football was "a fool" and the college president who let him was "encouraging brutality and a spirit of crime." *The Illustrated Sporting News* of 6 February 1904 called this a "twisted viewpoint" that proved Taylor fit only for "embroidery, knitting and other 'elegant accomplishments.'"

32. Emily Grant Hutchings, "Types of Beauty as Decided by Art," in *The Women's Athenaeum*, I, 88–89. She gives a complete outline of the ideal woman on 97–98, specifying the relative measurements to be applied to all parts of the body.

33. Minna Gordon Gould, "Physical Action and Beauty," in *The Women's Athenaeum*, I, 214–19. In the same volume, Catharine E. Beecher wrote in detail on "Physical Education and Physiology," 253–87.

34. Mary Coolidge Fish, "Physical Education and 'The Body Beautiful,'" in *The Women's Athenaeum*, I, 202–13. The emphasis on the value of movement broadly suggested the need to reform dress for women, and also for men, albeit less dramatically.

35. See Tomkins, *Merchants and Masterpieces*, 49–58. The quotation on Victorian art is from Gregory Hedberg, quoted in Green, "Re-creation of Olympus," 48–57.

36. "Beauty in Art and Nature," *Women's Athenaeum*, I, 182–83.

37. Fitz, "Problems of Physical Education," 27–28.

38. Deming, "College Boating in the Sixties," 416–19.

39. Sargent, *Physical Education*, 58, 104.

40. Pettigrew, *Animal Locomotion*, 1–2.

41. Adam, *Sandow on Physical Training*, 2–3. Walter Camp underscored the need for "constant waste and repair," so that the death of cells and even human beings became positive and life-giving. Camp and Deland, *Football*, 308.

42. Adam, *Sandow on Physical Training*, 12–15.
43. Walker, "College Athletics," 18.

CHAPTER EIGHT

1. Howells is quoted in Noble, *The Eternal Adam*, 78.
2. See Isaacs, *Jock Culture U.S.A.*, passim, and Smith, "Ty Cobb, Babe Ruth and the Changing Image of the Athletic Hero," 73–85. Wecter, *The Hero in America* refers to only two sports heroes — swimmer Gertrude Ederle and golfer Bobby Jones. Nor does Wecter distinguish between heroes of character and heroes of action, which is important to Isaacs and pertinent to the present argument.

It is tantalizing that secular heroism in America varied inversely with religious enthusiasm. In the seventeenth century, for example, military heroism seems to have been almost nonexistent in New England; but it became important in the 18th century when human agency vied with divine favor in explaining military success. This tendency appears to have strengthened in the 19th century. See Ferling, "The New England Soldier," 26–45.

3. Turner, *Reckoning with the Beast*, passim; Gardner is quoted in Barker-Benfield, *The Horrors of the Half-Known Life*, 297.
4. Noble, *The Eternal Adam*, 35.
5. Jung, *Answer to Job*, especially 165–80.
6. Isaacs, *Jock Culture U.S.A.*, passim, offers not merely a thematic presentation of topics pertaining to American sport but a variety of themes roughly conforming to the interests of the differing constituent groups mentioned in this study. In this way, Isaacs, like many other authors, unconsciously replicates the complex structure of sport in the very organization of his book.
7. Concerning Todd, see Barker-Benfield, *The Horrors of the Half-Known Life*. Regeneration and renewal were the reciprocal of Todd's penchant for conserving energy, which showed itself in his antimasturbation literature. The egoism and willfulness which Barker-Benfield sees in Todd recall the unrealistic "American Adam," described by Noble in *The Eternal Adam*, whose concentration on independence and perfectionism drive him away from all contact with real human society. Stearns, *Be a Man!* sees males in the nineteenth century experiencing great anxiety over their relationship toward women. As the product of a strategy of avoidance, sport functioned in part as a form of initiation in an anthropological sense and of acculturation in a sociological sense.
8. See, for example, Shiels, "The Feminization of American Congregationalism, 1730–1835," 46–62.
9. As Noble suggests in *The Eternal Adam*, the dominance of the sexual "beast" in man ran as a consistent theme in the works of such writers as William Dean Howells, Stephen Crane, and Theodore Dreiser. On the fear of "willfulness," see, for example, McLoughlin, "Evangelical Child-Rearing in the Age of Jackson," 21–34.
10. See Morison, *From Know-How to Nowhere*, 150. Frederick Law Olm-

sted also feared the raw frontier as a danger requiring mediation before it could benefit man. See Lewis, "Frontier and Civilization in the Thought of Frederick Law Olmsted," 385–403.

11. Concerning man's feeling that he was a part of nature and of the animal order, see Turner, *Reckoning with the Beast*.

Selected Bibliography

PRIMARY SOURCES: BOOKS

Adam, G. Mercer, ed. *Sandow on Physical Training.* New York: J. Selwin Tait, 1894.

Adams, Brooks. *The Law of Civilization and Decay, An Essay on History.* New York: Macmillan, 1896.

_____. *The Theory of Social Revolutions.* New York: Macmillan, 1913.

Adams, Henry. *The Degradation of the Democratic Dogma.* New York: Macmillan, 1919.

Alexander, John. *Boy Training.* New York: Association Press, 1911, 1912.

"An Old Boy," *Notes for Boys (and Their Fathers) on Morals, Mind, and Manners.* Chicago: McClurg, 1888.

Atwater, W.O. *A Respiration Calorimeter with Appliances for the Direct Determination of Oxygen.* Washington: Carnegie Inst., 1905.

_____. *Methods and Results of Investigations on the Chemistry and Economy of Food.* Bulletin 21, U.S. Dept. of Agriculture, Office of Experiment Stations [mid-1880s].

_____, and F.G. Benedict. *An Inquiry Regarding the Nutritive Value of Alcohol.* Washington: GPO, 1902.

Bain, Alexander. *Mind and Body.* New York: D. Appleton, 1879.

_____. *The Senses and the Intellect.* New York: D. Appleton, 1894.

George M. Beard. *Eating and Drinking, A Popular Manual of Food and Diet in Health and Disease.* New York: Putnam's, 1871.

_____. *Sexual Neurasthenia [Nervous Exhaustion]. Its Hygiene, Causes, Symptoms and Treatment, with a Chapter on Diet for the Nerves.* (Posthumous manuscript ed. A.D. Rockwell). New York: E.B. Treat, 1884.

_____. *The Symptoms of Sexual Exhaustion, Sexual Neurasthenia.* Baltimore: Practitioner Pub. Co., 1880.

Berenson, Senda. *Basket Ball for Women*. New York: American Sports Pub. Co., 1880.

Bloomer, Dexter C. *Life and Writings of Amelia Bloomer*. Boston: Arena, 1895.

Bourne, Randolph. *The World of Randolph Bourne*, ed. Lillian Schlissel. New York: Dutton, 1965.

Butts, Edmund L. *Manual of Physical Drill, U.S. Army*. New York: D. Appleton, 1914.

Camp, Walter, and Lorin F. Deland. *Football*. Boston: Houghton Mifflin, 1896.

Cheley, F.H. *Stories for Talks to Boys*. New York: Association Press, 1920.

Cobb, Ty, with Al Stump. *My Life in Baseball, The True Record*. Garden City, N.Y.: Doubleday, 1961.

Collier, Price. *England and the English from an American Point of View*. New York: Scribner's, 1916.

Combe, Andrew. *Observations on Mental Derangement*. Boston: Marsh, Capen & Lyon, 1834.

Combe, George. *Notes on the United States of North America During a Phrenological Visit*. 2 vols. Philadelphia: Carey & Hart, 1841.

Crowther, Samuel, and Arthur Ruhl, *Rowing and Track Athletics*. New York: Macmillan, 1905.

Edwards, Richard Henry. *Popular Amusements*. New York: Association Press, 1915.

Eggleston, Edward. *The Transit of Civilization*. New York: D. Appleton, 1914.

Elliott, Maud Howe. *This Was My Newport*. Cambridge, Mass.: Mythology Co., A. Marshall Jones, 1944.

Evers, J.J., and H.S. Fullerton. *Touching Second: The Science of Baseball*. Chicago: Reilly, 1910.

Fiske, G. Walter. *Boy Life and Self-Government*. New York: Association Press, 1910, 1912.

Fletcher, Horace. *The A.B.–Z. of Our Own Nutrition*. New York: Frederick A. Stokes, 1903.

Gill, C. *The Evolution of Christianity*. London: Williams & Norgate, 1883.

Gilman, Charlotte Perkins. *Women and Economics*. Boston: Small, Maynard, 1898.

Gladden, Washington. *Applied Christianity, Moral Aspects of Christianity*. Boston: Houghton Mifflin, 1886.

_____. *Social Salvation*. Boston: Houghton Mifflin, 1902.

Hall, B.H. *A Collection of College Words and Customs*. Cambridge, Mass.: John Bartlett, 1856.

Hartt, Rollin Lynde. *The People at Play, Excursions in the Humor and Philosophy of Popular Amusements.* Boston: Houghton Mifflin, 1909.

Hill, Lucille Eaton. *Athletic and Out-Door Sports for Women.* New York, Macmillan, 1903.

Huntington, F.D. *Home and College.* Boston: Crosby, Nichols, Lee, 1860.

James, William. *The Will to Believe and Other Essays.* New York: Dover, 1956 [rpts. of variously dated essays].

_____. *The Writings of William James,* ed. James J. McDermott. New York: Random House, 1967.

Jenkin, A.E. *Gymnastics.* New York: Frederick A. Stokes, 1891.

Jenks, Jeremiah W. *Life Questions of High School Boys.* New York: Association Press, 1908, 1910.

Kaempffert, Waldemar, ed. *The Book of Modern Marvels.* New York: Leslie-Judge, 1917.

Kent, Charles Foster, and Jeremiah W. Jenks. *Jesus' Principles of Living.* New York: Macmillan, 1920.

Klein, Felix. *In the Land of the Strenuous Life.* Chicago: McClurg, 1905.

Lea, Homer. *The Valor of Ignorance.* New York: Harper, 1909.

Lodge, Henry Cabot. *Early Memories.* New York: Scribner's, 1913.

_____. *Speeches and Addresses, 1884–1909.* 2d ed. Boston: Houghton Mifflin, 1892, 1909.

London, Jack. *Game.* New York: Macmillan, 1912.

MacDonald, Charles Blair. *Scotland's Gift, Golf, Reminiscences, 1872–1927.* New York: Scribner's, 1928.

MacFadden, Bernarr. *The Physical Culture Cook Book.* New York: MacFadden Publications, 1924.

Marey, E.J. *Animal Mechanism: A Treatise on Terrestrial and Aerial Locomotion.* New York: Appleton, 1879.

Martin, Frederick Townsend. *The Passing of the Idle Rich.* New York: Doubleday, 1911.

Mathews, Shailer. *The Social Teachings of Jesus.* New York: Macmillan, 1910.

Mathewson, Christy. *Pitching in a Pinch; or, Baseball from the Inside.* New York: Stein & Day, 1977 [1912].

Muir, John, *Our National Parks.* Boston: Houghton Mifflin, 1901.

Münsterberg, Hugo. *American Traits from the Point of View of a German.* Boston: Houghton Mifflin, 1901.

Muybridge, Eadweard. *Animal Locomotion: The Muybridge Work at the University of Pennsylvania.* New York: Arno, 1973 [1888].

_____. *Animals in Motion*, ed. Lewis Brown. New York: Dover, 1957 [1887].

_____. *The Human Figure in Motion*. New York: Dover, 1955 [1887].

Nearing, Scott, and Nellie M.S. Nearing. *Woman and Social Progress*. New York: Macmillan, 1914.

Nissen, Hartvig. *ABC of the Swedish System of Educational Gymnastics*. Boston: Educational Pub. Co., 1892.

Paret, J. Parmly, ed. *The Women's Book of Sports*. New York: Appleton, 1901.

Patten, Simon. *The Social Basis of Religion*. New York: Macmillan, 1911.

Pavlov, Ivan. *Lectures on Conditioned Reflexes*. New York: International Pubs., 1928.

Peabody, Francis Greenwood. *Jesus Christ and the Social Question*. New York: Macmillan, 1920.

Pettigrew, J. Bell. *Animal Locomotion or Walking, Swimming, and Flying With a Dissertation on Aëronautics*. New York: Appleton, 1888.

Rauschenbusch, Walter. *Christianity and the Social Crisis*. New York: Macmillan, 1907.

_____. *Christianizing the Social Order*. New York: Macmillan, 1912.

_____. *The Social Principles of Jesus*. New York: Association Press, 1912.

Robinson, Clarence C. *The Wage-Earning Boy*. New York: Association Press, 1912.

Roosevelt, Theodore. *American Ideals*. New York: Putnam's, 1902 [1897].

_____. *Applied Ethics*. Cambridge, Mass.: Harvard Univ. Press., 1911.

_____. *The Winning of the West*, I. New York: Putnam's, 1889.

_____. *The Works of Theodore Roosevelt*. 16 vols. New York: Collier, 1905.

Ross, Edward Alsworth. *Social Psychology, An Outline and Source Book*. New York: Macmillan, 1923.

Sandow, Eugene. *Life Is Movement, The Physical Reconstruction and Regeneration of the People*. London: National Health Press [c1910].

Sargent, Dudley Allen. *An Autobiography*. Philadelphia: Lea & Febiger, 1927.

_____. *Physical Education*. Boston: Ginn, 1906.

Schmidt, F.A., and Eustace H. Miles. *The Training of the Body*. New York: Dutton, 1901.

Sheldon, Henry D. *Student Life and Customs*. New York: Appleton, 1901.

Sizer, Nelson. *Forty Years of Phrenology*. New York: Fowler & Wells, 1882.

Spalding, Albert G. *America's National Game.* New York: American Sports Pub. Co., 1911.

Stevens, George Barker. *The Teaching of Jesus.* New York: Macmillan, 1902.

Taylor, Frederick W. *Scientific Management.* New York: Harper, 1947.

Van Rensselaer, Mrs. John [May] King. *Newport, Our Social Capital.* Philadelphia: Lippincott, 1905.

_____. *The Social Ladder.* New York: Holt, 1924.

Veblen, Thorstein. *The Theory of the Leisure Class.* New York: B.W. Huebsch, 1919.

Weyand, A.M. *American Football, Its History and Development.* New York: Appleton, 1926.

The Women's Athenaeum. 15 vols. New York: Macmillan, 1912.

Y.M.C.A., Social Service Commission, *Social Services Message.* New York: Association Press, 1913.

PRIMARY SOURCES: ARTICLES

Allen, Joseph Dana, and William Beach Olmsted. "Schoolboy Athletics in American Schools." *The Illustrated Outdoor News* 6 (24 Feb. 1906), 2.

"The Amateur." *Outlook* 103 (8 Feb. 1913), 293–95.

"Athletics and Morals." *Atlantic* 113 (Feb. 1914), 149–52.

Atkinson, Edward. "The Food Question in America and Europe." *Century* 33 (Dec. 1886).

Atwater, W.O. "The Chemistry of Foods and Nutrition." *Century* 34 (May 1887), 59–74.

Bancroft, W.A., et al. "The Crisis in Rowing." *Harvard Graduates' Magazine* 3 (Sept. 1894), 30–36.

Barney, Elizabeth C. "The American Sportswoman." *Fortnightly Review* 56 (Aug. 1894), 271.

Beasley, N.B. "Baseball: a Business, a Sport, a Gamble." *Harper's Weekly* 58 (11 April 1914), 27.

Bissell, Mary T. "Athletics for City Girls." *Popular Science Monthly* 46 (Dec. 1894), 145–53.

Boller, B.F. "Physical Training." *Mind and Body* 7 (April 1900), 26.

Bourne, Randolph. "The Undergraduate." *The New Republic* 5 (25 Sept. 1915), 197–98.

Brewster, G.O. "Boxing—As a Game." *Harper's Weekly* 54 (June 1910), 25.

Bruce, H.A. "Baseball and the National Life." *Outlook* 104 (17 May 1913), 104–7.

_____. "The Psychology of Football." *Outlook* 96 (5 Nov. 1910), 541–45.

Burton, Marion. "Hats and Boots for the Sportswoman." *The Illustrated Sporting News* 2, (9 Jan. 1904), 18–19.

Bushnell, Edward R. "Colleges and Schools." *The Illustrated Outdoor News* 7 (Nov. 1906), 146.

_____. "Football Prospects of the East's 'Big Six.'" *The Illustrated Sporting News* 5, (16 Sept. 1905), 4.

_____. "The Minor Colleges' Gridiron Outlook." *The Illustrated Outdoor News* 5 (30 Sept. 1905), 2.

_____. "With the College Athletes." *The Illustrated Outdoor News* 6 (20 Jan. 1906), 17.

_____. "With the College Athletes." *The Illustrated Sporting News* 6 (27 Jan. 1906), 17.

"Business Side of Baseball." *Current Literature* 53 (Aug. 1912), 168–72.

Butler, E.H. "Obvious Athlete." *Atlantic* 113 (March 1914), 422–26.

_____. "Shall Football Be Ended or Mended?" *Review of Reviews* 33 (Jan. 1906), 71–72.

Camp, Walter. "Athletic Extravagance in Training, in Playing, and in Describing." *Outing* 26: 81.

_____. "General Prospects of Yale's Football Champions." *The Illustrated Outdoor News* 5 (14 Oct. 1905), 11.

_____. "Harvard's Rowing Invasion of England." *The Illustrated Sporting News* 7 (11 Aug. 1906), 8.

_____. "Industrial Athletics: How the Sports for Soldiers and Sailors Are Developing into Civilian Athletics." *Outlook* 123 (11 June 1919), 252–53.

_____. "Lawn-Tennis, the Queen of Games." *Century* 80 (Aug. 1910), 545–57.

Casey, J.P. "Our Greatest American Game." *Independent* 61 (16 Aug. 1910), 375–78.

Chadwick, Henry. "Old Time Baseball." *Outing* 38 (July 1901), 420–22.

"Close of the Baseball Season." *Current Literature* 49 (Nov. 1910), 494–97.

Clurman, M.J. "Is It Not Time for Parents to Act." *Ladies' Home Journal* 28 (Sept. 1911), 5.

Colton, A.E. "What Football Does." *Independent* 57 (15 Sept. 1904), 600–607.

"Comment and Criticism." *Journal of the Military Service Institution of the United States* 12 (May 1891), 662–70.

_____. *Journal of the Military Service Institution of the United States* 13 (Nov. 1892), 1182–86.

Courtney, Charles E. "Teaching College Men the Art of Rowing." *The Illustrated Sporting News* 5 (29 April 1905), 2.

Curry, Duncan. "Yachting as a Sport for the People." *The Illustrated Sporting News* 3 (16 July 1904), 10–11.

Cushing, P.M. "Playing for What There Is in It." *Outing* 54 (Sept. 1900), 733–40.

Daniels, C.M. "How American Swimming Was Revolutionized." *The Illustrated Outdoor News* 6 (31 March 1906), 2.

Darling, Eugene A. "The Effects of Training." *Harvard Graduates' Magazine* 9 (Dec. 1900), 198–203.

_____. "Medical Supervision of Athletes." *Harvard Graduates' Magazine* 9, 190–96.

Davenport, H.C. "Modern Cave Man." *Collier's* 45 (11 June 1910), 19.

"D-e-e-lighted to Hear it." *The Illustrated Sporting News* 2 (9 April 1904), 2.

de Koven, Mrs. Reginald. "Bicycling for Women." *The Cosmopolitan* 19 (Aug. 1895), 392–94.

Deming, Clarence. "College Boating in the Sixties." *Outing* 44 (July 1904), 416–19.

"Dogs of High Degree and Their Titled Mistresses." *The Illustrated Sporting News* 2, 7 (May 1904), 8–9.

Donworth, A.B. "Gymnasium Training in the Army." *Journal of the Military Service Institution of the United States* 21 (Nov. 1897), 508–15.

Downey, George. "The Middle West's College Baseball Champions." *The Illustrated Outdoor News* 7 (23 June 1906), 6.

Edwards, William H. "What the Year Has Brought Forth at Princeton." *The Illustrated Outdoor News* 6, (11 Nov. 1905), 11.

Ehinger, C.E. "Report to the Executive Committee of the North American Gymnastic Union." *Mind and Body* 7 (Nov. 1900), 195–98.

Emmons, Robert W., II. "Needed Football Reforms." *Harvard Graduates' Magazine* 3 (March 1895), 318–22.

Evans, R.D. "Why Athletics Should Be Fostered in the Navy." *The Illustrated Sporting News* 5 (22 July 1905), 5.

"An Encyclopedia of Sport." *Outing* 59 (March 1912), 705.

Finlay, J.R. "The Abuses of Training." *Harvard Graduates' Magazine* 2 (March 1894), 322–29.

Foote, Morris C. "Military Gymnastics." *Journal of the Military Service Institution of the United States* 12 (March 1891), 243–45.

Foster, Thomas. "Why Our Soldiers Learn to Box." *Outing* 72 (May 1918), 114–16.

"Fox Hunting in an Automobile." *The Illustrated Outdoor News* 6 (13 Jan. 1906), 10.

Fullerton, H.S. "Fans." *American Magazine* 74 (Aug. 1912), 462–67.

———. "Hitting the Dirt." *American Magazine* 72 (May 1911), 3–16.

Fyffe, H.H. "What the Prize-Fight Taught Me." *Outlook* 95 (13 Aug. 1910), 827–30.

Gardiner, A.P. "The Graduate Athletic Association." *Harvard Graduates' Magazine* 6 (Mach 1898), 344–51.

Garrigues, Henry J. "Woman and the Bicycle." *The Forum* 20 (Jan. 1896), 582–87.

Gettell, Raymond G. "The Value of Football." *American Physical Education Review* 22 (March 1917), 139–42.

Godkin, E.L. "The Athletic Craze." *The Nation* 19, (7 Dec. 1893), 422–23.

———. "Athletics and Health." *The Nation* 19 (20 Dec. 1894), 457–58.

———. "Glorification in Athletics." *The Nation* 55 (1 Dec. 1892), 406–7.

"A Great Athletic Body." *The Illustrated Sporting News* 2 (5 Dec. 1903), 2.

Greeley-Smith, Nixola. "New York Women and the Art of Fencing." *The Illustrated Sporting News* 2 (9 Jan. 1904), 4–5.

Green, Charles W. "Looking After Baseball Players' Physical Side." *The Illustrated Outdoor News* 7 (28 July 1906), 2.

Greenleaf, R.W. "Student Diet at Harvard." *Harvard Graduates' Magazine* 2 (Dec. 1893), 171–83.

Gulick, Luther H. "New Athletics." *Outlook* 98 (15 July 1911), 597–600.

Hall, Edwin H. "The Money Rule in Athletics." *Harvard Graduates' Magazine* 12 (June 1904), 537–39.

———. "The Pitfall of Athletics." *The Nation* 78 (17 March 1904), 2020.

Hall, G. Stanley. "Some Relations Between Physical and Mental Training." *Proceedings of the American Association for the Advancement of Physical Education*, 1894, No. 2, pp. 30–37.

Handley, L. de B. "The Outdoor Swimming Season of 1906." *The Illustrated Outdoor News*, "Blue Ribbon Number" (Nov. 1906), 132–33.

Hemenway, Augustus, et al. "Important Suggestions on Athletics, Being the Report of the Committee on Physical Training, Athletic Sports, and Sanitary Condition of Buildings." *Harvard Graduates' Magazine* 6 (Dec. 1897), 191–96.

Herrick, Christine Terhune. "Schoolgirl Athletes on the Track and Field." *The Illustrated Sporting News* 1, (6 June 1903), 14–15.

Higginson, Thomas Wentworth. "Saints, and Their Bodies." *Atlantic Monthly* 1 (March 1858), 582–85.

Hough, Theodore. "A Review of Swedish Gymnastics." *Mind and Body* 7 (May 1900), 50–51.

"How Uncle Sam Has Created an Army of Athletes." *Scientific American* 120 (8 Feb. 1919), 114–15.

Hutchins, C.P. "Reconstructing the Game of Football." *The Illustrated Outdoor News* 6 (23 Dec. 1906), 2.

Hutchinson, W.H. "Exercise and Its Dangers." *Harper's Monthly* 114 (March 1907), 601–7.

———. "Real Danger of Athletics." *Outing* 57 (Nov. 1910), 168–73.

Inglis, William. "Apotheosis of La Boxe." *Harper's Weekly* 56 (31 Aug. 1912), 22–23.

"Intellectuality of the New Pugilism." *Current Opinion* 54 (Feb. 1913), 130–31.

"Is Athletic Training Overdone?" *The Illustrated Sporting News* 2 (5 March 1904), 2.

"Know Baseball, Know the American." *American Magazine* 76 (Sept. 1913), 94.

Lang, F.S. "The Problem of Professional Rowing Coaches." *The Illustrated Outdoor News* 6 (5 May 1906), 2.

Lardner, R.H. "Cost of Baseball." *Collier's* 48 (2 March 1912), 28.

Lucas, J.P. "Commercializing Amateur Athletics." *World Today* 10 (March 1906), 281–85.

Lyon, H.M. "In Reno Riotous." *Hampton* 25 (Sept. 1910), 386–96.

McKenzie, R. Tait. "Building the Physical Side of College Men." *The Illustrated Sporting News* 5 (12 Aug. 1905), 4.

Manice, Caroline F. "Women and Their Relation to Outdoor Recreation." *The Illustrated Sporting News* 2 (7 May 1904), 6.

Merrill, G.E. "Is Football Good Sport?" *North American Review* 177 (Nov. 1903), 758–65.

Metzger, Sol. "Who Will Win the Intercollegiate Regatta of 1906?" *The Illustrated Outdoor News* 7 (23 June 1906), 9.

Meylan, George L. "Harvard University Oarsmen." *Harvard Graduates' Magazine* 12 (March 1904), 362–76.

"Mishaps of the Football Campaign." *The Illustrated Sporting News* 2 (5 Dec. 1903), 2.

"Modish Raiment for the Sportswoman." *The Illustrated Sporting News* 2 (7 May 1904), 16.

"A Mutiny with a Moral." *The Illustrated Sporting News* 2 (30 April 1904), 2.

"National Game." *Outlook* 102 (19 Oct. 1912), 329–30.

"National Rifle Tournament." *The Illustrated Sporting News* 5 (9 Sept. 1905), 6–7, 10–11.

Needham, R.B. "The College Athlete." *McClure's* 25 (June 1905), 115–28, and 25 (July 1905), 260–73.

"Objections." *Current Literature* 40 (Jan. 1906), 21–25.

O'Hagan, Anne. "The Athletic Girl." *Munsey's Magazine* 25 (Aug. 1901), 734–35.

Orth, Albert. "The Pitcher's Viewpoint of the Game of Baseball." *The Illustrated Sporting News* 5 (23 Sept. 1905), 2.

Osborn, E.B. "The Revival of Boxing." *Nineteenth Century* 70 (Oct. 1911), 771–81.

"The Outreachings of Athletics." *The Nation* 60 (28 March 1895), 235–36.

Paine, Elizabeth. "Athletics at Women's Colleges — Bryn Mawr." *The Illustrated Sporting News* 3 (9 July 1904), 6.

———. "Athletics in Women's Colleges — Mount Holyoke." *The Illustrated Sporting News* 3 (6 Aug. 1904), 4.

———. "Physical Training in Women's Colleges — Smith." *The Illustrated Sporting News* 2 (4 June 1904), 3.

Paine, Ralph D. "Columbia's Athletic Prospects." *The Illustrated Sporting News* 2 (26 March 1904), 4–5.

———. "Harvard's Athletes for 1904." *The Illustrated Sporting News* 3 (14 May 1904), 22.

———. "Why Baseball is the Greatest American Pastime." *The Illustrated Sporting News* 3 (18 June 1904), 5–6, 17.

Paret, J. Parmly. "Importing Canadian Professionals for Ice Hockey." *The Illustrated Outdoor News* 6 (27 Jan. 1906), 8.

Parkhurst, C.D. "The Practical Education of the Soldier." *Journal of the Military Service Institution of the United States* 11 (Dec. 1890), 946–50.

"Penn. State — Athletic Stars of Pennsylvania — Mercersburg." *The Illustrated Outdoor News* 6 (21 April 1906), 12.

"The Point of View." *Scribner's* 19 (June 1896), 783–84.

Potter, Isaac B. "The Bicycle Outlook." *The Century Magazine* 52 (Sept. 1896), 786.

"President Roosevelt in Yellowstone Park." *The Illustrated Sporting News* 1 (4 July 1903), 8–13, 22.

"Prize Fight Moving Pictures." *Outlook* 95 (16 July 1910), 541–42.

Putnam, Henry W. "Required Gymnastics at Harvard." *Harvard Graduates' Magazine* 6 (March 1898), 309–14.

"Recent Prize-Fight." *Outlook* 95 (16 July 1910), 550–51.

Reeve, Arthur. "What America Spends for Sport." *Outing* 57 (Dec. 1910), 300–8.

_____. "World's Greatest Athletic Organization." *Outing* 57 (Oct. 1910), 106–15.

Richards, Eugene L. "College Athletics." *Popular Science Monthly* 24 (Feb. 1884), 446–53.

Richardson, Sophia. "Tendencies in Athletics for Women in Colleges and Universities." *Popular Science Monthly* 50 (Feb. 1897), 517–26.

Roosevelt, Theodore. "Degeneration and Evolution." *North American Review* 161 (July 1895), 96–109.

_____. "'Professionalism' in Sports." *North American Review* 151 (Aug. 1890), 187–91.

_____. "Recent Prize-Fight." *Outlook* 95 (16 July 1910), 550–51.

Sandys, Edwyn. "The Place That Woman Occupies in Sport." *The Illustrated Sporting News* 2 (21 Nov. 1903), 11.

Sanford, Ward. "Girls in Athletics." *The Illustrated Sporting News* 1 (13 June 1903), 2.

Sangree, Allen. "How a Big League Baseball Team Is Prepared." *The Illustrated Sporting News* 2 (26 March 1904), 6.

Sargent, Dudley Allen. "Ideals in Physical Education." *Mind and Body* 8 (Dec. 1901), 221–26.

_____. "The Hemenway Gymnasium: An Educational Experiment." *Harvard Graduates' Magazine* 3 (Dec. 1894), 169–80.

_____. "Strength Tests and the Strong Men of Harvard." *Harvard Graduates' Magazine* 5 (June 1897), 513–25.

Smith, Minna Gould. "Women as Cyclers." *Outing* 2 (June 1885), 318.

"Snobbery of Sport." *Independent* 74 (6 Feb. 1913), 277–78.

Sports Periodicals, ed. Donald J. Mrozek and Arne Richards. Westport, Conn.: Greenwood Press, 1977 [reprints of a series of turn-of-the-century journals].

"The Sportswoman." *The Illustrated Sporting News* 2 (6 Feb. 1904), 16.

Stauffer, Nathan P. "Why George Woodruff Went to Carlisle." *The Illustrated Outdoor News* 5 (28 Oct. 1905), 4–5.

Stearns, A.E. "Athletics and the School." *Atlantic* 113 (Feb. 1914), 145–48.

_____, and T.L. Browne, "Schoolboy Athletics from the Master's Viewpoint." *The Illustrated Outdoor News* 6 (7 April 1906), 2.

Steele, James L. "How the National Game Developed." *Outing* 44 (June 1904), 333–36.

Stevenson, William G. "Physiological Significance of Vital Force." *Popular Science Monthly* 24 (April 1884), 760–63.

Stewart, C.A. "Athletics and the College." *Atlantic* 113 (Feb. 1914), 153–56.

Stewart, C.D. "United States of Baseball." *Century* 74 (June 1907), 307–19.

Stillman, J.M. "The Source of Muscular Energy." *Popular Science Monthly* 24 (Jan. 1884), 377–87.

"The Strenuous Relatives of President Roosevelt." *The Illustrated Outdoor News* 7 (1 Sept. 1906), 7, 17.

Strong, Richard. "Great Britain's Famous Women of the Hunt." *The Illustrated Sporting News* 5 (20 May 1905), 8–9.

Taussig, F.W. "A Professor's View of Athletics." *Harvard Graduates' Magazine* 3 (March 1895), 305–11.

Ten Eyck, James A. "Relative to Crew Rowing — Sculls versus Sweeps." *The Illustrated Sporting News* 5 (27 May 1905), 239.

Thayer, Frederick W. "Harvard's Loss of Athletic Prestige." *Harvard Graduates' Magazine* 1 (Oct. 1892), 31–37.

Thomas, Roy A. "Teaching Baseball — Major League Comment." *The Illustrated Outdoor News* 7 (12 May 1906), 6.

Thwing, C.F. "Ethical Function of Football." *North American Review* 173 (Nov. 1901), 627–31.

_____. "Football: Is the Game Worth Saving?" *Independent* 54 (15 May 1902), 1167–74.

"Two Views of Athletics for Women." *The Illustrated Sporting News* 2 (14 Nov. 1903), 5.

van Allen, William Harman. "Vital Statistics of College-Bred Men." *Harvard Graduates' Magazine* 5 (Sept. 1896) 39–42.

Walker, Francis A. "College Athletics." *Harvard Graduates' Magazine* 2 (Sept. 1893), 2–4.

Weir, H.C. "Men and the Dollars Behind It." *World Today* 17 (July 1909), 732–61.

White, John S. "The New Athletics." *Proceedings of the American Association for the Advancement of Physical Education*, 1889, No. 3, pp. 46–52.

White, John Williams. "The Constitution, Authority, and Policy of the Committee on the Regulation of Athletic Sports." *Harvard Graduates' Magazine* 1 (Jan. 1893), 209–31.

Whitney, Caspar. "Is Football Worth While?" *Collier's* 44 (18 Dec. 1909), 13.

Williams, W. Mattieu. "The Chemistry of Cookery." *Popular Science Monthly* 24 (April 1884), 773–80.

"Wisconsin's Athletic Girls." *The Illustrated Sporting News* 2 (7 May 1904), 6.

"Women and Basketball," *Mind and Body* 7 (May 1900), 60.

"The Younger Experts' Newport Tennis Duel." *The Illustrated Outdoor News* 7 (8 Sept. 1906), 13.

SECONDARY SOURCES: BOOKS

Adorno, Theodor. *Prisms*, trans. Samuel Weber and Shierry Weber. London: Neville Spearman, 1967.

Alberts, Robert C. *The Good Provider, H.J. Heinz and His 57 Varieties.* Boston: Houghton Mifflin, 1973.

Allen, Frederick Lewis. *The Great Pierpont Morgan.* New York: Harper, 1949.

Ariès, Phillippe. *Western Attitudes toward Death: From the Middle Ages to the Present*, trans. Patricia M. Ranum. Baltimore: Johns Hopkins Univ. Press, 1974.

Arrington, Leonard. *Great Basin Kingdom, An Economic History of the Latter-Day Saints.* Cambridge, Mass.: Harvard Univ. Press, 1958.

_____, and Davis Bitton. *The Mormon Experience, A History of the Latter-Day Saints.* New York: Knopf, 1979.

Bannister, Robert C. *Social Darwinism, Science and Myth in Anglo-American Thought.* Philadelphia: Temple Univ. Press, 1979.

Barker-Benfield, G.J. *The Horrors of the Half-Known Life, Male Attitudes toward Women and Sexuality in Nineteenth-Century America.* New York: Harper, 1976.

Berkin, Carol Ruth, and Mary Beth Norton. *Women of America.* Boston: Houghton Mifflin, 1979.

Betts, John R. *America's Sporting Heritage, 1850–1950.* Reading, Mass.: Addison-Wesley, 1974.

Bledstein, Burton J. *The Culture of Professionalism, The Middle Class and the Development of Higher Education.* New York: Norton, 1976.

Boorstin, Daniel J. *The Americans, The National Experience.* New York: Random House, 1965.

Bowers, John Z., and Elizabeth F. Purcell. *Advances in American Medicine.* New York: Josiah Macy, Jr., Foundation, 1976.

Boyle, Robert H. *Sport — Mirror of American Life.* Boston: Little, Brown, 1963.

Bradley, Hugh. *Such Was Saratoga.* New York: Doubleday, 1940.

Brohm, Jean-Marie. *Sport — A Prison of Measured Time.* London: Ink Links, 1978.

Brousseau, Ray, ed. *Looking Forward.* New York: American Heritage, 1970.

Brown, Norman O. *Life Against Death, The Psychoanalytical Meaning of History.* Middletown, Conn.: Wesleyan Univ. Press, 1959.

Caillois, Roger. *Les jeux et les hommes.* Paris: Gallimard, 1958.

Chafe, William Henry. *The American Woman, Her Changing Social Economic, and Political Roles.* New York: Oxford Univ. Press, 1972.

Chandler, Alfred D. *Strategy and Structure: Chapters in the History of Industrial Enterprise.* Cambridge, Mass.: M.I.T. Press, 1962.

Clifford, John Garry. *The Citizen Soldiers, The Plattsburgh Training Camp Movement, 1913–1920.* Lexington: Univ. Press of Kentucky, 1972.

Cosmas, Graham. *An Army for Empire, The United States Army in the Spanish-American War.* Columbia: Univ. of Missouri Press, 1971.

Cremin, Lawrence A. *The Transformation of the School: Progressivism in American Education, 1876–1957.* New York: Knopf, 1961.

Curti, Merle. *The Social Ideas of American Educators.* New York: Scribner's, 1935.

Davies, John D. *Phrenology, Fad and Science: A 19th-Century Crusade.* New Haven: Yale Univ. Press, 1955.

Davis, Elwood Craig, ed. *Philosophies Fashion Physical Education.* Dubuque, Iowa: Brown, 1963.

Delamont, Sara, and Lorna Duffin. *The Ninetenth-Century Woman.* London: Croom Helm, 1978.

Edelstein, Tilden G. *Strange Enthusiasm, A Life of Thomas Wentworth Higginson.* New Haven: Yale Univ. Press, 1968.

Ekirch, Arthur A. *Man and Nature in America.* New York: Columbia Univ. Press, 1963.

Flink, James J. *The Car Culture.* Cambridge, Mass.: M.I.T. Press, 1975.

Frazer, Sir James George. *The Golden Bough, A Study in Magic and Religion.* New York: Macmillan, 1935.

Frederickson, George M. *The Inner Civil War, Northern Intellectuals and the Crisis of the Union.* New York: Harper, 1965.

Gardner, Joseph L. *Departing Glory, Theodore Roosevelt as ex-President.* New York: Scribner's, 1973.

Giedion, Siegfried. *Mechanization Takes Command, A Contribution to Anonymous History.* New York: Oxford Univ. Press, 1948.

Greven, Philip. *The Protestant Temperament, Patterns of Child-Rearing, Religious Experience, and the Self in Early America.* New York: Knopf, 1977.

Guttmann, Allen. *From Ritual to Record.* New York: Columbia Univ. Press, 1978.

Hagedorn, Hermann. *The Boys' Life of Theodore Roosevelt.* New York: Harper, 1918.

———. *Leonard Wood, A Biography.* New York: Harper, 1931.

Hartman, Mary, and Lois Banner, eds. *Clio's Consciousness Raised.* New York: Harper Colophon, 1974.

Hays, Samuel P. *Conservation and the Gospel of Efficiency, The Progressive Conservation Movement, 1890–1920.* Cambridge, Mass.: Harvard Univ. Press, 1959.

Hendricks, Gordon. *The Life and Work of Thomas Eakins.* New York: Grossman, 1974.

———. *The Photographs of Thomas Eakins.* New York: Grossman, 1972.

Hofstadter, Richard. *Anti-intellectualism in American Life.* New York: Knopf, 1970.

———. *Social Darwinism in American Thought.* New York: Braziller, rev. ed. 1959 [1944].

Holliman, Jennie. *American Sports, 1785–1835.* Philadelphia: Porcupine Press, 1975 [1931].

Hopkins, C. Howard. *History of the Y.M.C.A. in North America.* New York: Association Press, 1951.

Hoyt, Edwin P. *The Vanderbilts and Their Fortune.* Garden City, N.Y.: Doubleday, 1962.

Huizinga, Johann. *Homo Ludens: A Study of the Play Element in Culture.* Boston: Beacon, 1955 [1944].

Hutchinson, William R. *The Transcendentalist Ministers, Church Reform in the New England Renaissance.* Boston: Beacon, 1965.

Isaacs, Neil D. *Jock Culture U.S.A.* New York: Norton, 1978.

Jones, Howard Mumford. *The Age of Energy, Varieties of American Experience, 1865–1915.* New York: Viking, 1971.

Jung, Carl Gustav. *Answer to Job,* trans. R.F.C. Hull. London: Routledge & Kegan Paul, 1954.

———. *The Archetypes and the Collective Unconscious,* trans. R.F.C. Hull. Princeton, N.J.: Princeton Univ. Press, 1969.

Kern, Stephen. *Anatomy and Destiny, A Cultural History of the Body.* Indianapolis: Bobbs-Merrill, 1975.

Kett, Joseph F. *Rites of Passage, Adolescence in America, 1790 to the Present.* New York: Basic Books, 1977.

King, Willford I. *The Wealth and Income of the People of the United States.* New York: Macmillan, 1915.

———, Wesley C. Mitchell, Frederick R. McCauley, and Oswald W. Knauth. *Income in the United States, Its Amounts and Distribution 1909–1919.* New York: Harcourt, Brace, 1921.

Kohn, Hans. *American Nationalism, An Interpretive Essay.* New York: Macmillan, 1957.

271

———. *The Idea of Nationalism, A Study of Its Origins and Background.* New York: Macmillan, 1944.

Lane, Jack C. *Armed Progressive, General Leonard Wood.* San Rafael, Calif.: Presidio, 1978.

Lasch, Christopher. *The Culture of Narcissism, American Life in an Age of Diminishing Expectations.* New York: Norton, 1978.

———. *Haven in a Heartless World, The Family Besieged.* New York: Basic Books, 1977.

Lears, T. Jackson. *No Place of Grace, Antimodernism and the Transformation of American Culture, 1880–1920.* New York: Pantheon, 1981.

Lévi-Strauss, Claude. *The Savage Mind.* Chicago: Univ. of Chicago Press, 1968.

Lifton, Robert Jay. *The Woman in America.* Boston: Beacon, 1967.

Lucas, John A., and Ronald A. Smith. *Saga of American Sport.* Philadelphia: Lea & Febiger, 1978.

McBride, Paul. *Culture Clash—Immigrants and Reformers, 1880–1920.* San Francisco: R and E Research Associates, 1975.

McIntosh, Peter. *Fair Play, Ethics in Sport and Education.* London: Heinemann, 1979.

Martin, Frederick Townsend. *The Passing of the Idle Rich.* Garden City, N.Y.: Doubleday, Page, 1911.

Marx, Leo. *The Machine in the Garden, Technology and the Pastoral Ideal in America.* New York: Oxford Univ. Press, 1964.

Mathews, Mitford, ed. *A Dictionary of Americanisms.* Chicago: Univ. of Chicago Press, 1951.

Miller, Perry. *The New England Mind, The Seventeenth Century.* New York: Macmillan, 1939.

Morison, Elting E. *From Know-How to Nowhere.* New York: Basic Books, 1974.

Nash, Roderick. *Wilderness and the American Mind.* New Haven: Yale Univ. Press, 1967.

Noble, David W. *The Eternal Adam and the New World Garden.* New York: Braziller, 1968.

O'Connor, Richard. *The Golden Summers, An Antic History of Newport.* New York: Putnam's, 1974.

Persons, Stow. *The Decline of American Gentility.* New York: Columbia Univ. Press, 1973.

———, ed. *Evolutionary Thought in America.* New York: Braziller, 1956.

Potter, David. *People of Plenty, Economic Abundance and the American Character.* Chicago: Univ. of Chicago Press, 1954.

Pringle, Henry F. *Theodore Roosevelt, A Biography.* New York: Blue Ribbon Books, 1931.

Putnam, Carleton. *Theodore Roosevelt, The Formative Years, 1858–1886.* New York: Scribner's, 1958.

Redmond, Gerald. *The Caledonian Games in Nineteenth-Century America.* Rutherford, N.J.: Fairleigh Dickinson Univ. Press, 1971.

Rosenfeld, Morris, et al. *The Story of American Yachting.* New York: Bramhall House, 1958.

Runte, Alfred. *National Parks, The American Experience.* Lincoln: Univ. of Nebraska Press, 1979.

Ryan, Mary P. *Womanhood in America, From Colonial Times to the Present.* New York: New Viewpoints, 1975.

Sabo, Donald F., Jr., and Ross Runfola. *Jock, Sports and Male Identity.* Englewood Cliffs, N.J.: Prentice-Hall, 1980.

Satterlee, Herbert L., Jr. *J. Pierpont Morgan, An Intimate Portrait.* New York: Macmillan, 1939.

Schaap, Richard. *An Illustrated History of the Olympics.* New York: Knopf, 1963.

Schmitt, Peter J. *Back to Nature: The Arcadian Myth in Urban America.* New York: Oxford Univ. Press, 1969.

Spahr, Charles B. *An Essay on the Present Distribution of Wealth in the United States.* New York: Crowell, 1896.

Stannard, David E., ed. *Death in America.* Philadelphia: Univ. of Pennsylvania Press, 1975.

_____. *The Puritan Way of Death, A Study in Religion, Culture, and Social Change.* New York: Oxford Univ. Press, 1977.

Stearns, Peter N. *Be a Man! Males in Modern Society.* New York: Holmes & Meier, 1979.

Sutton, Ann, and Myron Sutton. *Yellowstone, A Century of the Wilderness Idea.* New York: Macmillan, 1973.

Thomas, Keith. *Religion and the Decline of Magic.* New York: Scribner's, 1971.

Tomkins, Calvin. *Merchants and Masterpieces, The Story of the Metropolitan Museum of Art.* New York: Dutton, 1970.

Troyat, Henri. *Daily Life in Russia Under the Last Tsar,* trans. Malcolm Barnes. Stanford, Calif.: Stanford Univ. Press, 1979 [1961].

Turner, James. *Reckoning with the Beast, Animals, Pain, and Humanity in the Victorian Mind.* Baltimore: Johns Hopkins Univ. Press, 1980.

Tyler, Alice Felt. *Freedom's Ferment, Phases of American Social History from the Colonial Period to the Outbreak of the Civil War.* New York: Harper, 1961 [1944].

Wecter, Dixon. *The Hero in America, A Chronicle of Hero-Worship.* New York: Scribner's, 1972 [1941].

White, Morton G. *Social Thought in America: The Revolt Against Formalism.* New York: Viking, 1949.

Wiebe, Robert H. *The Search for Order, 1877–1920.* New York: Hill and Wang, 1967.

Zborowski, Mark. *People in Pain.* San Francisco: Jossey-Bass, 1969.

SECONDARY SOURCES: ARTICLES

Allison, Lincoln. "Batsman and Bowler: The Key Relation of Victorian England." *Journal of Sport History* 7 (Summer 1980), 5–20.

Betts, John R. "The Impact of Technology on Sport in the Nineteenth Century." *Journal of Health, Physical Education, and Recreation.* (Nov.–Dec. 1969), 89–90.

———. "The Technological Revolution and the Rise of Sport, 1850–1900." *Mississippi Valley Historical Review* 40 (Sept. 1953).

———. "Sporting Journalism in 19th Century America." *American Quarterly* 5 (Spring 1953), 39–56.

Bradshaw, Ted K. "Trying Out the Future." *The Wilson Quarterly* 4 (Summer 1980), 75.

Bridenbaugh, Carl. "Baths and Water Places of Colonial America." *William and Mary Quarterly* 3 (April 1946), 151–81.

Buchholtz, C.W. "The National Park as a Playground." *Journal of Sport History* 5 (Winter 1978), 21–36.

———. "No Trail Too Steep: The Dream and Reality of Recreation in Our Western National Parks." *Journal of the West* 17 (July 1978), 96–110.

Cantwell, Robert. "They Led the Life of Riley." *Sports Illustrated,* 19 Nov. 1973, 106–28.

Chance, Gilbert. "Fast Horses and Sporting Blood." *Delaware History* 11 (Oct. 1964), 149–81.

Conron, John. "'Bright American Rivers': The Luminist Landscapes of Thoreau's *A Week on the Concord and Merrimack Rivers.*" *American Quarterly* 32 (Summer 1980), 144–66.

Danforth, Brian. "Hoboken and the Affluent New Yorker's Search for Recreation, 1820–1860." *New Jersey History* 95 (Autumn 1977), 133–44.

Danoff, Eric. "The Struggle for Control of Amateur Track and Field in the United States." *Canadian Journal of the History of Sport and Physical Education* 6 (May 1975), 43–85.

Dunning, Eric. "The Structural-Functional Properties of Folk-Games and Modern Sports: A Sociological Analysis." *Sportwissenchaft* 3. *Jahrgang* 1973/3, 215–32.

Edelman, Melvin L. "Academicians and Athletics: Historians' Views of American Sport." *The Maryland Historian* 4 (Fall 1973), 123–42.

Elias, Norbert, and Eric Dunning. "The Quest for Excitement in Unexciting Societies." *The Cross-Cultural Analysis of Sports and Games*, ed. Gunther Luschen. Champaign: Univ. of Illinois Press, 1970.

Fielding, Lawrence W. "Sport as a Training Technique in the Union Army." *The Physical Educator* 34 (Oct. 1977), 145–52.

Geldbach, Erich. "The Beginning of German Gymnastics in America." *Journal of Sport History* 3 (Winter 1976), 236–72.

Green, Maureen. "Re-creation of Olympus in high, heroic days of Victoria's reign." *Smithsonian* 9 (Dec. 1978), 48–57.

Guttmann, Allen. "On the Alleged Dehumanization of the Sports Spectator." *Journal of Popular Culture* 14 (Fall 1980), 275–82.

Hammond, Richard. "Progress and Flight: An Interpretation of the American Cycle Craze of the 1890s." *Journal of Social History* 5 (Winter 1971), 235–57.

Jable, J.T. "Pennsylvania's Early Blue Laws: A Quaker Experiment in the Suppression of Sport and Amusements, 1682–1740." *Journal of Sport History* 1 (Fall 1974), 107–21.

Levenstein, Harvey, "The New England Kitchen and the Origins of Modern American Eating Habits." *American Quarterly* 32 (Fall 1980), 369–86.

Lewis, Guy. "The Military Olympics at Paris, France, 1919." *The Physical Educator* 31 (Dec. 1974), 172–75.

———. "The Muscular Christianity Movement." *Journal of Health, Physical Education and Recreation*, May 1966, 27–28, 42.

———. "Theodore Roosevelt's Role in the 1905 Football Controversy." *Research Quarterly* 40 (Dec. 1969), 717–24.

———. "World War I and the Emergence of Sport for the Masses." *The Maryland Historian* 4 (Fall 1973), 109–22.

Lewis, Robert. "Frontier and Civilization in the Thought of Frederick Law Olmsted." *American Quarterly* 29 (Fall 1977) 385–403.

Loomis, C. Grant. "The Captive B'ar in California Amusements." *Western Folklore* 8 (Oct. 1948), 336–41.

Loy, John W. "The Nature of Modern Sport: A Definitional Effort." *Quest Monograph 10* (May 1968), 1–15.

MacDonald, Donald. "The Linville Highland Games and the Gathering of the Clans." *North Carolina Folklore* 6 (Dec. 1958), 36–37.

Mayer, H. "Puritanism and Physical Training." *International Review of Sport Sociology* 8 (1973), 37–51.

Meikle, Jeffrey L. "'Over There': Arthur Conan Doyle and Spiritualism." *The Library Chronicle of the University of Texas at Austin,* New Series (Fall 1974), 23–37.

Miller, David Cameron. "Kindred Spirits: Martin Johnson Heade, Painter; Frederick Goddard Tuckerman, Poet; and the Identification with 'Desert' Places." *American Quarterly* 32 (Summer 1980), 167–85.

Moore, John Hammond. "Football's Ugly Decades." *Smithsonian Journal of History* 2 (Fall 1957), 49–68.

Moss, George. "The Long Distance Runners of Ante-Bellum America." *Journal of Popular Culture* 8 (1974), 370–82.

Mrozek, Donald J. "The Image of the West in American Sport." *Journal of the West* 17 (July 1978), 3–14.

Nash, Roderick. "The American Invention of National Parks." *American Quarterly* 22 (Fall 1957), 49–68.

Northam, Janet, and Jack W. Berryman. "Sport and Urban Boosterism in the Pacific Northwest." *Journal of the West* 17 (July 1978), 53–60.

Orians, G. Harrison. "The Origin of the Ring Tournament in the United States." *Maryland Historical Magazine* 36 (Sept. 1941), 263–77.

Park, Roberta J. "The Attitudes of Leading New England Transcendentalists toward Healthful Exercise, Active Recreation and Proper Care of the Body: 1830–1860." *Journal of Sport History* 4 (Spring 1977), 34–50.

———. "'Embodied Selves': The Rise and Development of Concern for Physical Education, Active Games and Recreation for American Women, 1776–1865." *Journal of Sport History* 5 (Summer 1978), 5–41.

Paxson, Frederic L. "The Rise of Sport." *Mississippi Valley Historical Review* 4 (Sept. 1917), 143–68.

Rader, Benjamin G. "Modern Sports: In Search of Interpretations." *Journal of Social History* 13 (Winter 1979), 307–21.

———. "The Quest for Subcommunities and the Rise of American Sport." *American Quarterly* 29 (Fall 1977), 355–69.

Riesman, David, and Reuel Denny, "Football in America: A Study in Cultural Diffusion." *American Quarterly* 3 (Winter 1951), 309–25.

Schleppi, John R. "'It Pays': John H. Patterson and Industrial Recreation at the National Cash Register Company." *Journal of Sport History* 6 (Winter 1979), 20–28.

Smith, Leverett. "Ty Cobb, Babe Ruth and the Changing Image of the Athletic Hero." *Heroes of Popular Culture,* ed. Marshall Fishwick. Bowling Green, Ohio: Bowling Green Univ. Popular Press, 1972.

Smith, Ronald A. "The Rise of Basketball for Women in Colleges." *Canadian Journal of the History of Sport and Physical Education* 1 (Dec. 1970), 18–36.

Smith-Rosenburg, Caroll, and Charles Rosenburg. "The Female Animal: Medical and Biological Views of Woman and Her Role in Nineteenth Century America." *Journal of American History* 40 (Sept. 1973).

Tobin, Gary Allan. "The Bicycle Boom of the 1890s: The Development of Private Transportation and the Birth of the Modern Tourist." *Journal of Popular Culture* 7 (Spring 1974), 838–49.

Vondracek, Felix J. "The Rise and Development of Athletic Sports in the United States: 1860–1900." *The Quarterly Journal (North Dakota Quarterly)* 23 (Fall 1932), 46–58.

Wangensteen, O.H., and S.D. Wangensteen, "Lister, His Books, and Evolvement of His Antiseptic Wound Practices." *Bulletin of the History of Medicine* 48 (Spring 1974), 100–128.

Wiles, R.M. "Crowd Pleasing Spectacles in 18th Century England." *Journal of Popular Culture* 1 (1967), 90–105.

Willis, J., and R. Wettan. "Social Stratification in New York City Athletic Clubs, 1865–1915." *Journal of Sport History* 3 (Spring 1978).

Willoughby, David P. "When Sandow Visited California." *Pacific Historian* 15 (Spring 1971), 72–77.

Woods, Alan. "James J. Corbett: Theatrical Star." *Journal of Sport History* 3 (Summer 1976), 162–75.

Index

About the Book and Author

Few observers of American life today would doubt that sports occupy a prominent place in our society, but equally few have examined the origins of the country's greatest passion. Probing our history, culture, and consciousness, Professor Mrozek shows how sports gained national acceptance and became as standard as fried chicken and church on Sunday.

Today's boom has its roots in the period 1880–1910. As Mrozek shows, forgotten as well as famous public figures and athletes helped shape the modern craze. They included nutritionist Horace Fletcher, strongman Eugene Sandow, journalist Elizabeth Paine, and such familiar personalities as Teddy Roosevelt, Henry Cabot Lodge, and John Muir.

A national interest in sports could develop only after the governing classes had ceased to oppose organized games. Thereafter many forces worked on the public mind. National unification after the Civil War, changes in the role of women, and increases in leisure time all played a part. Other contributing trends were interest in an energetic lifestyle, the beginnings of a youth culture, and a generalized need for acceptable ways of expressing sexuality and sensuality. Mrozek's wide-ranging book paints a lively and compelling portrait of the American people in quest of sport.

Donald J. Mrozek teaches history at Kansas State University.